Agatha Christie

and

Shrewd Miss Marple

Before she
was famous:
The young
Agatha in 1912

Other books written or
edited by Peter Keating
include:

Autobiographical Tales (Priskus Books)

Kipling the Poet (Secker & Warburg)

Rudyard Kipling, *Selected Poems* (Penguin)

Marie Corelli, *The Sorrows of Satan* (Oxford World's Classics)

*The Haunted Study: A Social History of the
English Novel 1875-1914* (Secker & Warburg)

Matthew Arnold, *Culture and Anarchy and other Selected Prose* (Penguin)

Into Unknown England 1866-1913:Selections from the Social Explorers
(Fontana)

Elizabeth Gaskell, *Cranford* and *Cousin Phillis* (Penguin)

The Working Classes in Victorian Fiction (Routledge)

Working-Class Stories of the 1890s (Routledge)

Arthur Morrison, *A Child of the Jago* (MacGibbon & Kee)

Agatha Christie

and

Shrewd Miss Marple

Peter Keating

Agatha Christie with her
notebook in 1946

© Peter Keating, 2017

Published by Priskus Books

A CIP catalogue record for this book is available from the British Library.

ISBN 978-0-9926507-3-5

Book layout and cover design by Clare Brayshaw

Miss Marple drawing by Gilbert Wilkinson *The Royal Magazine*, December 1927.

Prepared and printed by:

York Publishing Services Ltd
64 Hallfield Road
Layerthorpe
York YO31 7ZQ

Tel: 01904 431213

Website: www.yps-publishing.co.uk

ARMCHAIR DETECTIVE Agatha Christie wrote 66 detective novels

CRIME QUEEN A portrait of Agatha Christie from about 1960

Contents

Preface

In October 1961 the *Sunday Times* published a 'talk' between Agatha Christie and Julian Symons on the subject of 'The Gentle Art of Murder.' Symons was a good choice for the job. Christie was known to dislike being interviewed and when she did give in under pressure she tended to be uncooperative. But she had already met Symons as fellow members of the Detection Club, and although he would only ever have considered himself a casual acquaintance, she agreed, rather grudgingly, to the interview. 'I suppose that as it is you it will be all right,' she wrote to him. Unlike many other writers of detective stories at the time, Symons admired Christie's work, especially the Hercule Poirot novels of the 1930s, the best of which he regarded as established classics of the genre and superior to those featuring Miss Marple. Even so, he had a sticky time keeping things going and the interview proved to be fairly innocuous, with nothing notable being said about the art of murder, gentle or otherwise. Yet something significant did emerge. When Symons tried to talk about Poirot he was surprised to be told that Christie could no longer 'bear' him. He resisted the temptation to push the matter further. There seemed no point in doing so, it being all too obvious that Christie far preferred Miss Marple to Poirot. So much so that Christie herself, Symons wrote, 'radiates a sort of shy benevolence, suggesting her own Miss Marple.'

There was a deeper issue at work here, something that no one could possibly have known about at the time, though perhaps Symons caught it intuitively. Christie was over seventy years old when the interview took place, and never before had she felt such a strong personal tie with Miss Marple or been so committed to her. There were still many books to come from Christie, among them several Poirot novels which would, unfortunately, turn out to be rather half-hearted efforts, faint shadows of his past achievements. In sharp contrast, Miss Marple's future was bright. A new Miss Marple was being prepared for publication while Christie was talking to Symons and three more, as yet unwritten, were to follow during the next decade. These four novels would take Miss Marple into new fictional territory and firmly reinforce her popularity, immediately and in the future. For Christie they marked a culminating point in her lifelong struggle to come to terms with Miss Marple, a moment she had long hoped for but had probably begun to believe would never come.

The main aim of *Agatha Christie and Shrewd Miss Marple* is to trace the history of the complex relationship between Christie and Miss Marple, between author and character, in all of its various stages, from its origins in the chaos of Christie's notorious 'disappearance' in 1926 through to her intense personal involvement in the final trilogy of Miss Marple novels. It is a book that has taken an exceptionally long time to reach completion, having gone through several versions, each markedly different from the one it displaced. Some of the delays can be blamed on the usual difficulties, personal and practical, that inevitably upset any writer's timetable, and some are attributable to that special kind of absorbing affection that Christie's novels seem to inspire in so many of her readers. But in this particular case it was primarily the subject, Agatha Christie herself, that caused the occasional discouragements, rethinks and about-turns. For a writer who has always been regarded as proverbially simple and unproblematic, Christie can be exceptionally difficult to come to terms with.

This is largely because of the very special image of her that has descended to us. It is of a natural storyteller with a genius for devising ingenious puzzles; wonderfully entertaining, of course, and hugely popular, but otherwise capable of being defined only in negative terms. Her novels are seen as clever but lacking depth, clearly deficient in any literary intelligence or ability, and failing to offer any serious interest in politics, society, criminology, the drastic changes in twentieth-century British life that were taking place all round her, or, it can often seem, in anything at all, except the manufacture of tricksy plots to explain away unconvincing murders. The novels are also often accused of carrying more than a whiff of class condescension, snobbery and racism. And all of these objections to her and her work are expected to be accepted unquestioningly even though, as has been pointed out so often, she has a vast and devoted readership made up of people of different nations, classes, and every level of education and literary sensitivity.

Nor does this popularity show any sign of slowing down. Her phenomenal sales figures often seem to have taken on a life of their own, as though they are the only thing of lasting interest about her. But there is nothing about Christie of the explosive best-seller whose great fame and vast sales usually decline abruptly at death and quickly settle to rest in a largely hidden corner of literary history. This was to be the fate of Marie Corelli and Hall Caine. They are worth singling out among many possibilities because when Christie was born in 1890 they were not only the two leading best-selling British novelists of the time but pioneers of their kind as well. How many readers do their books have now? How many people even know their names? Christie's position is nothing remotely like theirs. More than forty years after her death, both she and her books can still be regarded undeniably as 'best-sellers.' Yet at the same time, and incongruously so, she remains an author who is hugely read, greatly loved, widely admired, and critically ignored.

The peculiar nature of Christie's reputation has been well expressed by Alison Light, one of the few literary critics to allow the work serious consideration, in her book *Forever England*. Light notes there is something about Christie that 'seems to mark her out for an especially cold shoulder and the particularly gratuitous insult.' She continues: 'It is an extraordinary fact, given the centrality of her work to British cultural life, that no self-respecting British critic has ever written at decent length about her.' These observations come from 1991, and the situation has hardly changed since. It is true that Christie is now attracting more academic attention, but this is largely of a specialist nature and so far has done little to answer the central cultural and literary issues raised by Light.

To render the situation all the more strange, we know from the biographies of Christie that the outstanding personal qualities she possessed are completely at odds with all the critical negativity. She was an extremely intelligent, largely self-educated woman, driven by a restless curiosity, well-informed on an exceptionally large number of subjects, a more than merely talented musician and singer, well read in literature of the past and present, and knowledgeable about modern painting. In addition, I would want to emphasize that she kept herself well up-to-date on changes in criminal legislation and on the dramatic social and political transformation of Britain in the twentieth cemtury. She was also fascinated by Freudianism, and developed a passion for psychological interpretations of Shakespeare's plays. All of these interests find their way, and a generally unacknowledged way at that, directly or indirectly into the novels. The common critical view of her as nothing more than simple teller of quirky murder mysteries, simply won't do. It can just as well be argued, as it will be here, that she was, in fact, a skilled, self-conscious, allusive and increasingly self-referential writer.

But, of course, it has not proved possible to communicate convincingly much of this kind of positive information about her because it is only ever allowed to take second place to what is so widely regarded as the one, all-important event of her life. For anyone who would like to see more attention given to the novels themselves, the amount of space devoted to the disappearance, whether in serious biographies or the generally far from serious media, is bound to feel disproportionate. It can also be distracting, and irritating. Not that it can be set entirely to one side, for my purposes at least. After all, Christie herself was profoundly affected by it, in a whole variety of important ways, for the rest of her long life. And, while it is no intention of mine to enter into the controversies that can still be provoked by mention of the disappearance, it is a key part of the argument of the present book that we are indebted to it directly for the creation of Miss Marple and indirectly for the subsequent development of her fictional career.

What needs particularly to be understood about the impact those infamous eleven missing days have had on Christie's reputation is the way they drove her so totally in upon herself. She obviously vowed that she would never talk or write about them, and she kept her word. Although she describes the break-up of her marriage to Archie in her autobiography, she does so without mentioning the disappearance at all. The inevitable result of her persistent silence was that the true events, whatever they may have been, became all the more mysterious and fascinating to investigators, leaving the field wide open for conjecture.

If Christie's vow of silence had applied only to this particular part of her life, then it might possibly have been contained, even closed off. Instead, she extended it in the most extreme way to include her participation in virtually any form of personal publicity. As Julian Symons found out, even late in her life Christie remained uninterviewable. If what she said was going to be published, she took care to say nothing that might possibly matter. She adopted the same intransigent attitude towards her books, the art and practice of writing, and her personal opinions on just about everything.

Many of her friends were astonished that she could even consider writing her autobiography, but they soon found out that *An Autobiography* is a masterpiece of concealment, even deception. Its narrative is managed so skilfully that it is sometimes impossible to know whether what is being said is true, false or deliberately misleading. Given all of this, it is understandable that negative attitudes towards her life and work were allowed to flourish; that most literary critics were encouraged to follow Christie's own example in seeming to believe there was nothing worth saying about her work; and that her millions of devoted readers simply got on with reading and greatly enjoying the novels.

The approach I have taken in *Agatha Christie and Shrewd Miss Marple* is that of a literary and social historian with something more than a passing interest in psychoanalyis. This has permitted me to set her work within contexts that are rarely taken into account. The structure of the book has been determined by the life and career of Miss Marple. I have examined in considerable detail how much we know and do not know about her, just what kind of literary character she is, and the irregular, apparently spasmodic nature of Christie's involvement with her. A key element in that involvement is the manner in which the Miss Marple novels change over the span of Christie's life, far more so than those of Hercule Poirot. One result of the particular method I have used is that I have been able, incidentally as it were, to offer solutions to a number of hitherto long-standing and eagerly disputed questions among Miss Marple's many admirers.

Although I regard the Miss Marple novels as of more substantial literary and biographical interest than is usually allowed, I have tried to be careful of seeming to make exaggerated critical claims for them. Christie was pre-eminently a writer of detective stories, and I have kept this firmly in mind. Her main concern was to perfect and develop a particular type of detective story, not to claim for it a higher literary status. This ambition of Christie's I have respected and tried to clarify. At the same time I have not restricted myself to a consideration of the cleverness or otherwise of the detection in her novels with a view to ranking them accordingly, this often being the only issue about her work which is considered. Rather, I have constantly asked what kind of detective novel was Christie trying to write, even what kind of detective novel did she *think* she was trying to write because, as we have just seen, she long ago stopped offering any guidance or help on such matters. I have sought to deal with the problems this creates by carefully placing Miss Marple within Christie's overall life and work and supporting my claims with detailed studies of individual novels. I am aware that the results can sometimes seem startling. This is not, however, due to any critical outrageousness on my part. It is simply a matter of looking carefully at what is actually there in the books and placing it within an appropriate context, whether social historical or pyschoanalytical. For me, personally, the truly surprising thing is to disover the small amount of attention that has been paid to how much *is* actually there in the novels.

There is another difficulty in trying to analyse Christie's novels which is slightly different from her refusal to say anything revealing about them. This is the fact that she was both a prolific and a highly spontaneous writer. She herself often explained the coexistence of these two qualities by saying that most of the hard work was done before she began any actual writing. In other words, she prepared much of the novel in her mind and then transferred it, often at remarkable speed, to paper. The need to consider more closely what exactly Christie meant by this has been prompted by John Curran's recent edition of Christie's working notebooks. This material had already been drawn upon by Christie's biographers, but Curran has now made it readily and valuably available for anyone to use, and I for one have taken grateful advantage of that opportunity. Isn't what we have, here in the notebooks, the hard work that Christie did before sitting down to write?

Well, yes and no! What we find abundantly in the notebooks are possible story lines, names of characters, and plot patterns, together with Christie's many refinements and changes of mind. These were often set down haphazardly and over many years. It is strong evidence not only of how carefully Christie plotted her novels but also of an irregular, inconsistent approach to the task that can seem disturbingly random. This, however, was probably not the whole case. In *Agatha Christie's Secret Notebooks*, Curran argues that randomness *was* her method, 'how she worked, how she created, how she wrote.' This is surely correct. Drifting in between the notes and the novels, as it were, was a mysterious, undefinable spontaneity that contributed a very special tone and vigour to the finished article. Many of the ideas and techniques that I draw attention to in *Agatha Christie and Shrewd Miss Marple* – intellectual speculation, political and social opinions, oblique references to national issues, all kinds of allusions and ambiguities, the determination to answer her critics albeit indirectly – were not confided to the notebooks. They belonged to those same areas of life that Christie would never have thought of mentioning in public. But they are there in the novels all right. They are a further integral part of the hard work of the mind that flowed from Christie in a remarkably spontaneous, often unplanned, unanticipated manner, and can only be fully understood by being teased out of the novels.

This is far from being the first book devoted to Miss Marple, and it is unlikely to be the last. Anne Hart led the way in 1985. She was followed by Marion Shaw and Sabine Vanacker (1991), James Cresswell (2006) and Isabel Anders (2013). Their approaches are all different from each other, as mine is from theirs. I have benefitted from these books, and also found encouragement in those few other critics, whether or not I share their views, who have taken the line that Christie's work deserves to be treated more positively than it generally is. They include especially Alison Light, Gillian Gill, and the late Julian Symons. I am greatly indebted to Christie's excellent biographers – Janet Morgan, Jared Cade, and Laura Thompson – for details of her life. To Jared Cade there are due other, specific thanks.

Cade's *Agatha Cristie and the Eleven Missing days* is concerned primarily with the disappearance, but it was a different aspect of the book that impressed me when I first read it.

I was already interested in trying to establish links between Christie and Miss Marple and had quickly discovered that, at that time, one of the difficulties in making any serious progress was the absence of reliable bibliographical information, something that is mentioned a little more fully in chapter two of the present book. Cade obviously felt the same. He had not only hunted down the correct first publication and serialization details of much of Christie's early work, but proceeded to demonstrate how essential they were in establishing a trustworthy chronology of her life. A request to Jared Cade for further bibliographical advice on tracing the first publication of Miss Marple's short stories was met with great kindness and generosity. I am extremely grateful to him.

As yet, and as one would expect, virtually no serious textual work has been done on Christie's novels. When quoting from or referring to the novels, I have used for convenience and consistency, the 'Crime Collection' edition of Christie's novels published in twenty four volumes by Paul Hamlyn, 1969-72. For the relatively few novels which were still to have their first publication after the Crime Collection had appeared, I have turned to the readily available HarperCollins editions, hardback or paperback. Unless otherwise indicated, all statements in the present book attributed to Christie herself are taken from *An Autobiography*, first published by Collins in 1977. This is yet another of her books that would certainly, and perhaps revealingly as well, benefit from some informed textual and biographical editing.

Peter Keating
March 2017

Chapter 1

What's in a name?
Hercule, Jane, Ariadne and Agatha

> He knew all about Miss Marple. Everybody
> in St. Mary Mead knew Miss Marple; fluffy and
> dithery in appearance, but inwardly as sharp and
> as shrewd as they make them.

These are the thoughts of Sergeant Cornish, the policeman in charge of law and order in the tiny village of St. Mary Mead, as he confronts Miss Jane Marple and her visiting friend Mrs McGillicuddy in *4.50 from Paddington* (1957). Mrs McGillicuddy has a murder to report and what sounds like a very tall story to tell. Sergeant Cornish would like to persuade her that she must have been dreaming and send her gently on her way, but he needs to be careful. Mrs McGillicuddy's reliability is vouched for by Miss Marple, and there is no point in trying to persuade *her* that a good friend has made a mistake. Miss Marple may appear to be just another old woman, as gullible and unreliable as the rest of them, but when murder is involved she has the annoying reputation of usually being right.

She has lived in St. Mary Mead for much of her long life and presumably Sergeant Cornish will be used to seeing her about the village and hearing her praised or mocked by his senior officers. So when he says that along with everyone else in St. Mary Mead he knows 'all about her,' what does he mean? The answer is, very little more than we are told here.

He is aware of there being two Miss Marples, and that they appear to contradict each other, with the 'fluffy and dithery' outward appearance providing no guide at all to her inner shrewdness. Even those two conflicting images are merely observed or reported characteristics, fixed marks of identity. Of the woman behind them, of her inner thoughts

1

and feelings and how she came to be both dithery and shrewd he will know virtually nothing. His ignorance is shared not only with the other inhabitants of St. Mary Mead but with Christie's countless readers as well. Miss Marple may be one of modern fiction's most endurable characters and far and away its most celebrated woman detective, but she is also an unknown quantity and has to be treated with caution. Christie made sure of that.

A comparison with Hercule Poirot, Christie's other world-famous literary detective, is revealing.

About him, Christie was not in the least reticent. There was no alternative. He had been Christie's starting point as a professional writer, the principal cause of her early success, and he would remain the financial base of it throughout her career. Poirot's first case in Britain, *The Mysterious Affair at Styles*, was also Christie's first-published novel. It had appeared in 1921 though written several years earlier in the middle of the First World War while her husband Archie was serving in France and she was working at a hospital dispensary in Torquay.

Styles was not her first attempt at writing fiction, and the desire to write a detective novel was far from new. According to Christie's well-known account in *An Autobiography* (1977) the ambition stretched back to the days when she and her sister Madge had been enthusiastic readers of popular late Victorian and Edwardian detective fiction. Madge was eleven years older than Agatha; bright, keen on books, and with aspirations of her own to be a published writer. For many years she was an influential model for her younger sister. Under Madge's guidance, their reading of detective stories wasn't allowed to slip into the passive entertainment it so often is, but became unusually intense, critical, and self-educational. They discussed in detail the plots of the books they most enjoyed, identifying clues, reconstructing murder riddles, and comparing favourite authors. In the process they turned themselves, in Christie's own words, into 'connoisseurs of the detective story.' Following one of these analytical sessions, Agatha said how good it would be to write a detective story of her own. Madge was discouraging. She replied that she herself had once had the same thought, but decided it would be too difficult, so what chance could there be of her little sister succeeding? Christie took Madge's attitude as a personal snub, and thus 'the seed had been sown.'

By the time Christie came to write *Styles* her understanding of how different types of detective stories worked was impressive, with the discussions between the sisters bolstered by years of her own wide reading. She already had a grasp of much of the theory: it now needed to be applied.

This she did by dissecting the component parts of her favourite detective stories, considering in turn motive, method, plot, range of characters, and settings. Whatever she found artistically uninviting she discarded, what appealed to her she took over or adapted. The author she studied with the greatest care and to whom she was most indebted, was Arthur Conan Doyle whose Sherlock Holmes stories she had begged Madge to read to her long before she could read them for herself. She modelled Poirot quite consciously on Holmes, and presented him with his own Dr Watson or 'stooge' as Christie later liked to describe this kind of supporting role, in the form of Captain Hastings. At the start Hastings was also Poirot's chronicler just as Watson had been Holmes's.

It was important that Poirot should be marked out by certain notable physical and personal characteristics. These had to be as distinctive as those of Holmes, though also very different. Poirot thus came into existence as a settled type, fixed and known, an instantly identifiable character. As there were large numbers of Belgian refugees in Britain at that time, Christie decided to make him a French-speaking Belgian. It was a smart topical move on Christie's part, though a constant cause of national misidentification for Poirot himself. Translations of French detective novels and English novels featuring detectives with French names had been widely popular with British readers for some years, a trend that Christie was happy to pick up on. Her detective's first name, she decided, should be 'grand' in the manner of Sherlock Holmes, and because he was small in stature she settled, as a mild joke, on Hercules. She already had Poirot in mind as a surname, though without, as far as she was aware, knowing why. It was a pity it didn't go very well with Hercules, but it did with Hercule. 'Hercule Poirot. That was all right – settled, thank goodness.' This is Christie's own brisk account of the process. There have been attempts to find originals for Hercule Poirot, and perhaps she was unconsciously influenced in her choice of his first name, though not much else.[1] What she made of that name was entirely her own doing. It was to give her detective real distinction. The surname was less important: as Christie herself explained, it had only to blend in euphonically with the all-important first name. But although at the time Christie may have felt that the matter was settled, over the years she would be forced to return to it again and again, cheerfully and discontentedly, positively and negatively.

In the foreword she wrote for *The Labours of Hercules* (1947) Christie has Poirot being visited by an academic friend, Dr Burton, a classical scholar and Fellow of All Souls. Burton is not the first person to wonder why Poirot's 'Christian' name should be so pagan, but he toys with the thought and suggests that it may represent a widespread tendency of parents to give to their children names that can seem fun when they are babies but embarrassingly inappropriate when they grow up. He makes gentle fun of Poirot by inventing a playful 'imaginary conversation' in which the mothers of Poirot and Holmes are portrayed sitting together sewing or knitting 'little garments' and testing on each other rather esoteric first names for their babies to come: 'Achille, Hercule, Sherlock, Mycroft.' Burton is not entirely to the point with Conan Doyle. Sherlock and Mycroft appear to have been early English and/or Irish surnames with no classical or pagan connections, and Conan Doyle's originality lay in using them as first names. It is, perhaps, this that Burton has in mind. He is, though, spot on with Hercule. It is the French version of the Roman Hercules which is, in turn, derived from the Greek mythological hero Heracles, a semi-divine strong man and athlete, his superhuman muscular strength demonstrated in popular images by the gigantic club he wields. In something of a contrast to his reputation for brute force, Hercules was also known as a friend of mankind who was obliged, because of the jealousy of Zeus's wife Hera, to resolve a countless number of apparently insoluble 'labours.' Over the years these became reduced to twelve, a tradition that Christie follows.

Achille is the French version of Achilles, the Greek warrior who defeats the Trojan Hector in battle. It is the name given to Poirot's twin brother, a shock for the reader devised by Christie to equal the moment when Sherlock Holmes reveals that he has a brother called Mycroft. Achille

Poirot appears only once (or does he?) in *The Big Four* (1927). When Dr Burton asks Poirot whether it is true that he had a brother called Achille, Poirot replies guardedly: 'Only for a short space of time.' That deliberately ambiguous answer can be taken as Christie's as well.

While there is nothing inherently peculiar in naming a child Hercule or Hercules, Dr Burton's general point about doting parents is reasonable enough. Christie, as we have seen, deliberately chose an incongruously grand name for her small detective, and, sure enough, this particular Hercules grows up to be a physically unprepossessing short man, with an egg-shaped head, flamboyant moustaches, green eyes, a foppish taste in clothes, and a fastidious reluctance to indulge in any kind of physical activity. Poirot recognizes the justice of Burton's case, but consoles himself with the thought that the great classical hero was nothing 'but a large muscular creature of low intelligence and criminal tendencies.' Still, Hercules had also been a great solver of problems even if of a grossly physical kind, and Poirot wisely decides to concentrate on this and turn Hercules' reputation around in order to demonstrate the superiority of modern intellect to ancient physical force. He does so by transforming the Christian/pagan contrast into 'an ingenious and amusing conceit' in which the twelve tasks carefully selected and carried out by Hercule Poirot all become labours of the mind.

In addition to the peculiarity of his first name, Poirot follows Holmes in many other ways as well. He is intensely proud of his powers of detection and aware of his superiority to most professional police officers. This personal pride does not prevent both Holmes and Poirot from being entirely classless when it comes to taking on cases. It is the personal challenge that matters most to them. Christie also followed Conan Doyle in making Poirot considerably more mind than body and not personally much interested in sex. Both men carry with them throughout life the dominatant memory of just one rather vague ideal woman.

Further, they are both so distrustful of fresh air that they are capable of solving problems by hardly moving from their rooms, though the chaotic comfort of Holmes's Baker Street apartment is far removed from the modernist principles of stark symmetrical elegance favoured by Poirot in Whitehaven Mansions. As with Sherlock Holmes, it is the superiority of

Poirot's analytical mind or his 'little grey cells' that sets him apart from other people. The phrase was Christie's own coinage and first used in *Styles*, though virtually everything else about Poirot was suggested by Holmes.

From the start the reader was provided with sufficient details of Poirot's early life to grasp immediately who he was and where he came from. We first see him recently arrived in England from Belgium together with other refugees during the First World War and being reunited with Captain Hastings, a friend from less troubled times. He already has behind him a distinguished record of service in the Belgian police, and looks forward, eventually, to retiring to an English village in order to cultivate vegetable marrows. This unlikely ambition he is shown pursuing and abandoning in *The Murder of Roger Ackroyd* (1926), though twenty years later in that playful foreward to *The Labours of Hercules* Poirot is still shown to have a yearning to experiment with the flavour of what Dr Burton scornfully describes as 'those great swollen green things that taste of water.'

By this time the marrows had little real significance because Christie had long since decided that although *Roger Ackroyd* had been a great success as a work of detective fiction, Poirot himself was not suited for village life. At the same moment she may well have also registered the idea of salvaging the village setting. Miss Marple didn't yet exist. She was still unformed, unplaced and unnamed. But Christie was not the kind of author to waste a good fictional idea and when, a little more than a year on from *Roger Ackroyd* Miss Marple did make her literary debut, the village environment so recently evacuated by Poirot was there ready and waiting for her.

Giving up on his rural idyll Poirot returns with relief to the metropolitan world. For a few years before his horticultural experiment in the country he had shared fairly modest lodgings in London with Hastings. These had provided the setting for the first Poirot novels and a large number of the early short stories. It was also the time of his rise to wealth and fame in England as a 'consulting detective,' as he is described in *The Big Four*. In only the second of the full-length novels, *The Murder on the Links* (1923) Hastings falls in love, marries and moves with his wife to Argentina. Left alone, Poirot sets himself up in an ultra-modern London flat/office, looked after by a valet or 'gentleman's gentleman' (whose name Christie rather awkwardly spells Georges when Poirot is speaking and George when used in the third-person narrative), and managed by a super-efficient, plain-looking secretary Miss Lemon. Occasionally, and arbitrarily, Hastings returns from Argentina to help out, leaving his wife to manage their ranch. This casual arrangement obtained until *Curtain* (published in 1975 shortly before Christie's death) when Hastings was fully and finally reunited with a now dying Poirot.

Over the years, and in spite of remaining outwardly and obviously a foreigner, Poirot is shown to be entirely at home in both the modern city and country house life. He becomes a celebrated figure in English society, with an exceptionally large social range of friends and clients. These include not only high-ranking members of the police force, the CID and even Special Branch, but also representatives from the worlds of business, the theatre and arts, the professional classes, wealthy dilettantes, and nobility. He does not, however, further distinguish himself by regularly helping out the royal families of Europe. That remained the province of Sherlock Holmes and was, anyway, a less likely option for a private detective after the First World War had so drastically changed the map of Europe.

Once Christie had provided Poirot with a stable character and social position, further details of his life could simply emerge as and when required, as is the case with most other serial heroes. Gradually we learn about his relatively poor family background and large number of siblings, including the probably mythical twin brother Achille. We are also provided with information about his career as a detective in Belgium, some of his early cases, his strong Catholic faith, and his idiosyncratic taste in dress, food and drink.

Something like half of Christie's prolific output was dedicated to Poirot. He features in thirty-five novels and more than fifty short stories. Furthermore, Poirot's hold on Christie was not only lifelong but consistent as well. He was there at the very start of her career and still around at the end. Within that period of more than half a century it was unusual for there to be a spell of longer than two years during which Christie's devoted readers were not presented with a new Poirot novel.

* * *

There was no such consistency or regularity as far as Miss Marple was concerned. She had twelve novels and twenty short stories dedicated to her, and these appeared spasmodically, spread over much of Christie's career, usually published in small groups with long, apparently random, gaps between. One observable division is that a majority of the short stories were published early on, while most of the novels were written much later. It was, though, in those short stories that Miss Marple made her debut.

They were published originally as two separate batches of six stories in popular magazines between late 1927 and early 1930. The last of these short stories led directly into Miss Marple's first full-length novel *The Murder at the Vicarage* which was published in October 1930. Two years further on all of the early short stories were collected together in volume form as *The Thirteen Problems* (1932). Miss Marple then largely disappeared from public view. Over the next decade, the only indication that she hadn't been entirely forgotten was one short story called 'Miss Marple tells a Story.' That Christie was continuing to think of Miss Marple at all has recently been revealed by John Curran in his examination of Christie's working notebooks. When planning *Death on the Nile* (1937) it seems that Christie considered this, one of the most exotic of her novels, as a possible vehicle for Miss Marple. Curran tells us that a question mark was placed against the initial mention of Miss Marple, and understandably so.[2] It was, of course, Poirot who was eventually to take that celebrated trip up the Nile on the S.S. Karnak and Christie didn't turn her mind again to Miss Marple until early in the Second World War when two novels, *The Body in the Library* (1942) and *The Moving Finger* (1943), appeared in quick succession. At the same time four new short stories were published in *The Strand Magazine*.[3] There were only ever to be two more Miss Marple short stories, both of which were written for special occasions: 'Sanctuary' in 1954 and 'Greenshaw's Folly' six years later.

In addition to *Library* and *Moving Finger*, Christie revealed in her autobiography that 'during the first years of the war,' at a time when she feared she might not survive the German bombing raids on London, she wrote a further Miss Marple novel that would later become *Sleeping Murder*. Nothing was generally known about its composition at the time. The manuscript was locked away together with that of Poirot's 'last case' *Curtain*. The intention was that both novels would be published posthumously. The Miss Marple was left 'by deed of gift' to her second husband Max Mallowan, the Poirot to Rosalind Hicks, the daughter from her first marriage. Although Christie was to live for many years after the end of the war, the original plan was only slightly relaxed in order to allow *Curtain* to appear in 1975. Christie died in 1976 and, as planned, the Miss Marple novel was published shortly after her death. Christie had first called it *Murder in Retrospect* but early on had been obliged to change the title. It became *Cover her Face*. Then in 1964 P.D.James had coincidentally used that same title for her debut novel and the long-concealed *Cover her Face* was renamed once again, this time and finally as *Sleeping Murder*.[4]

In spite of this burst of wartime activity Miss Marple seemed to disappear yet again, with the first of her post-war novels, *A Murder is Announced*, not appearing until 1950. But from then on she was treated consistently. *They Do It With Mirrors* was published in 1952. It was followed by *A Pocket Full of Rye* (1953), *4.50 from Paddington* (1957) and *The Mirror Crack'd from Side to Side* (1962), with a final trilogy of Miss Marple novels still to come: *A Caribbean Mystery* (1964), *At Bertram's Hotel* (1965) and *Nemesis* (1971).

For a writer as prolific as Christie, and someone who was always willing to meet public demand as long as it was a matter of spending more hours at her desk and didn't involve any public appearances, the way in which the Miss Marple novels were published was uncharacteristically fitful. It is as though she was suffering from some kind of psychological resistance, an unwillingness to fully acknowledge Miss Marple or to move forward with her until she had the character safely settled in her own mind and was certain she could control her. In contrast to Poirot, Christie seemed reluctant to provide any personal information at all about Miss Marple.

The fundamental differences between the two detectives are epitomized by their carefully chosen names. As with Poirot, it was Jane Marple's first name that Christie wanted to stress. In linguistic terms, her surname, like Poirot's, was relatively unimportant, though of huge personal significance to Christie. Janet Morgan has explained that Marple Hall was the name of a large house in Cheshire not far from Abney Hall, the home of Christie's now married sister Madge. Christie would have known of Marple Hall from her frequent visits to her sister, and she was sufficiently struck by the unusual name to use it in an early draft of one of the Harley Quin stories 'The Dead Harlequin' which was collected in the volume *The Mysterious Mr Quin* published in April 1930. In the working draft of the story she had used Marple as the name of the family and their country house, but by the time the story was collected in volume form both names had been changed to Charnley. Marple was now transferred to a very different batch of stories which Christie was starting to work on at roughly the same time.[5] The personal connection is particularly significant because Abney Hall played an important part in Christie's disappearance. It was where she was taken by Archie after he collected her from the Harrogate Hydro in December 1927 and from where the family medical certificate was issued stating that she had been suffering from amnaesia, a view given apparent authenticity by a public statement from two doctors. The transfer of the name Marple from the Quin to the Miss Marple stories was an act that locked Jane Marple for ever into Christie's own private history.

While the full relevance of the surname would have been apparent only to Christie, Jane was as deliberate a choice as Hercule had been. Miss Marple is given one of the most ordinary and unheroic of names, a clear movement away from the pagan and the exotic. It has similarities to Christie's own name in that Agatha and Jane have both come to be regarded as quintessentially English: they also both carry connotations of goodness or graciousness as well as ordinariness and moral stability. However, by the time Christie created Miss Marple, the name Jane had taken on a slightly different and distinct image of its own. The spinster detective living in an obscure village, spending her days closely observing her neighbours' everyday behaviour and building her methods of detection on what she sees around her is a classic 'plain' Jane. Not ugly or unattractive, but commonplace. There seems to be no agreed source for the phrase that is now so strongly proverbial, but one of its likely sources does connect Miss Marple with an illustrious fictional predecessor.

Charlotte Bronte had chosen both the forename and surname of Jane Eyre to indicate contrasting qualities in her fictional heroine. Lacking the physical glamour to be a romantic lead, a role that is not conventionally open to a plain Jane, she survives and triumphs through the strong reserves of spirit, air, or 'Eyre' that are hidden within her. Whether or not Christie had these allusions consciously in mind, by 1927 when Jane Marple made her appearance, the phrase plain Jane was in common use and would have been instantly recognized as perfectly applicable to the spinster detective. She is someone whose remarkable qualities are all internal, hidden away until brought openly into play.

The name Jane was also, like that of Agatha, falling out of fashion because it had begun to carry an air of either dusty or formidable Victorian propriety, something, of course, that would be pleasing rather than worrying to Miss Marple. The little we do learn of Miss Marple's early life, in sharp contrast to that of Poirot, confirms at every point the ordinariness and respectability of her existence, and most of the information comes not, as it does with Poirot, from the author, but from either Miss Marple's own random and infrequent reminiscences or those of friends and acquaintances. This information emerges haphazardly and only when it is required either to provide a starting point for one of her cases or to justify the setting of a novel. We would never have known, for instance, that Miss Marple had an aunt who was married to the Canon of Ely if those relatives had not once taken the young Jane Marple to stay at Bertram's Hotel. This is something we learn only in the early 1960s when Christie wanted to write about crime in London and was looking for an excuse to send Miss Marple off to the metropolis. Miss Marple's curiosity to see whether the hotel she had enjoyed staying in as a young girl was still as she remembered it provided Christie not only with a convenient plot device but also a neat entry to the manipulation of memory that is a main theme of the novel.

In addition to the Canon of Ely and his wife, a fairly large number of uncles, aunts, nephews and cousins, are referred to at various times. Some of these seem to be well placed socially or financially, but the references to them are vague. Apart from the feeble niece who is helped out by Miss Marple in 'The Thumb Mark of St Peter,' Raymond West is the only one of them to appear in the novels and short stories. Even his connection is rather unclear and used by Christie mainly as a convenient plot device. In the post-war years Miss Marple is genuinely hard up and in order to move beyond St. Mary Mead, as it became increasingly important to Christie that she should, then financial help was needed. This is readily provided by Raymond West and his wife. It is thanks to their generosity that Miss Marple can convalesce on the south coast of England and in the Caribbean, stay at the fashionable Bertram's Hotel and also in the Wests' London flat. In these relatively exotic locations Miss Marple becomes involved in some of her most famous cases. There is no doubt about Raymond's affection for his aunt, and he is present as far back as 1927 to play a significant part at Miss Marple's debut, but it is never made clear what there may have been in their past relationship to encourage him to behave in the generous way he does. He is, presumably, the son of Miss Marple's only sister who is mentioned in the early short story 'The Four Suspects.' There we are told that she and the young Jane had once been taught together by a German governess, another past experience that is only invoked to help Miss Marple solve a mystery. Otherwise the sister, who isn't even named, would probably not have been introduced at all. And, of course, the reader is never actually told she was Raymond's mother.

In financial terms, the Marple family would have been comfortably off, though by no means wealthy. At the age of sixteen, whatever the nature of Jane's early education, we learn that it was enhanced by a year spent in Florence where she became friends with two American sisters. They are later married and transformed into Carrie Louise Serrocold and Ruth Van Rydock in *They Do It With Mirrors*, once again in order to set the story going and to provide it with contrasting strands. The now enormously wealthy and vain Mrs Van Rydock also reveals the surprising information that back in those younger days she had wanted to be a nun and adds, more believably, that 'you were going to nurse lepers, Jane.'

That seems a not unlikely ambition for the young Miss Marple because apart from having the Canon of Ely as an uncle, and another uncle who we learn quite coincidentally was a Canon somewhere else, Ruth Van Rydock remembers the young Jane as a 'pink and white English girl from a Cathedral Close.' Some commentators have taken these references to mean that Miss Marple's own father would have held a similar post in the church, and perhaps he did. But all we ever truly learn about him, apart from his occasional quoted words of advice to his daughter, is that he visited the Paris Exhibition which was opened in 1889. On what was presumably a different occasion, we are also told that Jane herself was once taken to Paris by her mother and grandmother.

The most fruitful of Miss Marple's memories, at least as far as providing helpful information about her character, involve the young men she might possibly have married. There were two of these. The first, recalled in *Bertram's* when she was 'such a silly girl in many ways,' caused her to 'cry herself to sleep for at least a week.' Or rather, it was her mother who caused the tears by nipping the young Jane's 'friendship so firmly in the bud.' And a good job too, Miss Marple came to believe. When she runs across the man in later years she finds him 'quite dreadful.' The second suitor, who is remembered in *Caribbean* had been 'unexpectedly warmly welcomed by her father' – the clumsy 'unexpectedly' looks significant – and was encouraged to call. But this time Miss Marple was not interested. He wasn't dreadful, just dull, 'very dull.' Miss Marple would have been in her late teens when these potential love affairs came and went, and they are all we ever learn about the romantic side of her life. Even so, it is more than we are told about her years as a young and a middle-aged woman. One moment she is 'such a silly girl,' the next an elderly lady. In between we have fifty-odd years of complete blankness.

Except for one striking exception. Several times Miss Marple refers to her considerable experience of nursing, and always as though it has some emotional meaning for her. 'I am used to sick people,' she confides in *Nemesis*. 'I have had a good deal to do with them in my time.' There are are no grounds to believe she ever worked as a nurse for her living, and, indeed, good historical reasons to suppose it highly unlikely that she would ever have done so. Nor can we assume that, like Christie, she served as a nurse during the 1914-18 war. It therefore seems likely that the nursing experience she refers to was domestic. This would mean there were two possible explanations for her spinsterhood. When she was young her marriage prospects were low because she was too bright and sharp for the men who showed an interest in her, while as she grew older much of her life was spent caring for her sick parents. Even this is, as usual, supposition.

The only aspect of Miss Marple's mysterious existence that Christie ever appeared concerned about was her age. Here was a problem shared with Poirot. Christie herself soon came to believe it had been a mistake to introduce Poirot as someone who had already enjoyed a full career in Belgium. As his new life in England advanced he became, in real terms, older and older while his personality remained fixed. There was no literary reason why this should have worried Christie. Serial heroes are not necessarily required to age at all. Some do, some don't. It depends entirely on the attitudes of their authors and whether they are willing or able to handle an ageing and therefore necessarily changing central character. Christie, though, was worried by it. She had brought about what she felt were narrative problems for herself by having to return time and again to a character whose age was fixed at some indeterminate point in the distant past.

At all times excessively cagey about Miss Marple, Christie soon began to feel herself in danger of repeating the mistake she had made with Poirot. In the first stories the question of Miss Marple's age didn't matter because she simply needed to be an old woman. As long as Christie had no long-term plans for Miss Marple no change was needed. She could stay as she was; not only old but fairly static as well. But after a while it became clear to Christie that she did want to write in a more expansive way about Miss Marple and to do so she would have to modify the original limiting image. The difficulty was that unlike Poirot who could appear in novel after novel as sprightly, dapper and essentially ageless, Miss Marple actually needed to be thought of as old. Not quite as old as she had been at the beginning, but still old. After all, her image relied heavily on her being solidly mid-Victorian, with appropriate views on everything from literature and painting to how 'gentlemen' should be entertained. These characteristics were all retained while her physical appearance was gradually adapted to fit someone of her age and class in the twentieth century. Over the years she became more physically active, taller and thinner, and appropriately dressed in good-quality functional clothes, shoes and gloves. When Crump, the surly Butler at Yewtree Lodge in *A Pocket Full of Rye* (1953) answers the door to Miss Marple he sees, 'a tall, elderly lady wearing an old-fashioned tweed coat and skirt, a couple of scarves and a small felt hat with a bird's wing.' She carries with her a 'capacious handbag' and 'an aged but good quality suitcase.' Trained to recognize 'a lady' when he sees one, Crump immediately treats Miss Marple with respect.

The ladylike qualities that Crump responds to have nothing to do with money or social position. Miss Marple has neither. Rather, they are again expressive of a respectable Victorian upbringing that had valued above all things honesty, religion, outward control, and authority. As James Cresswell observes, the recurrent description of her as upright or straight-backed denotes moral as well as physical characteristics.[6] Such qualities allow her to gain entry to places and situations that might otherwise be barred to her. That, though, is about all they can do.

For everything else she grew to depend increasingly on qualities more commonly associated with age than class. Or, more precisely in Miss Marple's world, with that classless and irritating being, an old 'pussy.'[7] She knits compulsively, has white 'fluffy' hair, blue eyes which vary from 'faded' to 'severe' according to circumstances, becomes easily confused, is inclined to 'flutter' and 'flute,' gossips whenever she gets the chance, and studies the garden of any house she visits for what it can tell her about the moral state of the owners.

Although these would come to be regarded as Miss Marple's natural defining characteristics, they are not always genuine. Often they are conscious ploys, strategies employed to enable her to gain time or knowledge when investigating a case. The knitting and gardening serve many narrative and structural purposes. They are used by her to draw attention away from her formidable intelligence, while the knitting is also symbolic of the detective slowly creating a meaningful pattern out of mystifying events. In the later novels it takes on the judgmental function of the spinning of fate or destiny, even evoking at times the gruesome *tricoteuses* of the French Revolution as Miss Marple slowly and surely draws a murderer towards the gallows.

It is largely through the conscious, often symbolic, manipulation of these generic personality traits – the knitting, fussing, fluting, absent-mindedness, gossip, and dedication to gardening – that Christie is so successful in preventing us from realizing that we know hardly anything of any substance about Miss Marple. Instead of providing a detailed or even skeletal biography or family background, Christie concentrated on creating for Miss Marple a generalized, manageable, subtly fluctuating old age. While doing so, she also reserved the right to draw attention to how impossibly aged Miss Marple must actually have been.

'Why I do believe that's old Jane Marple,' exclaims Lady Selina Hazy in *Bertram's*. 'Thought she was dead years ago. Looks a hundred.' Lady Selina, whose own age is given as sixty-five, is not the only character in these late novels perplexed by Miss Marple's longevity. One year earlier in *Caribbean* Mr Rafiel had responded to Miss Marple's demand that they join forces to prevent a further murder taking place with a bewildered: 'You're about a hundred and I'm a broken up old crock.' In fact, the estimates of Lady Selina and Mr Rafiel are on the generous side. As Christie herself had noted, Miss Marple was 'born at the age of sixty-five to seventy,' so by the mid-1960s, and allowing for the difficulties always involved in attempts to date Christie's novels, her age could have been anywhere between one hundred and three and one hundred and eight.

As the years went by Christie began to enjoy the joke about the indeterminate age of her two famous detectives and especially that of Miss Marple. *Nemesis* (1971) opens with Miss Marple reading the obituary column in *The Times* and indulging in a little of Lady Selina Hazy's competitive nature: 'Elizabeth Quantril. Eighty-five. Well, really! She had thought Elizabeth Quantril had died some years ago. Fancy her having lived so long … nobody had expected *her* to make old bones.' But at this point, Elizabeth Quantril's bones would have been youthful compared with those of Miss Marple. A few weeks further on when she joins the coach party she surveys her companions and decides that two of them are 'about seventy' and can therefore 'roughly be considered as contemporaries of her own.' *Very* roughly it must be said. At this moment in time as she sets off by coach to solve her final case Miss Marple's thoughts could reasonably have been fixed on celebrating her one hundred and fifteenth birthday.

* * *

One of the many links between Agatha Christie and Conan Doyle was that both authors soon came to feel a personal dislike for the literary detectives who had brought them fame and wealth. Doyle tried to make sure he wouldn't have to have anything more to do with Sherlock Holmes by killing him off after two series of stories, but popular outrage at this act of authorial murder forced him to bring Holmes back to life.

Christie didn't follow Doyle in trying to get rid of Poirot once and for all. She was no doubt aware that any attempt to write him out of her life would probably have been no more successful than Doyle's had been to rid himself of Holmes. But although she decided to stand by Poirot, she did so reluctantly and increasingly at a distance. She also became more and more irritated by some aspects of the personality she had, as she now came to believe, given him rather thoughtlessly at the beginning. Coming into existence as a fully formed type had tended to make him unchangeable and therefore problematic. Christie made this point herself in a newspaper article in 1938: 'Why – why – why did I ever invent this detestable, bombastic, tiresome little creature? … there have been moments when I've disliked M. Hercule Poirot very much indeed, when I have rebelled bitterly against being yoked to him for life.'[8]

Much of the trouble was caused by the way Poirot's grandiloquent pagan name clashed so incongruously with his physical and personal characteristics. In novel after novel Poirot's pomposity, foppishness, arrogance, conceit, and absurd fussiness in dress and manners are portrayed quite openly by Christie as insufferable. The unattractive nature of such qualities soon became an essential feature of his character.

The result was that the famous detective, with his high morality, Catholic religion, openly proclaimed infallibility, constant denigration of the loyal Hastings, and readiness to deliver a pompous lecture to anyone who disgrees with him, often comes over as a slightly absurd or comic figure, although far more so in the books than on television or in the cinema. Of course the other side is also given. Poirot has an appealing quaintness and can be charming and sympathetic. Although he is often extremely patronizing to Hastings this doesn't stop Poirot genuinely missing him once he had gone. There are also cases in which Poirot's humanity allows him to relax his usually inflexible attitude to murder. Even so, Christie's satirical tone and her constant critcism of him, make it clear that human sympathy is a quality Poirot notably lacks. Allowing him to survive was almost as risky as finishing him off entirely, and it took a remarkable artistic balancing act by Christie to be able to express so frankly her own dislike for Poirot without this destroying him entirely in the minds of his many devoted readers.

What aggravated this narrative difficulty was that once Hastings had gone Poirot was left starkly alone, in the spotlight, mourning the loss of his dear, dim-witted friend, but with no straight man with whom he could interact, no one to whom he could unselfconsciously display his intellect and vanity. Hastings might be brought back now and then, and Inspector Japp could be relied on to be around when needed, but these were not really solutions. Poirot simply couldn't continue to be left alone on the stage all of the time, exposed and vulnerable. He would quickly become grotesquely pompous, overbearing, too ridiculous. The only alternative was to provide him with a new companion.

Those of Christie's readers who shared this view were eager to advise her what to do. The solution they favoured was clear. They urged her to bring Poirot and Miss Marple together. Successful individually, united they would surely be invincible.

Unsurprisingly, Christie did not like the idea. In the *Autobiography* she treats it in her customary tactful, though dismissive manner. The two detectives, she explains, were both 'stars' in their very different worlds, with contrasting personalities and attitudes. Why *should* they meet? They would not get on well together. The deeper reason, though, Christie kept to herself. Uniting the two detectives would have involved artistic and personal compromises of a kind impossible for her to tolerate. She had worked hard at keeping the two apart from each other so that if she should decide to write more about Miss Marple it would be possible to do so without trapping herself in the kind of restrictions she had long ago imposed on Poirot.

And although she held back from making the point herself, she had already created a female companion for Poirot, someone she had been careful to make very different from Miss Marple, though still someone that Christie and her readers could delight in.

Ariadne Oliver had appeared in a couple of the Parker Pyne stories before being given a larger role in *Cards on the Table* (1936). She is a friend of Poirot's rather than a companion and the two are shown to get on well together, even though from the beginning her presence served to act as an oblique criticism of the overweening Belgian. *Mrs* Oliver, as she is always called, though no information about a marriage or a husband is ever given, was to serve in part as a mouthpiece for views and opinions of Christie's own that she was unwilling to voice openly. In placing her as Poirot's companion Christie knew exactly what she wanted of Mrs Oliver. It is surely significant that following Christie's perennial concern with age – her own, Poirot's and Miss Marple's – she was determined to avoid making an error over it this time. Whatever Mrs Oliver's oddities and eccentricities, she is actively middle-aged, definitely not old.

Nor was she to be placed in a position where she could possibly trespass on any future role to be taken up by Miss Marple. To ensure this, she is linked with Poirot in being given a grand classical or pagan 'Christian' name. In Greek legend, Ariadne was the daughter of Minos, the King of Crete and is best remembered in classical mythology for using a ball of thread to help Theseus find his way out of the labyrinth, the lair of the fearful Minotaur. As the solver of one of the most famous of mythological riddles Ariadne Oliver has impeccable detective credentials, and in this she also recalls Hercule/Hercules. Here again her surname is comparatively normal, though 'Oliver' does carry legendary (and indeed proverbial) connotations from having been one of Charlemagne's most celebrated paladins or knights.

The mock-heroic allusions here were clearly convenient for Christie in a variety of ways. The two women are shown to share a large number of physical, career and personality traits, though without Mrs Oliver ever becoming Christie's *alter ego* in any straightforward way. The most notable link between them is that Mrs Oliver is a writer of very popular novels which feature an idiosyncratic, immediately identifiable foreign detective. He is a Finn called Sven Hjerson, and is loathed by Mrs Oliver. Asked in *Mrs McGinty's Dead* (1952) how she invented the personal characteristics that have made him so popular, she replies, in a frustrated tone virtually identical to Christie's on Poirot: 'How do I know? … How do I know why I ever thought of the revolting man? I must have been mad. Why a Finn when I know nothing about Finland? Why a vegetarian?'

Mrs Oliver's role in the novels is, however, more complex than this kind of immediate reflection of Christie herself might suggest. For every moment when she can be accepted as a spokeswoman for Christie, there is another when she behaves or speaks in ways that Christie would never have condoned. Mrs Oliver is, notably, both a feminist and an ardent believer in the existence of female intuition. Christie, who thought that feminists were misguided and that the idea of women having some intuitive power special to them was ridicuous, enjoyed setting Mrs Oliver's outspoken support on such matters against her own more cynical view. This kind of duality is apparent throughout the Ariadne Oliver novels and allows her to serve not only as a humorous brake on Poirot's excesses but also to speak in variety of ways, from the direct to the cryptic, on Christie's behalf. And some of the allusions can come over as very cryptic and personal indeed, as in this comment from *Cards on the Table* (1936) which is offered quite gratuitously: 'A Welsh name! I never trust the Welsh! I had a Welsh nurse and she took me to Harrogate one day and went home having forgotten all about me.' At such moments we see that one important function served by Mrs Oliver was that she could be used as an early expression of the narrative playfulness to which Christie became increasingly drawn as her career progressed.

The seven novels which feature Mrs Oliver are, with the exception of *The Pale Horse* (1961), pre-eminently Poirot's novels, not hers. She is mainly a supporting character, a foil to Poirot without ever becoming too close to him or in any way like Hastings. Immensely attractive though Mrs Oliver is (and good fun as well) Poirot always remains in control of their shared exploits. Further, she is everything that Miss Marple isn't. A rumbustious, self-opinionated, flamboyant, apple-munching career novelist, she is able to interact with Poirot in ways that would have been completely beyond the ordinary yet wise and mysterious spinster of St. Mary Mead. Christie must have considered Mrs Oliver in these terms, especially as she was introduced into the Poirot novels in the very middle of the 1930s when Miss Marple was being held in abeyance and Christie remained undecided about how she should use her or whether she would ever use her again.

* * *

Following the initial flurry of activity in the years 1927 to 1932, Christie's involvement with Miss Marple became slow, fitful, almost non-existent without ever disappearing entirely. It was an intensely personal, ambiguous relationship, and in spite of the years of apparent neglect, affectionate. Nothing that Christie ever wrote about Miss Marple would contain as much as a hint of the criticism and sarcasm that was heaped regularly on Poirot. Nor was there any of the good-natured humour associated with Mrs Oliver. Yet warm as it was, Christie's personal approach to Miss Marple was also edgy and insecure; sometimes a source of comfort, sometimes of anguish. Occasionally it seems as though Christie might have regretted forming the relationship at all. And perhaps she did. For although the two women have many characteristics, attitudes and values in common, and increasingly so as the years passed, there was always to be one fundamental, carefully maintained, and extremely important, division between them.

In the portrayal of Miss Marple not only is there barely a hint of anything in her past life that might help explain how she became the woman she is, there is also apparent a clear assumption that no such knowledge is needed. Miss Marple gets along very well as she is without a past. No doubt this was a piece of convenient wish-fulfilment on Christie's part. For at the centre of her own life there was the 'disappearance,' that one huge event that everyone knew of but nobody knew anything about. There was plenty of speculation and conjecture about what might have gone on and why, but no reliable information available at all. It was once widely believed, and to a large extent still seems to be, that once that mystery was solved everything about Christie would be explained, or at least understood. But the only person who could possible satisfy this intense curiosity was Christie herself and she stubbornly refused to offer any help. Whatever had happened would remain her very own secret and guarded obsessively to prevent it from escaping her control.

Christie's habit of treating Miss Marple with extreme caution as though any frank discussion of her might reveal private confidences best kept hidden, is very much part of this extreme touchiness about all aspects of her own private life, and often her public life as well, that developed after the disppearance. She herself acknowledged the events of that time

21

as having brought about a sharp change in her personality. She claimed that her life-long shyness had been rendered chronic by her treatment at the hands of the press. It certainly appears true that the shy, though also vivacious and fun-loving young woman that Christie had once been, now became hypersensitive about all aspects of her private life. Unfortunately the reaction went even further than this. It came to embrace virtually everything that could be considered in any way remotely personal, including her writing and career, as well as her views on society, life, politics, art, literature and everything else.

The case of Miss Marple epitomizes the dilemma that Christie had created for herself as well as the difficulties involved in overcoming it. She must, surely, have been conscious, to some extent or other, of the intimate connection between her own life and that of Miss Marple. If not, why was she always so defensive on the subject, unwilling for many years to engage fully with Miss Marple yet apparently not able to to leave her alone? By the time a sustained willingness to write about her did emerge in the 1950s Christie had long been guarding her fictional creation with a shield of half-truths and misinformation that satisfied nobody and merely encouraged more speculation. Complete silence clearly wasn't practicable, though it might have made more sense. After all, the village detective's origins and early development were tied inextricably to that period of Christie's life that she herself would happily have wiped entirely from her memory.

Chapter 2

Enter Miss Marple:
'The Tuesday Night Club'

The trouble that Christie took to distance herself from Miss Marple was extreme to the point of being paranoiac. Not only was she generally unwilling to talk about Miss Marple, she didn't even like to acknowledge that she had played any active part in creating her. She preferred to claim that Miss Marple had crept up on her unobserved, furtively, surreptitiously, taking possession. She described the process as having involved no deliberation, no advance planning, no conscious will. In *An Autobiography*, the most celebrated female detective in literary history is described as having 'insinuated' herself 'so quietly' into Christie's life that her moment of arrival was barely noticed. Even recalling the publication of the first Miss Marple novel, *The Murder at the Vicarage*, failed to stir Christie's obstinate memory: 'I cannot remember where, when or how I wrote it, why I came to write it, or even what suggested to me that I should select a new character – Miss Marple – to act as the sleuth in the story.'

It was not always possible for her to be so forgetful. Elsewhere in the *Autobiography* she acknowledged that Miss Marple must have owed something to her two mid-Victorian grandmothers who were known within the family as Auntie-Grannie and Granny B. They were sisters and lived in different parts of London, Auntie-Grannie (who was comfortably-off) in Ealing which Christie remembered as having 'all the romance of a foreign country,' and Granny B. (who was relatively poor) in Bayswater. Every Sunday, at Auntie-Grannie's imposing house, they would entertain relatives and their eccentric circle of friends, or the 'Ealing cronies' as Christie dubbed them, to a massive 'midday dinner.'

Afterwards, they all slept for a 'at least an hour' and when the guests had departed the sisters had tea. Granny B. then went home. The young Agatha would often attend these gatherings and was clearly influenced by them. Here, she may well have picked up some hints for a future Miss Marple. No doubt she was also encouraged to develop both her romantic view of the Victorians and her life-long passion for food.

In addition to the Ealing connection, it was Christie herself who proposed Caroline Sheppard in *The Murder of Roger Ackroyd* as a possible forerunner of Miss Marple, and Christie again who went much further than this to suggest that her portrayal of the village community in *Roger Ackroyd* must have meant that she had many of the characters who would eventually people St. Mary Mead 'lined up below the borderline of consciousness, ready to come to life and step out on to the stage.' Such an admission would normally seem to indicate a high degree of self-awareness in an author, but not Christie. She was still happy to insist that when she started to write *Vicarage* she had no idea what made her think of Miss Marple as the central character, and then, just a few paragraphs after making *that* assertion, refer to having published a group of Miss Marple short stories three years before the novel. There is no awareness of any inconsistency in these or other similar statements, and no way of knowing whether they can be attributed to a faulty memory or deviousness. The reader is simply left to assume that Miss Marple was little more than the arbitrary product of one of Christie's occasional flurries of writing activity. It was an easy enough assumption for an author as prolific as Christie to get away with.

After the prolonged composition and publication of *Styles*, books and stories flowed from her in an apparently unstoppable, barely considered manner. They were impressively varied as well. Poirot was her mainstay, represented by a very large number of short stories, but she did not focus exclusively on him. Nor was it yet obvious that he was destined for massive popularity or that Christie would continue to write so much about him.

Along with the Poirot short stories she was writing thrillers of the kind associated with Edwardian bestsellers like Edgar Wallace and E. Phillips Oppenheim. This was something she would always enjoy doing, even though she displayed little real talent for it. One of the lasting features of these rambling narratives, so different from the tightly constructed detective stories at which she came to excel, was Christie's early engagement with young, highly intelligent characters, notably women, who were drawn from the fun-loving iconoclastic side of the 1920s. Her bright young married couple Tommy and Tuppence Beresford who were introduced in *The Secret Adversary* (1922) and were to recur throughout her career as detectives and special agents, belong here. And so, from the best of her thrillers *The Man in the Brown Suit* (1924), does Anne Beddingfield, the prototype of a number of aggressively independent, feisty young women who would feature in some of Christie's later and more celebrated novels.

Christie's industriousness in the opening years of the 1920s might seem to indicate that she had adjusted effortlessly to literary professionalism, but the haphazard nature of her work also suggests that she had yet to settle on a definite path. She was working off the unsatisfactory contract she had signed with Bodley Head and aware that once this was done she would have the freedom to secure much better terms. Meanwhile she was feeling her way as an author, testing out various possibilities. With periodical editors seeking from her as many short stories as she was capable of writing, a demand she was ony too willing to meet, it seems hard to believe that she might still have considered herself as mainly a wife and only secondly a writer. But she liked to claim that this was the case, and it was possibly true, early on at least. Certainly at this time the unevenness of her work as well as its diversity can be taken to mean that she was moving with events rather than dictating them, taking up what came to hand, at best seeking to discover what kind of literary talent she had or, perhaps, whether she had much literary talent at all.

That doubt was resolved decisively in June 1926 with the publication of *The Murder of Roger Ackroyd*. It was a commercial and a controversial triumph, a detective novel of a standard far above anything she had written before; unexpected, challenging, set expertly within a skilfully realized village community; challenging to the reader; a dramatic monologue of outrageous daring. To the present day it is accepted as a landmark in the history of detective fiction. It firmly established Christie as a major talent and dispelled any lingering doubts she may have felt about her ability as a writer. It also marked the apotheosis of Hercule Poirot.

So prominent did he now become in Christie's career that most of the other detectives she introduced in the 1920s never even began to challenge his prominence. They attracted admiring readers, as did virtually everything Christie ever wrote, but they lacked the secure commercial identity of a Poirot. This did not matter much to Christie who turned to them mainly as private pleasures. Mr Parker Pyne's exploits were employed for a special kind of light romantic short story; Tommy and Tuppence provided an occasional outlet for thrillers with a gentle domestic tone; while Harley Quin and Mr Satterthwaite allowed Christie to express her long fascination with the *Commedia dell'Arte* and to speculate on artistic and philosophical matters. Even today it is difficult to read any of these books without feeling them to have been personal to her in ways that the Poirot novels never were.

At the start she probably thought of Miss Marple in much the same way as these other miscellaneous literary detectives, a character in a story that could follow the example of *Roger Ackroyd* by being set in a small village of the kind she felt had proved unsuitable for Poirot. Christie didn't even need to create a new leading character to be her village detective. After all, she had Caroline Sheppard ready to hand and was fully aware of it. As things turned out, however, Caroline Sheppard was never to appear in Christie's fiction again. She was quite suddenly displaced by Miss Marple who came into being a short time after *Roger Ackroyd*. And Miss Marple was a very different type of character from Caroline Sheppard.

* * *

The publication of *Roger Ackroyd* should have made 1926 a year of personal triumph for Christie. It turned out to be a prolonged nightmare, engaging her in distressing personal and public experiences that would, literally, haunt her for ever. It is now reasonable to assume there will never be an explanation of what exactly happened to Christie at this time that is capable of satisfying everyone interested in the issue.[1] Nor is it my intention to rehearse those long-standing disputes. But as they were the immediate setting for the emergence of Miss Marple, it is necessary to offer here a brief outline of the main events, uncontroversially so I trust.

In the summer that *Roger Ackroyd* was published, Archie told Agatha he had fallen in love with a woman called Nancy Neele. He wished to marry her and asked Agatha to agree to a divorce. There was some half-hearted talk of them staying together, but by December any thoughts of reconciliation felt pointless and Archie left Styles, their house in Sunningdale that had been named after Agatha's first published novel. On the evening of Friday 3 December, Agatha also left Styles. Her abandoned car was found the following morning, with no indication of what had happened to her. She seemed to have disappeared without trace and there were press and police campaigns to find her. After ten days of massive publicity she was identified as a guest staying at the Hydropathic Hotel in Harrogate, Yorkshire, under the name of Mrs Neele. On 14 December Archie came to Harrogate and identified his wife.

For many commentators, at the time and since, the family argument that Agatha had been suffering from amnesia lacked any serious credibility. The favoured alternative theory was that Agatha had faked the disappearance, some said to spite her husband, others to gain publicity for her work or to test out the plot of a new novel. It would have been easy for people at the time to accept this kind of explanation. The fiendishly clever *Roger Ackroyd* was much in the public mind and there was open speculation that nothing was beyond the ingenuity of the person who could write such a book! Even before the disappearance, some reviewers had been keen to pronounce it dishonest for having flaunted the fair-play rule that was assumed to govern detective fiction. What chance for her now? Agatha Christie, the inventor of the most teasing puzzle yet to fascinate the world of detective fiction had herself become an equally strange, fascinating mystery.

While public interest flourished, the private aspects of the affair were settled with surprising speed. The divorce was granted in April 1928 and finalized six months later. Archie and Nancy Neele were quickly married. Totally unprepared for the situation in which she now found herself, Christie was forced to build a new life of a kind that would earlier have seemed alien to her. She never spoke publicly about the disappearance and she never wrote openly about it. If others insisted on trying to explain it they would have to do so without her help or encouragement. Inevitably her intransigence served only to feed the mystery that had begun on the evening of 3 December 1926 when she drove away from Styles in the 'grey bottle-nosed Morris Cowley' car that, encouraged by Archie, she bought with her own money and loved initially, and ironically, for the liberating effect it promised to have on her everyday life.

The image of herself in the period immediately following the break with Archie that Christie wanted future generations to accept is presented with deceptive care in *An Autobiography*. It is of someone utterly lonely, abandoned, betrayed, hunted down by a ferocious pack of press wolves, and forced by financial hardship to honour publishing contracts in which she no longer had any faith. She claimed especially to loathe the two books she was currently working on: *The Mystery of the Blue Train*, the intended follow-up to *Roger Ackroyd*, and *The Big Four*, a collection of earlier Poirot adventures hastily cobbled together for publication in volume form. One of the main reasons why the break-up of her marriage was so devastating to her is to be found in her absorbing evocation, also in the *Autobiography*, of what courtship and marriage meant to young women of her background in Edwardian England. It helps explain why Christie makes no attempt to interpret her personal situation in positive rather than negative ways. She was keen to emphasize what had been lost and totally unwilling to recognize that new opportunities might have emerged or that there was any possibility of a fresh life ahead to be worth embracing.

Yet, in spite of her calculated attempts in the *Autobiography* to present a contrary view, the line that Christie actually followed was extremely positive, though grudgingly and resentfully taken, as though she wanted nothing to do with any of it. The depression was real enough, and so were the indications of a strong recovery. Late in 1928, shortly after the divorce had been finalized, Christie took the sudden decision to travel alone on the Orient Express to Baghdad. Even in the relatively liberated 1920s it was a daring thing for an attractive divorced woman to do. It was on this trip that she met the archaeologist Max Mallowan. The two were married in 1930 and Christie entered into an entirely different way of life.

It may well be, as we have been told constantly by commentators, that Mrs Mallowan, the woman, would never cease to love Archie

Christie and was always to regret that she hadn't worked harder to save her first marriage, yet there also seems little doubt that Agatha Christie the burgeoning writer and artist gained far more than she lost by the divorce. Her second marriage brought her personal security, travel, new scenes, fresh ideas and atmosphere for her fiction, inspiration for many of her finest books, and a degree of intellectual stimulation from Max and his academic colleagues that she welcomed and made good use of in her work. Little of this would ever have come to her from Archie.

And what was true of the active nature of Christie's personal response to her depressed state following the break with Archie applied also to her situation as a writer. As has often been recognized, she could not possibly have been as worryingly short of money as she claimed, and while it is completely understandable that she should have disliked the books she was working on at that time her position as far as publishing was concerned was far more manageable than she made it out to be. She was now rebuilding her writing career from a position of acknowledged success and, admittedly, some public notoriety as well. In addition to the comfortable sales of her novels, newspaper editors were eager to obtain serial rights from her, and the money they offered was very substantial indeed. Nor was she in any sense being left to settle these financial and publishing issues by herself. The days of her being taken advantage of by an unscrupulous publisher were gone. She now had the support of an experienced agent and a leading publisher. *Roger Ackroyd* had proved to her that she possessed the talent to be a professional author, and the split from Archie forced her to accept that position.

Christie's immediate response to the terrible personal crisis of 1927 was to indulge in one of the frenzies of writing that always accompanied personal crises in her life. The customary industriousness increased spectacularly. First, she cleared away the two books she would always love to hate. *The Big Four* was the only Christie title to be published in 1927, while *The Blue Train* was finally published early in the following year. Even as these dispiriting tasks were being completed she had begun a series of literary experiments. She turned back to Tommy and Tuppence with *Partners in Crime*, continued to develop Mr Harley Quin, wrote a play and a thriller, and *Giant's Bread* (1930), the first of the series of novels written under the pseudonym Mary Westmacott. The work of this time has the appearance not only of having been written arbitrarily but also of being published in the same way. So much so that Janet Morgan, even when working from Christie's own papers, has admitted to finding it difficult to establish a reliable order of composition for the books and stories which appeared in 1930.[2]

Poirot was left out of this creative flurry though his absence was more than made up for by the introduction of Miss Marple. Not only was she Christie's most important literary achievement in the few years immediately following the disappearance, she is also the character whose creation is most intimately indebted to that time of personal obscurity and pain.

That this has never been sufficiently recognized is due largely to the difficulty identified by Janet Morgan of fixing reliable dates of composition for works of this period. The dates of the first publication of her short stories have also been uncertain. It has long been common for even otherwise responsible writers on Christie to refer to *The Murder at the Vicarage* as though it marked the first appearance in print of Miss Marple and to the short stories as though they were only published after the novel. Even when the stories are properly acknowledged as preceding *Vicarage*, there is often an accompanying vagueness about where, as well as when, they were actually published: sometimes the details are ignored, sometimes the stories are attributed to entirely wrong magazines. On a point of accuracy alone it is worth getting the facts straight, and, owing to recent research, this is now less of a problem.[3]

Bibliographical accuracy, though, is not the only issue at stake. Far more is involved. Miss Marple was not just a part of this particular spell of literary activity. She played a leading role in it. And, as far as Christie's recovery is concerned, an inspirational one. Without the disappearance we might never have had Miss Marple at all.

Christie must have started writing about her by the summer of 1927 or even earlier that year. This would have been within six months of the disappearance having been resolved. She continued to write about Miss Marple in a thoroughly businesslike manner through the spells of depression, the wrangling over divorce proceedings, the distasteful revisions to *The Blue Train*, any psychotherapy she may or may not have undergone, the divorce itself, Archie and Nancy's marriage, her adventurous trip to the Middle East, her meeting with and marriage to Max Mallowan, and even for up to two years after she had become Mrs Mallowan.

Yet it was during this extraordinarily traumatic yet fertile time of approximately five years from 1927 to 1932, that, according to the account given in *An Autobiography*, Miss Marple was 'insinuating' herself so quietly into Christie's consciousness that her arrival went virtually unnoticed!

Christie's dislike of *The Blue Train* has always been acknowledged by her biographers to be especially revealing of her frame of mind at this turning point in her life, and rightly so. Barely concealed by the sensational murder, is a story of casual love affairs, unhappy marriages, divorce, and the difficulty of choosing between reliable and unreliable suitors. All of this is easily related to Christie's own situation while she was struggling to write the book. So is the nature of the heroine, Katherine Grey, an attractive single woman of thirty-three who is suddenly released from her tedious life as a paid companion to an elderly widow Mrs Harfield and strikes out on her own. The small details of Katherine's life before she attains independence are of particular interest. She is living in a village in Kent. Mrs Harfield's forename we learn near the close of the book is Jane, which need not be significant, but the name of the village has to be. It is called St. Mary Mead, and it would soon be requisitioned by Christie to become the permanent home of Miss Jane Marple.

Very soon! Indeed, the crossover of village names seems to indicate that Christie was beginning to think about Miss Marple while she was still hurriedly working on *The Blue Train* early in 1927. After all the delays, *The Blue Train* was eventually serialized in *The Star* newspaper in Febraty 1928 before being published in book form the following month.[4] The first Miss Marple story had appeared the previous December. This means that in the topsy-turvy world of Christie's publications at this time, the Miss Marple stories (and *her* St. Mary Mead) actually began appearing in print before *The Blue Train* (and Katherine Grey's St. Mary Mead).

Christie seems to have regarded the St. Mary part of the name as generic for English villages: much earlier she had made Styles St. Mary the village base of her first novel. The priorities, though, are clear. Styles St. Mary would reappear just once again in Christie's fiction, many years later in *Curtain*, so that it could serve as the setting of Poirot's last as well as his first case in England. St. Mary Mead in Kent was never to be heard of again, but it was transferred to a different unnamed county not all that far away and established as Miss Marple's home village. Katherine Grey was to disappear as well, though not before she begins to develop an attitude that would become a Miss Marple trademark: 'Oh, dear,' Katherine thought to herself, 'how extraordinarily alike the world seems to be everywhere! People were always telling me things in St. Mary Mead, and it is just the same thing here.' The St. Mary Mead that was a central preoccupation of Christie's mind for the next five years was already being tested as a training ground for Miss Marple. Even so, whatever the similarity of the names, the mood was quite new. *The Blue Train* would always be associated by Christie with personal humiliation and loss; Miss Marple with rehabilitation and growth.

* * *

The now named and domiciled spinster detective made her debut in a story called 'The Tuesday Night Club' which was published in the Christmas number of *The Royal Magazine* in December 1927. This was the first anniversary, virtually to a day, of Christie's disappearance. Five further Miss Marple stories were then published consecutively in the *Royal*, one a month until May 1928. In the following year Christie wrote a further batch of six Miss Marple short stories which were published between December 1929 and May 1930, once again month by month, though in a different magazine, this time *The Story-Teller*.

The tone of 'The Tuesday Night Club' is totally unlike the frenetic atmosphere of *The Blue Train*. The story opens quietly, domestically, with the air of something of a set piece, as though being presented on stage. Miss Marple is at home in her handsome cottage in St. Mary Mead, situated in an unspecified spot in the Home Counties: 'The room was an old one with broad black beams across the ceiling,' and 'furnished with good old furniture that belonged to it.' She is entertaining guests invited by her nephew, the very superior modern novelist Raymond West who is visiting Miss Marple together with his fiancée, an assertive modern painter called Joyce Lemprière who will eventually marry Raymond: he actually proposes to her during one of these early stories. When they are married, Joyce conventionally changes her second name to West, and, less conventionally, her first name to Joan, presumably because of a memory lapse or change of mind on Christie's part. The principal guest is Sir Henry Clithering, a recently retired Commissioner of Scotland Yard. He is meeting Miss Marple for the first time, but will quickly become a great admirer and make himself indispensable to her career as a detective. Also present are Dr Pender, a clergyman, and Mr Petherick a solicitor. These are the characters who feature in the first batch of six stories.

Miss Marple herself is introduced sitting 'erect' in a 'big grandfather chair' presiding over her guests rather than caring for them. Her dress is described with the kind of attention usually given to historical costumes:

> Miss Marple wore a black brocade dress, very
> much pinched in round the waist. Mechlin lace was
> arranged in a cascade down the front of the bodice.
> She had on black lace mittens, and a black lace cap
> surmounted the piled-up masses of her snowy hair.

She is knitting 'something white and soft and fleecy' and viewing the guests 'with faded blue eyes, benignant and kindly.' Later she is shown with 'an old lace fichu draped round her shoulders.' Raymond, we are told, admires his aunt's personality which he sees as being at one with her home, and on this he certainly seems to be right. This Miss Marple is both very old and very stately, set regally on her grandfather chair, framed by the seasoned wood of an ancestral home. She is not only Victorian in manner. In some respects she actually *is* a reflection of Queen Victoria, the aged monarch much as she was presented iconically during her last years, seated here in a throne-like stance, dressed in heavy black.[5]

This image was deliberately antiquated. After all, the year of publication was 1927 and the story was not being offered in any way as historical.

The old-fashioned element was further reinforced by Gilbert Wilkinson's illustrations of Miss Marple that accompanied the stories in *The Royal Magazine*. His was the first ever visual image of her. Wilkinson kept faith with the historical pose, but lessened the image of Victorian severity by giving Miss Marple eyes that are large and expressive rather than faded, and thin tight lips that are very clearly controlling inner thoughts. She is kindly, but knowing or quizzical rather than benignant, and totally in control of the proceedings.

Prompted by Raymond's speculation on 'what class of brain' is most successful at unravelling some of the mysteries of life that otherwise seem to remain unexplained, the guests agree to form themselves into a club which will meet weekly to consider mysteries of this kind. Each of them in turn has to outline a mystery they have come across personally and the others will try to advance a solution to it. It's really little more than a party game, but as Joyce points out the participants make up a 'representative gathering,' one that is particularly fitted to play this particular game. Between them they represent literature, art, the police, the law, medicine, and religion. Miss Marple is the only one of them who doesn't have any kind of professional qualification. At first Joyce thinks that fussy, aged, unmarried Aunt Jane will be no good at their game or even interested in taking part in it and tries to sideline her.

But Miss Marple insists and offers as her special kind of qualification the 'insight into human nature' that has come to her from living for so many years in St. Mary Mead. The game is started by Sir Henry, fittingly so as being the only person present connected professionally with crime and detection. One by one the mysteries are aired, the guests confess themselves bewildered, and Miss Marple intervenes to provide the solution. Gradually her aloof image drops away and we have revealed the more mundane, common-sense approach of the future solver of much larger problems: 'Well, my dear … human nature is much the same everywhere, and, of course, one has opportunities of observing it at close quarters in a village.'

There were some eighteen months between the close of the first six stories (May 1928) and the start of the second (December 1929). The same basic game-playing pattern as before is followed except that the venue shifts away from Miss Marple's rather oppressive cottage. The stagey setting was clearly felt to have served its limited purpose. The new meetings take place in the home of Colonel and Mrs 'Dolly' Bantry. Sir Henry Clithering is still present. He is visiting the Bantrys who are old friends. Seeking to entertain him, Dolly asks if there is anyone living locally he would like to meet. To her astonishment he names Miss Marple. 'Do you mean,' asks Dolly, 'you would like me to ask *her* to dinner?' The Bantrys hardly know Miss Marple except as the 'typical old maid of fiction … Quite a dear, but hopelessly behind the times' and can't understand how Sir Henry can have been so impressed by her on his earlier visit to the village. But they follow his wishes and the dinner party goes ahead.

In purely physical terms Miss Marple is much as she was in the earlier stories. When she arrives, she is still wearing her black lace mittens with the old lace fichu draped round her shoulders and a piece of lace over her white hair. The other guests, however, are new. Joining the Bantrys and Sir Henry are Dr Lloyd, a village doctor, and Jane Helier 'the beautiful and popular actress' who replaces Raymond and Joyce as a representative of the larger world of metropolitan sophistication. Once again the game of unsolved mysteries is played, and once again Miss Marple emerges the clear victor. The Bantrys' prejudice against her evaporates and in many of the later novels they are to be found, together with Sir Henry, among her very closest friends and admirers. After playing his part in this second batch of short stories, Dr Lloyd moved entirely out of Christie's fictional world while Jane Helier was to make only one further brief appearance, in the much later short story 'Strange Jest.'

The twelfth and last of the stories, 'The Affair at the Bungalow,' was published in *The Story-Teller* in May 1930. Christie, however, was far from finished with her new detective. In October of that same year Miss Marple made a triumphant appearance in her first full-length novel, *The Murder at the Vicarage* which was in turn followed by a new Miss Marple story called 'Death by Drowning.' It appeared by itself in *Nash's Pall Mall Magazine* in November 1931 and was then collected together with the earlier twelve Miss Marple stories and published as a kind of coda to *The Thirteen Problems* in June 1932.

This brought to a temporary close a body of work, produced consistently over a period of five years, that Christie had begun in a mood of personal despair following the break up of her marriage and the hated publicity provoked by her disappearance. Out of Christie's attempt to suppress her mood of personal desperation by confronting new experiences, there had come a flurry of experimental writing which included the creation of a literary character who would eventually become one of the world's most popular literary detectives.

Just how conscious Christie was of this creative process is unknowable. Yet some guiding drive or purpose there must surely have been, whether personal or public, conscious or subconscious, or, as seems most likely, a combination of all four. But as any answer would never come from Christie herself, it needs to be sought within the work she produced so intensely, compulsively, obsessively even, while refusing ever to provide any reliable information about what she felt or thought she was doing. In this case, any further understanding has to reside in the original batch of 'Tuesday Night Club' stories. To tease it out we need to return, from a different angle, to the question of what drew Christie to the idea of Miss Marple in the first place.

* * *

The central drama played out within the Tuesday Night Club is a classic early twentieth-century clash between the generations. At this time of intense personal insecurity Christie no doubt had, as she herself suggested, her mother, Auntie-Grannie, and Grannie B. much in mind, and it may be that Auntie-Grannie's physical appearance in particular made a distinct contribution to Miss Marple's initial visual image.[6] This apart, the creation of Miss Marple owes little more to Christie's close relatives than their general air of common sense and their unwillingness to take people at face value. In the *Autobiography* the two grandmothers are portrayed as very lively, even racy, urban, flirtatious and much concerned with spending money. None of this is remotely like the original Miss Marple who is dignified, calm, ladylike, necessarily careful with her money, and in possession of unshakeable moral standards and literary and artistic tastes, all of which are traditionally and conventionally mid-Victorian. She is a visible representative of a bygone age.

Several of the other guests are not a great deal younger than Miss Marple, and are personally sympathetic to her. But strikingly different from everyone else are Raymond West, the son of Miss Marple's shadowy unnamed sister, and Joyce Lemprière. They represent modern literature and painting and also a younger generation that is in every respect aggressively up to date and intolerant of the past, especially that of their mid-Victorian grandparents. Joyce Lemprière 'the artist, with her close-cropped black head and queer hazel-green eyes' might have been a description taken straight from D.H.Lawrence, a novelist that the young Christie had read with great enthusiasm. Raymond and Joyce both openly mock the Victorian artists and poets admired by Miss Marple. Their own work – his novels relentlessly 'unpleasant,' her paintings aggressively non-figurative – epitomize the new artistic standards that have rendered their Victorian predecessors as naïve and outmoded as they assume Aunt Jane herself to be.

The mood of anti-Victorianism that is so powerfully present in the social and artistic values of the 1920s is often assumed to be a direct product of the First World War, but that is to oversimplify the historical situation. Certainly the war came to represent in the most appalling of ways the final death of Victorian idealism as well as the definitive formation of literary and artistic modernism, but the process was slow and tortuous, its roots stretching back into the last twenty years of Queen Victoria's long reign.[7] The writers and artists who established themselves so firmly as the leaders of the whole series of artistic revolutions by the 1920s – whether Joyce and Lawrence, Pound and Eliot, or Picasso and Braque along with hosts of other writers, painters, and musicians – were, in terms of birth and early upbringing, products of the last two decades of the nineteenth century and in revolt against everything their parents' generation represented.

In Britain, one of the most explicit attacks was delivered by Lytton Strachey, born in 1880, who in *Eminent Victorians* (1918) and *Queen Victoria* (1921) offered a collective portrait of the Victorians as fake, false, prudish, hypocritical. The term that came to describe the process, using a current piece of 1920s American slang, was 'debunking.' The mid-Victorians were the prime targets. For any self-respecting young person in the 1920s they could only be understood by first removing from them all their characteristic humbug, nonsense, 'bunk' or 'bunkum.' Raymond West and Joyce Lemprière are classic debunkers of the 1920s, and Miss Marple is the defending counsel for mid-Victorianism.

Agatha Christie herself was at one with the pioneering modernists in being born a late Victorian who survived the First World War to establish herself as a writer in the 1920s. She was their exact contemporary, though is not often thought of as such. In the culturally divisive language of the time which was itself a product of combative modernist attitudes, she would eventually come to be regarded as 'lowbrow' while they were 'highbrow.' Christie was very conscious of being classified in this way, and she was always strongly aware of the kind of denigration the label carried. Her resentment at it often found expression in irony or sarcasm. In her second marriage, she was acutely aware of being someone commonly thought of as a lowbrow united with a husband who was widely regarded as a highbrow. It was a situation, in its domestic context at least, she grew to accept and to regard with good, if double-edged, humour.[8]

It had not always been so. Together with her first husband, the handsome young war hero Archie, recreated idealistically as Tommy to her own Tuppence, she had been very much part of the bright-young-thing mood of the 1920s. She was drawn especially to the compulsive brittle irreverence that had, strange as it may now sound, much in common with Lytton Strachey and other members of the Bloomsbury Group. In her case, though, it was related more directly to P.G.Wodehouse, a writer she was always to admire and who returned her admiration. Christie's own contribution to the experimental literature of the 1920s took the form of the daringly modern narrative of *Roger Ackroyd*.

The impact of that book and Christie's subsequent work should not be underestimated or placed too easily in a totally separate category of light literature. The immediate literary atmosphere of the time, and of Christie working away experimentally at *Roger Ackroyd*, was far broader and more varied than that assumption allows, though it is true enough that its urgent combative tone was being dictated by literary Modernism.

Ulysses and *The Waste Land* had been published just four years before *Roger Ackroyd*, while *Mrs Dalloway* was published one year earlier and *To the Lighthouse* one year later. Aldous Huxley, the type of intellectually superior novelist, dealing with modern life in determinedly unpleasant ways, who could possibly have provided a hint for the kind of novelist portrayed by Christie in Raymond West, was already known for *Crome Yellow* (1921) and *Antic Hay* (1923), with *Point Counter Point* still to come in 1928. Joyce Lemprière stands for the equivalent movement in painting, a decisive shift away from representation in favour of abstraction. Miss Marple is fully aware of what is involved here and enjoys taunting Joyce with admiring references to Victorian painters. This was not Christie's own attitude. On the contrary, Christie's own early artistic interests, in painting and music as well as literature, were more in line with the Moderns than they would later seem to be. And why not? They were, after all, her very own generation and informed references to them are to be found scattered throughout her work.

Then, abruptly, late in 1926, everything fell apart as Christie herself became a victim of the pleasure-seeking, sexually liberated, iconoclastic 1920s. It is this that provides the basic context of the Victorian versus Modern clashes at the Tuesday Night Club. Yearning for some kind of stability Christie sets Miss Marple firmly and safely back with the mid-Victorians, while she herself balances the succeeding generations, unable and unwilling to condemn the Moderns yet not at all sure what exactly she can salvage from them. For Christie, Miss Marple was a retreat from the gaiety and pain of the age, even a retreat from youth itself. Although in one sense warmly reminiscent of Christie's mother Clara Miller and Auntie-Grannie and Grannie B., any incongruous personal connotations they may have had are withheld from Miss Marple. Instead, they are transformed into impersonal representatives of an unchanging and unchallenged morality. Miss Marple is the classic spinster, unmarried and with none of the disturbing clutter of marriage or divorce hanging about her, as it so obviously was at this time for Christie herself. Miss Marple is old, very old, as old as Queen Victoria, with no danger of her ever being thought of as sexually attractive, or of drawing upon herself any of the destructive trends of the twentieth century. Her own past is a comforting void, not up for discussion or dispute.

Her literary and artistic tastes are provocatively invoked in order to taunt the debunking modernism of Raymond West and Joyce Lemprière. At one point, Joyce expresses surprise that 'Aunt Jane' hasn't had anything to say about the case under discussion and asks whether she has an opinion. Miss Marple answers rather pettishly: 'You wouldn't like my opinion, dear. Young people never do, I notice. It is better to say nothing.' Joyce responds with a brisk: 'Nonsense, Aunt Jane; out with it.' And that's exactly what Aunt Jane does, 'it' being not only a complete solution to the current problem up for discussion but also a charge against Joyce and Raymond that they have been unable to see the truth for themselves because they are too 'credulous and easily gulled.'

And the attitudes operating here are present throughout the original six short stories. Raymond and Joyce are always sure they are right and, when tested against their ancient old-fashioned aunt, are always shown to be wrong. What they lack is wisdom. This can only come with age and experience of life, with a passion for watching and observing people, with a growth of tolerance and understanding. Miss Marple possesses all of these qualities and they will, eventually, turn her into a great detective. But here, at the start, she is first and foremost a defiant personification of Christie's lost stability, so unyielding that all fashions and trends, all modern creeds and beliefs, even the twentieth century itself, are obliterated by her.

That kind of stark superiority was perfect for the atmosphere of the Tuesday Night Club. It allowed Miss Marple to triumph over arrogant youth, and Christie to distance herself from all it represented. But the pose which would, understandably enough, have felt so immediately comforting to Christie was necessarily static and recognized as such. Queen Victoria-Marple may seem to know it all, but she will never convince others of her wisdom as long as she remains comfortably settled in her grandfather-chair throne. It is not enough for Miss Marple, however right she feels herself to be, simply to put down Raymond and Joyce. They can hardly be expected to take much notice of her or believe that she always knows better than them. In terms of the arts they practice they cannot be other than as they are, and it is notable that while Miss Marple may not like what they do, she is enormously proud of their achievements, especially the success of Raymond's novels. After all, they are firmly of their own time, blessed or cursed with its strengths and weaknesses, and theirs is the world in which Miss Marple will be obliged to operate if she is to have any future at all.

Her inherited Victorian wisdom must remain, but in order to be more widely accepted it has to be applied to ways of life that belong firmly to the twentieth century, to the present rather than the past. That is crucial, whether or not she is correct in her belief that the problems to be faced are much the same as they always have been. The game organized by Raymond and Joyce was a useful starting point for Christie, but it could never be a sufficient forum for Miss Marple. In order to move on it was necessary for her to prove herself in the real world; in effect, to be convincingly released from the confines Christie had imposed on her in these very first stories.

Chapter 3

Village Detection

For anyone observing the young Agatha Christie's career as it developed in the mid-1920s, the earliest Miss Marple stories could well have been regarded as a regrettable step backwards, a personal retreat from the narrative complexity of *Roger Ackroyd*, a denial of edgy modernity in favour of the more distant comfort of mid-Victorian values. It would have been a reasonable position to take, though not for long. As the Miss Marple short stories accumulate they mirror Christie's own rapid growth at this time. Just as the negative image of herself that she liked to promote following the break with Archie was quickly contradicted by a flurry of new writing, her sudden decision to take the Orient Express to Baghdad, and a second marriage, so, within the same period of time Miss Marple was transformed from a chair-bound relic of Victorian stability into a a very distinctive kind of twentieth-century detective.

Christie's initial concern was simply to establish a stable, recognizable image for Miss Marple, providing her with a setting within which she could effectively display the special skills she had revealed in those first stories. This was achieved with impressive speed. It is made immediately clear that Miss Marple's superiority to the other members of the Tuesday Night Club comes from the 'insight into human nature' she has gained from closely observing life over so many years in St. Mary Mead, and this claim is underpinned by the theory of 'village parallels.' Here are the basic qualities that were to serve her faithfully throughout her long career, though at the beginning the problems set up for her to solve are hardly worthy of her formidable personality. Too often they appear contrived and rely for their effect on supernatural or melodramatic tricks.

Nor, at first, did Miss Marple's explanations of how she solves the problems carry much conviction. The solutions she offers tend to rest less on any deep insight into human nature than on a large general knowledge that might well be available to anyone who has happened to live long enough. For no very good reason, Miss Marple alone appears able to give a culinary rather than a financial meaning to the phrase 'hundreds and thousands,' to remember having played with 'disappearing ink' as a child, and to know that a 'real' gardener wouldn't work on a Whit Monday. Within the first batch of stories, it is only in the 'The Bloodstained Pavement' that we find the chilling human viciousness that would come to underlie so much of Christie's best work. It was typical of Christie's astuteness that she quickly saw the potential of the basic plot in that particular story and kept it on hand to be reused more than once in the future.

Eighteen months later, in the second batch of stories, Miss Marple was outwardly much as she had been before; a very old woman dressed in the same out-moded manner though still the star of the show, more mentally alert and quicker on the uptake than anyone else. The problems set for discussion were once again being explored within the confines of a game-playing group and were, inevitably, to be solved retrospectively and conjecturally. But in many other respects there was a marked change of both tone and quality in the stories. The switch of venue from Miss Marple's gloomy cottage to the hospitality of the Bantrys' dinner table notably lightens the atmosphere, as also does the removal from the scene of Raymond and Joyce. With them goes the inter-generational conflict that had originally pre-occupied Miss Marple, and Christie herself. The dialogue is far fresher with the introduction of Jane Helier bringing further brightness and some well-handled dumb-blond glamour to the proceedings. She's also a striking contrast to Miss Marple, with nothing of the plain Jane about *her*.

Most impressive of all is a new awareness of what kind of game they are all playing. Raymond and Joyce's good-natured but rather adolescent competition with Aunt Jane now goes and everyone concentrates on the task in hand – telling stories. It's as though Christie herself, in post-Archie panic, had grabbed at the ancient idea of group storytelling without being fully aware of what she was doing. Now, picking up on the exercise, she is eager to point out the importance of the experiment she is involved in, stressing both the variety of stories offered and the different ways in which they can be told.

Colonel Bantry is encouraged to tell 'a ghost story' which he has personally experienced but doesn't really understand or believe in. This provides Miss Marple with an opportunity to demonstrate the slow and deeply private way in which her mind works. It is totally bewildering, and often deliberately so, to those around her; a pose or act of an apparently muddled old lady who is in fact skilfully holding her audience off until she herself is totally sure of her conclusion:

> It really depends on the primroses … I mean, Mrs Bantry said they were yellow and pink. If it was a pink primrose that turned blue, of course, that fits in perfectly. But if it happened to be a yellow one …

It was to be the first of many such performances in Miss Marple's career.

Dolly Bantry, who is being called on here to provide some specialist horticultural information to help solve her husband's ghostly tale, tries to back out of the game entirely. As a passionate gardener, her reading seems limited to bulb catalogues and she is terrified when called upon to tell a story: 'I've been listening to you all and I don't know how you do it: "He said, she said, you wondered, they thought, everyone implied" Well I just couldn't and there it is!' Her husband, happy that he has passed his own test, advises her with more than a touch of smugness: 'You're quite good at the facts, Dolly, but poor at the embroidery.' There's no alternative but to comply and Dolly does her more than adequate best. In 'The Herb of Death' her bumbling nervousness is transformed into a Christie masterclass on dinner-table dialogue as well as a murder mystery in tune with Dolly's very own personal interests.

As before, everyone in the group is challenged to tell a story of their own and to try to solve the uncompleted stories told by their companions, but there is now a much greater awareness among them of the different kinds of stories being told and of the nature of storytelling itself. 'Don't call me Mrs B,' Dolly rebukes Sir Henry. 'Scheherazade, then' he replies.

Here they are all obliged to be Scheherazades, even when, like Dr Lloyd, they are claiming a higher status for their narratives than mere fiction: 'You see, Miss Helier, this isn't a serial story. This is real life; and real life stops just where it chooses.'

In the first group of stories Miss Marple's contribution had been 'The Thumb Mark of St Peter.' It is of interest in that it reveals something of her personality, but the story itself relies for its effect on a rather feeble verbal quibble and allows her special abilities little scope. By the time of Miss Marple's next narrative, in the second batch of stories, Christie was far more sure of what she was doing and 'A Christmas Tragedy,' is a very different matter. Miss Marple is now placed so centre stage that she pretty well forgets to outline a problem for the others to discuss. Instead, she takes over completely as both narrator and detective, telling with cold-blooded confidence how she identified, manipulated, and trapped a murderer. She is even allowed to round off her story with an admission of the pleasure she can still feel at the part she played in getting the murderer hanged.

In contrast to Miss Marple's tightly controlled narrative, 'The Affair at the Bungalow' is a teasing, apparently rambling double take on the use of an unreliable, not to say duplicitous, narrator. The 'beautiful Jane Helier,' whose dumbness throughout has made her the butt of everyone else because of her seeming inability to master the simplest of narrative conventions, eventually reveals, in a mood of triumphant self-satisfaction, that while she may not be much of a storyteller she is a very good actress indeed. 'I didn't give myself away once, did I?' she asks an astonished Dolly after the group has broken up. And, it certainly seems as though she has fooled everyone. Except, of course, Miss Marple who has, it emerges, declined this particular chance to go public because of her fundamental belief that in an emergency 'women must stick together,' a stance that, once again, will reappear even more forcefully in her future career.

* * *

The Miss Marple of these later stories was clearly being prepared for her larger role in *The Murder at the Vicarage* which followed shortly after. She is now totally liberated from the Victorian image and no longer presented as though holding court, whether in her grandfather chair or at the Bantrys'dinner table. Her earlier costume is no longer featured, apart from a passing mention near the close of the novel of her arranging her lace fichu and fleecy shawl. Otherwise, we have a slightly younger, new-look Miss Marple who is described in a carefully neutral manner by Leonard Clement, the vicar of St. Mary Mead and the narrator of *Vicarage*, as 'a white-haired old lady with a gentle, appealing manner.' She lives alone in a cottage that has not only lost its brooding ancient atmosphere, but is given no special descriptive attention at all. When Colonel Melchett pays Miss Marple a visit, he is simply shown into a 'small drawing-room' that he feels is 'a bit crowded,' but with 'plenty of good stuff.' It is one of four similar cottages situated around the vicarage, all of which are inhabited by women, either spinsters or widows.

And it is as a member of this group that Miss Marple is introduced in *Vicarage*, one of a chorus of tea-drinking, scandal-spreading gossips consisting of herself, Mrs Price Ridley, Miss Wetherby, and Miss Hartnell. They are not an attractive group, and according to Griselda, the vicar's wife, the 'terrible' Miss Marple is the one of them to be most avoided. She is 'the worst cat in the village.' Eventually the vicar's more sympathetic view prevails and Griselda is won over, but for a while either of them could turn out to be right. This Miss Marple certainly relishes gossiping with her friends: 'Oh! My dear ... *I* think married ones are the worst. Remember poor Mollie Carter.' It is at moments like this that we can most easily catch Christie's memory of Caroline Sheppard in *Roger Ackroyd* as having been a possible model for Miss Marple. Not that she ever had quite the right qualities. In *An Autobiography* Caroline Sheppard is described as 'an acidulated spinster. Full of curiosity, knowing everything, hearing everything; the complete detective service in the home.' That is a pertinent enough summary of how Miss Marple is to function as a detective, though not of her personality. While the two characters share an intense interest in the daily experiences of village life, 'acidulated,' meaning sour or jaundiced, could only be applied to Caroline Sheppard. As far as the Miss Marple of *Vicarage* is concerned, she may be catlike but she is never acidulated.

Gradually even these traces of Caroline Sheppard disappear as Christie separates Miss Marple from her choral company. Her companions go on individually to reveal themselves as every bit as mean-minded as Griselda finds them to be. By the close of the book, though, Miss Marple has been sufficiently transformed to win over Griselda and earn a closing tribute from Leonard as 'really ... rather a dear.'

And so she is, though there is a larger issue here than the eradication of Caroline Sheppard's influence. The mean-mindedness had to be carefully removed from Miss Marple without destroying her love of gossip. This is as crucial a factor as her advanced age in helping to make of her 'a complete detective service in the home.' Her social world is very small and one that is shared overwhelmingly with other women in a similar situation to herself. It makes inevitable the choral quality employed initially by Christie. 'There's a lot of talk,' sighs Colonel Melchett struggling to get on with the investigation. 'Too many women in this part of the world.' Less diplomatically, Miss Cram, the lively young incomer and a natural target for the gossips, complains: 'Wicked it is, the way these old ladies go on down here. Say anything, they will.' What Christie needed to do was to separate Miss Marple from that kind of casual nastiness without eliminating entirely all of the inquisitive qualites it has helped breed in her. Nosiness and a love of gossip are accepted as natural to her advanced age and village background. Nurtured and used broadmindedly they become crucial to her as a detective.

It is much to the point that Christie belonged to the last generation of women writers who were not only able to use the language of spinsterhood and old maids unselfconsciously but who were also willing to continue to tolerate its presence in literature. She herself was strongly aware of the concern her parents' generation had shown with what they had described as 'redundant women' (i.e. the large number of unmarried women created by the social and gender restrictions of the Victorian period). As the relevance of that particular concept began to fade, it was replaced by the similar sounding though different phenomenon of 'surplus women' (i.e. women whose unmarried state had been forced upon them by the mass slaughter of young men during the First World War). Christie uses both of the terms in the Miss Marple novels, and it is of course possible that

Miss Marple herself might have been one of the redundant many, but that is not the point being made by Christie. For her, Miss Marple becomes a kind of fictional epitome of all of these historical changes, not only a culminating point of the spinster tradition but also, in most respects, its finale.[1]

One of the words used most often to describe Miss Marple is 'shrewd.' It is not applied only to her. As with several other favourite words, Christie tended to overuse it, indiscriminately so at times. But it does carry a particular resonance in Miss Marple's case. The meaning of the word has changed considerably over time. Today it is generally taken to imply approbation, even admiration, and is used to describe someone who possesses keen insight and a balanced judgement, as it is with Miss Marple. This particular meaning, though, became a generally accepted usage only in the nineteenth century. In earlier years it carried very different connotations. When Shakespeare writes: 'This young maid might do her a shrewd turn if she pleased' (*All's Well*, III, v, 67-8), he is offering not comfort but a warning: he means malicious or harmful. Shrewd was also often employed to describe a range of undesirable qualities or conditions such as sharp, piercing, mischievous, cunning. The noun, drawn from the same linguistic source as the adjective shrewd, is still familiar from Shakespeare's play *The Taming of the Shrew* as describing a woman who is nagging, spiteful, mean-minded. These various connotations go back long before Shakespeare. They were drawn from the physical characteristics of the shrew, the small mouse-like creature with a pointed nose and tiny eyes that was once regarded as hostile to human beings. According to the OED, in earlier times the human shrew would have been a man, someone wicked or malignant. Only later did it come to apply solely to witch-like or scolding women.

Although Miss Marple is never presented as malicious or spiteful, any more than acidulated, in *Vicarage* especially she does carry with her more than a touch of the old-style shrew. In addition to the gossip and casual nosiness she has a very sharp tongue and is quite capable of patronizing both Leonard and Griselda. The passion shared with her shrewish allies for what the vicar calls 'unsavoury reminiscences' is fed by constant observation of her neighbours. Throughout the novel she is fascinated by the possibility that Griselda may have been having an affair with Lawrence Redding, while her garden has such a notorious local reputation as a spy post that the two main suspects in the novel rely on it to establish alibis for themselves. But Miss Marple is up to that trick and cleverly double-crosses them: 'They go in together ... and ... I'm afraid they realize that I shan't leave the garden till they come out again!' When it's convenient for her usually excellent eyesight to fail she has always on hand a pair of powerful binoculars, justified, of course, by her well-known love of studying the habits of birds.

And, proud though she may appear to be of her Victorian modesty, and quick as she is to exploit it when convenient to do so, she greatly enjoys talking in ways that are far from any conventional view of Victorian old ladies. How can she be sure that Mrs Protheroe was unarmed? After all, she might have been carrying a pistol 'concealed – er – upon her person' the Chief Constable delicately suggests. Miss Marple puts him right with a certain amount of relish:

> My dear Colonel Melchett, you know what young women are nowadays. Not ashamed to show exactly how the creator made them. She hadn't so much as a handkerchief in the top of her stocking.[2]

She would always retain some of the less attractive qualities that she displays in *Vicarage* but they gradually become assimilated into a keen general alertness to, and comprehensive knowledge of, everything going on around her. And ultimately, her uncanny insight, however it may have been obtained, is justified by the use to which she puts it. There would even be hints in a jokey way of her having remained in touch with still darker forces: 'Darling, a hundred years ago you would certainly have been burned as a witch!' Lucy Eyelesbarrow murmurs affectionately to Miss Marple many years later in *4.50 from Paddington*. And so she could have been. It's precisely those qualities, and the uncertainty about her they provoke, that she has so knowingly nurtured and developed over the years. The one thing that worries her is how she would cope if 'a really big mystery came along.'

Now she knows. When Colonel Protheroe is shot in the vicarage it is the first murder to have taken place in St. Mary Mead for 'at least fifteen years.' Here is the big case Miss Marple has been waiting for, the opportunity to apply the theories she has been trying out on smaller events for all that time. The test is made available to her and passed triumphantly. It involves a classic ingenious riddle and a duplicitous, amoral murderer who is driven by greed and totally indifferent to the suffering of any innocent people caught up in his schemes. His capture satisfies both Miss Marple's intellect, or the 'logical certainty of her conclusions' as Colonel Melchett describes it, and her driving sense of high moral purpose.

Yet although *The Murder at the Vicarage* established a working pattern for Miss Marple, its tone was to be quite different from that of any of her subsequent cases. The dominant atmosphere within which she rids herself of the reputation for being the 'worst cat in the village' is light-hearted and fresh, at times irreverent, even *risqué* in a nineteen-twentyish manner. *Vicarage* is a youthful book and one in which an unusual number of young people actually appear, including Raymond West who makes a late entry into the novel and is described by the vicar as 'a rather exquisite young man.' It is a book of love affairs, broken marriages, runaway wives, much slangy coded talk of S.A. (Sex Appeal), and of the modern fashion for casual rather than lasting sexual relationships. As a mark of the relatively free spirit of *Vicarage* not all of the irregular relationships it portrays are by any means doom-laden or fated to end in murder. They are simply, nowadays, how things are.

Conscious of needing to live up to their bright-young-thing image, the young characters delight in saying shocking things and wearing shocking clothes. Miss Marple's close observation of Mrs Protheroe's stocking-tops is characteristic of the clever use made throughout the novel of modern fashions. So is the vicar's equally close observation of Gladys Cram's legs which he records 'were encased in particularly shiny pink stockings, were crossed, and I had every opportunity of observing that she wore pink striped silk knickers.' Dennis, the vicar's teenage nephew who lives at the vicarage, is always on hand to apply his impromptu bawdy rhymes to people and circumstances. Here they are addressed to Gladys Cram, the closing lines being diplomatically cut off, in music-hall style, by the vicar: 'Come fly with me, my bride to be. And at the Blue Boar, on the bedroom floor…' Dennis's natural ally at such moments and central to most of the fun in the book is Griselda. She is twenty years younger than her husband, 'distractingly pretty' and ironically named. At the start of the book, Leonard Clement muses that Griselda is in fact a most suitable name for a vicar's wife, though not for *his* wife.

The Griselda he has in mind is to be found in 'The Clerk's Tale,' one of Chaucer's *Canterbury Tales*. She is an exemplary wife, adapted from Boccaccio, who is so subservient to her husband's commands that she follows them unquestioningly however harsh or unfeeling they may be. It is not, however, Chaucer's Griselda who lands up in St. Mary Mead by marrying the vicar. To the delight of the village gossips, this Griselda can't cook and is a totally incompetent housekeeper. She teases and mocks the village spinsters, even allowing them to believe that she is posing in the nude for the local artist. She is also shown, openly and frankly, to be very happy sexually with her older husband.

The light, often humorous, tone of *Vicarage* no doubt owed much to having been written in the period of excited personal contentment that followed Christie's meeting with Max Mallowan. It was published just one month after their marriage and almost exactly three years after the first Miss Marple short stories had appeared. For the earliest readers of *Vicarage*, this would have been their introduction to Miss Marple. They could only have known of the existence of the short stories if they had happened to read them as published originally in *The Royal Magazine* and *The Story-Teller* as Christie was still to collect them together for publication in volume form as *The Thirteen Problems*. Before doing that she had to add to them the specially written thirteenth story 'Death by Drowning.'

It was a rather odd thing to do and we don't know what Christie was thinking of. It is possible that she simply wanted to justify the catchy title she already had in mind for a collection, but it's difficult to see why that should have mattered to her. Even if, for some personal compelling reason, she had felt obliged to write a thirteenth story, it would still have been easy enough for her to adapt the style of the new one to recreate the Miss Marple of the other stories. But this she clearly didn't want to do. When 'Death by Drowning' is placed in its proper context with *The Thirteen Problems* and *The Murder at the Vicarage*, it becomes plain that for Christie the thirteenth story was a matter of looking forward rather than back, a conscious tidying up of the Miss Marple material.

Sir Henry Clithering is once again visiting the Bantrys. Learning this, Miss Marple calls on him. Of course he remembers her admiringly and in what looks like a deliberate placing in context by Christie of this latest mystery he refers carefully to the earlier 'dozen unsolved and hypothetical cases' which they and the other participants had come together to try to solve. Now there are just the two of them and Miss Marple is taking the initiative. She is shown 'sitting in the drawing-room – very upright as always, a gaily coloured marketing basket of foreign extraction beside her.' A murder has been committed and, it seems, quickly solved, at least to the satisfaction of the local police. Too quickly in Miss Marple's opinion. Convinced that she knows who the true murderer is, she passes the information to Sir Henry and persuades him to intervene in the case. She then leaves everything to him, moving out of the story only to reappear towards the close in order to provide some essential local knowledge.

'Death by Drowning' thus asserts that the Miss Marple who closes *The Thirteen Problems* is no longer the armchair theorist of the earlier stories in the collection but the livelier, indeterminately aged figure of *The Murder at the Vicarage* with whom an interested reader would have been familiar by the time *The Thirteen Problems* was published. Christie did not go out of her way to draw attention to how different 'Death by Drowning' was from the rest of the stories in the collection but it obviously mattered to her that the change in Miss Marple's image should be clarified at this point. And the reason for that must surely have been that Christie had strongly in mind a possible future for Miss Marple as a more acceptable rival to the already famous Poirot. But, with Christie being Christie, what may at first seem an obvious explanation of a relatively slight biographical or bibliographical puzzle is pretty well bound to develop into a much larger mystery, as it does here.

For after having introduced Miss Marple so fully and carefully to the reading public, after having devoted a large part of five years to doing so, and even after having written 'Death by Drowning' in order to make clear, presumably, that the earlier stories had in certain important respects been superseded, Christie then put Miss Marple to one side and she was not to appear before the public again in any substantial way for a whole decade. In time, particular circumstances would demand modifications in Miss Marple's age, manner and abilities, but these were always to be relatively slight. The fundamental nature of her personality, environment, and methods of detection were all firmly established. In the five years embracing her disappearance, divorce and second marriage Christie had created a highly distinctive, new kind of literary detective. For now, it seemed as though Christie didn't quite know what to do with her, but when she did finally make up her mind on the matter she could at least be sure that Miss Marple would be in place, pretty well fully formed, and fit and ready to act out whatever role was handed to her.

* * *

Towards the close of *The Murder at the Vicarage*, excited at having finally demonstrated her ability to handle a real murder case, Miss Marple takes the opportunity to explain how she became a detective. It has nothing to do with any professional training or even a theoretical interest in what at a later date she describes as 'criminology.' This again is totally unlike Poirot. When he set out on his new career as a private detective in England he had behind him many years of professional experience in combating crime. All that Miss Marple can offer is a very ordinary life which she has turned to extraordinary advantage. The deductive skills she possesses come, she explains, from the accident of 'living alone … in a rather out-of-the-way part of the world' and choosing the study of 'Human Nature' as her 'hobby.' St. Mary Mead is her laboratory, its inhabitants and everyday events her specimens. These she studies, analyses and classifies as if under a microscope just 'as though they were birds or flowers, group so-and-so, genus this, species that.' In 'Death by Drowning' she had explained to Sir Henry Clithering that this kind of local information was best thought of as 'specialized knowledge' and some years later in *The Body in the Library* he recalls the phrase admiringly, saying that it applies just as well to a good deal of regular police work. Although these early experiments have given her considerable self-confidence, she is still sensible enough to appreciate that that may not be enough. Only when she gets the chance to apply her theories to 'a really big mystery' will she know whether her 'tiny working models' are, as she believes, much the same as the large-scale variety. This opportunity comes to her with the Protheroe murder.

Ordinariness is the key to Miss Marple's greatness as a detective and also to her originality as a literary character. In the short story 'The Companion,' Sir Henry Clithering laughingly accuses Miss Marple of having portrayed St. Mary Mead as 'a positive hotbed of crime and vice.' The tone is friendly, but his attitude is misguided in much the same way as the criticisms voiced by Raymond West whose anti-Victorianism is captured in two striking images. They are introduced very early and recur throughout the novels. 'I regard St. Mary Mead,' he announces in *Vicarage*, 'as a stagnant pool.' He means that it contains nothing of interest for a modern young man like himself and that his aunt cannot possibly have learned anything worthwhile from it. Miss Marple replies tellingly that if viewed under a microscope a drop of water from a stagnant pool will reveal itself as 'full of life.' More personally, in another early story, 'A Christmas Tragedy,' he is reported as accusing his aunt of having a mind 'like a sink.' Once again she has no difficulty turning this scornful image to her own advantage. After all, a sink is 'the most necessary thing in any house; but, of course, not romantic.'

That Raymond, in spite of his pride at understanding real life is actually a romantic is a countercharge of Miss Marple's that genuinely riles him. And so it should. His feeling of superiority over the Victorians rests on the belief put into popular twentieth-century currency by Lytton Strachey that an ingrained hypocrisy allowed them to deny the existence of the darker sides of life while at the same time remaining titillatingly obsessed with them. In contrast, the moderns face reality frankly and truthfully. Miss Marple takes an opposite view. For her the Victorians were not hypocritical. They were positively facing up to the reality of moral and physical squalor in a rapidly changing and expanding society. If they seemed preoccupied with such things it was in order to correct and improve them, while someone like Raymond is so busy writing enthusiastically about the darker sides of life that he is unable to recognize the wider social context to which they belong and therefore to appreciate any true change or reform.

As the Victorians' living representative, Raymond's criticisms are aimed directly at Miss Marple, and her responses to them are intensely personal and positive. It is *her* approach to crime that is realistic, *her* microscopic eyes that are capable of penetrating beneath the surface of village quiet. St. Mary Mead is no more lawless than other places, but its potential for crime and vice is just as great. Raymond's mistake is that he is too inclined to accept surface as reality, to notice only the scummy top layer of a pond or the well-maintained kitchen sink. In 'The Bloodstained Pavement' Miss Marple relishes the opportunity to return to Raymond and Joyce a little of the condescension they regularly heap on her: 'I hope you dear young people will never realize how very wicked the world is.'

For Miss Marple crime is not a separate, isolable activity, but a permanent element of human nature; and the forms it takes, as she asserts repeatedly, are 'much the same in a village as anywhere else.' Joyce Lemprière's assumption in 'The Tuesday Night Club' that as she has 'knocked about among all sorts and conditions of people' she must therefore 'know life as darling Miss Marple here cannot possible know it' is entirely unjustified, and Miss Marple resents it. If life really is much the same everywhere then what reason can there possibly be to believe that someone who has traipsed about the world and met lots of different people will necessarily have a greater knowledge of human nature than someone who has remained intelligently and sensitively where they have always have been and met relatively few people? To believe otherwise is merely another form of misguided romanticism that has no place in Miss Marple's realistic view of the world.

At the close of 'The Thumb Mark of St. Peter,' having been worsted in yet another contest, Raymond says: 'Well, at all events, Aunt Jane, there is one thing you don't know.' He is referring to what he expects to be his shock announcement that he has become engaged to Joyce, but he's wrong again. Miss Marple has noticed that after dinner he had taken Joyce out to admire the sunset down by the jasmine hedge and that is the spot 'where the milkman asked Annie if he could put up the banns.' Not much liking the comparison, Raymond is nevertheless assured that it is perfectly fair: 'Everybody is very much alike, really. But fortunately, perhaps, they don't realize it.' And here, right at the start, is the basis of Miss Marple's philosophy. It is simple, democratic, and open to anyone who is astute or interested enough to follow it through. Not that many people are capable of doing so.

The reason for this is that while they may be fundamentally similar, people vary greatly in their social, national and financial circumstances and become so obsessed with what are in effect external trappings that they fail to understand how closely they share many of their basic feelings and emotions with others, whether poor or rich, celebrated or obscure, proud or humble. 'Fortunately, perhaps,' Miss Marple observes, because these are the everyday illusions that make life bearable, and Miss Marple is highly unusual in aiming to live without illusions. Raymond likes to think that the marriage proposal of a successful novelist is different in kind from that of a village milkman, but it isn't, and how could it be? The circumstances of the people involved are clearly different, but not the experience itself. Raymond and the milkman is an early example of one of Miss Marple's 'tiny working models' which Sir Henry Clithering picks up on and describes, at first mockingly but later with great admiration, as 'village parallels.' They are a key part of the 'specialized knowledge' that encapsulates Miss Marple's view of life.

The prototype of the village parallel, announced in 'The Tuesday Night Club,' is the case of Mrs Carruthers's 'two gills of picked shrimps' which disappear so strangely. The solution to that mystery is never given and it lingers on as something of a joke because Miss Marple is ridiculed out of finishing the story. Still, she has many other parallels to pursue. A case of murder and false identity in 'The Companion' brings to mind: 'Mrs Trout. She drew the old age pension, you know, for three old women who were dead, in different parishes.' The systematic murder of easily duped wives in 'The Bloodstained Pavement' comes as no surprise to Miss Marple: 'There was Mrs Green, you know, she buried five children – and everyone of them insured. Well …' And, among many hidden sexual relationships, there is Mr Badger, the chemist recalled in 'The Herb of Death': 'He had a very young housekeeper – young enough to be not only his daughter, but his grand-daughter. Not a word to anyone … And when he died ...' Miss Marple's village parallels will be applied in the future to more spectacular cases, but they all serve to demonstrate that although the scale of crimes may vary, the human motives underlying criminal acts are much the same be it fraud or financial greed, sexual passion or jealousy, impersonation, perjury, deceit, betrayal, or murder. They are all there beneath the apparently stagnant surface of life in both the tiny hamlet and the big city, specimens to be examined and learned from, perfect working models ready to be enlarged and applied.

Miss Marple's work in applying these village parallels and other lessons she has learned from St. Mary Mead, is carried out alone. Solitariness is not only characteristic of her detection, but one of its most unusual qualities as well. From the beginning of modern literary detection, it had been assumed that the detective needed a partner, someone with an inferior or more mundane mind, who could act as willing companion and sounding board. The attraction of 'a duo' was that it avoided the very real danger of a narrative becoming a tedious monologue. Dupin had his unidentified chronicler, Holmes his Watson, Poirot his Hastings or Mrs Oliver.[3] But Miss Marple the aged spinster has no one. It is difficult not to believe that in this, as so often with Miss Marple, Christie was dramatizing her own artistic position, someone willingly isolated, accepting grudgingly the scorn so often applied to her work, labouring away silently, cleverly, skilfully; unappreciated, pushing on, never defending herself in public. Of course, this was not true of her personal life, but in the Miss Marple stories and novels the reader is never far from Agatha Christie the detached, isolated, misunderstood author.

Miss Marple's personal situation, from whatever angle one likes to view it, is extreme. There is no attendant chronicler of her deeds, no 'stooge,' husband or devoted admirer, no assistant (professional or amateur), and no family, apart from all those vague and distant relatives. Raymond is often around but he could never function as a reliable companion. She doesn't even have a close friend to work with. In *A Murder is Announced* Dolly Bantry offers to apply for the position but is told by Miss Marple that she won't do because she's incapable of keeping anything to herself. In the early days there had been the gossips and other village acquaintances, mainly professionals like Mr Petherick, Dr Haydock who turns up in several later novels, and, eventually, Griselda. In *4.50 from Paddington* she even draws on David West, the second son of Raymond and Joan, for information about railway timetables. Most surprisingly, there are a couple of sympathetic middle-aged women, Mrs Dane Calthrop and Mrs 'Bunch' Harmon, who are liked and trusted by Miss Marple.[4] Friends such as these are useful when specific help is needed, but they can't ease the loneliness which Miss Marple is often shown as experiencing. She is burdened by her astute, highly developed understanding of human nature which she is able to share only by solving whatever problem is absorbing her attention.

* * *

Nobody quite like Miss Marple had appeared in fiction before. She was not the first woman to feature in a detective novel. Nor was Christie the first woman to create one. Michelle B. Slung has estimated that by 1901 the adventures of some twenty fictional woman detectives had been published.[5] Not that any of these can challenge Miss Marple's originality. Who now remembers Dorcas Dene, Miss Van Snoop or Lady Molly of Scotland Yard? It's not unfanciful to see the 'Old Man in the Corner' who, along with Lady Molly was created by Baroness Orczy, as a possible influence on Miss Marple. Unnamed, seemingly immobile, always seated at a table in an ABC tea shop and obsessively unravelling a piece of string while he works out bewildering murder mysteries, Orczy's old man might well be seen as a male predecessor of the spinster detective fussing with the knitting that symbolizes her own mental activity. But if there was an influence at work here, it was local and static, and in no way lessens the singularity of Miss Marple.

And much the same has to be said, ultimately, of the American author Anna Katharine Green (1846-1935), even though if anyone created a prototype of Miss Marple, it is to her that the credit should go. Green made an early name for herself with *The Leavenworth Case* (1878) which featured a New York Police detective called Ebeneezer Gryce. It wasn't until *That Affair Next Door* (1897) that Miss Amelia Butterworth was introduced as an amateur foil to the professional detective. Miss

Butterworth lives in a New York flat, is comfortably off, and, owing to her 'lonely and single life' has little to do but interest herself in the activities of her neighbours by spying on them from behind her curtains. Gryce quickly comes to admire her sharp observation and analytical mind, and draws attention especially to her understanding of the minutiae of women's lives or to use Gryce's own words, of 'women's eyes for women's matters.' Christie certainly knew Green's work and she may well have have drawn unconsciously on aspects of Miss Butterworth's approach to crime in creating Miss Marple. The differences between the two women detectives, though, are also substantial.

In literary terms, Miss Butterworth belongs essentially to the more leisurely world of Victorian fiction rather than the crisply focused detective novel of the twentith century that Christie did so much to establish. Her multisyllabic name and close co-operation with Gryce as well as the cumbersome narrative and heavy dialogue all seem old-fashioned compared with the lightness and verve of Christie's fiction. In one area, though, Amelia Butterworth does look forward rather than back. Compared with with Miss Marple's old-fashioned English village, the dark apartment blocks and shadowy streets of her New York represent the world of detective fiction to come. Yet, curiously, this again, in terms of possible influence, is something that serves to distance the two female sleuths from each other rather than bring them closer together.

A far more direct influence on Miss Marple may have been G.K.Chesterton's Father Brown. Christie is known to have admired the Father Brown stories. They were around long before Miss Marple appeared on the scene, and there are striking similarities between the two detectives. In addition to acting alone, Father Brown's analytical mind is concealed by an outward appearance of fussy innocence. He is free to observe what is going on because nobody is ever willing to take seriously someone who looks so silly. Nor can they easily believe how a priest who can adopt the pose of what in 'The Blue Cross' Father Brown himself calls 'a celibate simpleton' could possibly know so much of the darker sides of life. Long hours spent in the confessional is the answer to that. Much the same is true of Miss Marple's illuminating lifetime spent in the confines of St. Mary Mead. This has made her extraordinarily cynical.

She believes that life is so fundamentally unpleasant that it is best left alone, unless you are the kind of person who feels obliged to confront it, as in their different ways she and Father Brown both are. She says repeatedly that she trusts no one, refuses to accept as true whatever she is told without corroborating evidence, never grants someone the benefit of the doubt, and always thinks the worst of people, until she has incontrovertible evidence that it would be wrong to do so. To outsiders the working of her imagination is unknowable, and, once again like Father Brown, inconceivably at odds with her simple appearance. To Inspector Craddock in *4.50 from Paddington* she admits that her 'process of reasoning' is 'not really original,' and in doing so acknowledges an influence. All she did, she explains, was to follow the example of the boy in Mark Twain who found the horse. He simply imagined where he would go if he were a horse, and then went there. Craddock gets the point. 'You imagined what you'd do if you were a cruel and cold-blooded murderer?' he says, 'looking thoughtfully at Miss Marple's pink and white elderly fragility.'

As several of her opponents testify, she is a 'terrifying' woman, ruthlessly unstoppable when needing to protect the innocent or trap the guilty. Her integrity is ultimately the only safeguard she has. With a change of gender and the America city transformed into an English village or market town, Raymond Chandler's 'down these mean streets a man must go who is not himself mean, who is neither tarnished nor afraid' could be a fitting evocation of Miss Marple.

Both Father Brown and Miss Marple disappear into the crowd and re-emerge, to everyone's surprise, with accusations and solutions. Outwardly they gain by appearing to be people whose views aren't worth consulting. Of course, it could be argued that Father Brown does in fact have a partner, and one who would render any earthly counterpart unnecessary. But then so does Miss Marple. Although she is not as staunchly affiliated to a religious faith as Father Brown, she regards her belief as crucial to her detective work.[6] As early as 'The Thumb Mark of St. Paul,' and deliberately challenging the 'modern young people' in her audience to laugh, she admits: 'when I am in really bad trouble I always say a little prayer to myself … And I always get an answer.' In her later adventures she becomes as much an agent of God and as militant a Christian as Father Brown himself.

All private detectives, however lofty a view of their own activities they may have and however distrustful they are of the official keepers of law and order, must ultimately rely, if they are to justify their deductions, on the existence of a reasonably efficient and smoothly functioning police force. It is the oddest of the many artificialities of literary detection that private detectives are allowed a degree of power and independence to hunt down the guilty that they would never have in real life. In more recent mystery fiction, as society has come to adopt a less idealistic view of its police forces, the private detective of fiction as he descends from Conan Doyle and Christie, has become increasingly (and inevitably) a member of the police, often semi-detached but no longer 'private.'

Even in earlier fiction some limits had to be imposed. After all, once a crime is solved, it is the police who are responsible for carrying criminals off, presenting the evidence against them, making sure they are brought to trial, and then locking them safely away. The police provide these standard services for Miss Marple, as for everyone else, and in addition they are, for her especially, an additional back-up service. Her solitariness puts her constantly in danger of attack. This she accepts. She is physically as well as morally courageous and on several occasions willingly puts her own life at risk. In *The Moving Finger* when Jerry Burton rebukes her for involving Megan in snaring the killer she snaps back at him: 'We are not put into this world, Mr Burton, to avoid danger when an innocent fellow-creature's life is at stake. You understand me?'

Even so, the violence common in many other detective and crime stories is largely avoided. After all, Miss Marple quite obviously lacks the physical strength possessed by her male equivalents or their assistants. Furthermore, being without an assistant she can't, in what looks like becoming a particularly tough case, follow Holmes's example and advise Watson to carry his revolver with him. So, when necessary, she uses the police to provide her with active support, still leading her solitary way in most of her investigations but aware that they are ready on hand to help her close off a case. It is not surprising that among the great literary detectives she is unusual in her admiration for the police and never disillusioned by them. With the exception of Inspector Slack, who serves as an early sparring partner, they generally respond by treating her with respect and admiration. This is ultimately due to the reputation she builds for herself which, in its turn, owes much to the police friends she has in very high places.

Impressed by Miss Marple's performances at the Tuesday Night Club, Sir Henry Clithering goes out of his way to learn more about her and with the shared experience described in 'Death by Drowning' he becomes her patron. He has retired from Scotland Yard, but he makes sure that his successors know about the remarkable Miss Marple. In case after case, once she has set everything in motion, she moves into an alliance with the police, overcoming their perfectly understandable doubts that this little old lady can possibly have anything to teach them, waiting for them to remember her earlier triumphs and the fulsome tributes that Sir Henry has spread through Scotland Yard.

The view of Miss Marple originally advanced by Dolly Bantry as being 'the typical old maid of fiction …hopelessly behind the times' persists throughout her career, not because that's what she actually is but because she quickly learns to use the image positively. It is often greatly to her advantage to be taken as the typical old maid of fiction. But no one in an official position is allowed to believe this if Sir Henry is on hand to put them right. Should the investigating officers in *A Murder is Announced* take any notice of the 'old pussy' who claims to have some relevant information? Of course they should, Sir Henry tells them. They'd be foolish not to. After all, he proclaims, neatly summing up pretty well all of her crucial qualities: 'She's just the finest detective God ever made. Natural genius cultivated in a suitable soil.'

Chapter 4

Rural life and Minimalism

'Are they not fresh and beautiful?' Dr Watson gushes to Sherlock Holmes in 'The Adventure of the Copper Beeches.' It's an 'ideal spring day' and the two men are looking out of a train window at the 'little red and grey roofs of the farm-steadings' set in the green fields of Hampshire. Holmes's response is unexpected, and grave. He replies that while Watson sees 'beauty' in the scene, he himself can think only of the 'impunity with which crime may be committed there.' When Watson protests, Holmes slaps him down: 'It is my belief, Watson, founded upon my experience, that the lowest and vilest alleys in London do not present a more dreadful record of sin than does the smiling and beautiful country-side.'

Watson is shocked by what he regards as Holmes's cynicism, but Miss Marple wouldn't have been. Even though she has probably had little, if any, personal experience of London's low and vile alleys, she would still have rushed to agree the general point with Holmes. In *A Caribbean Mystery*, Raymond West, feeling that his elderly aunt is too bound up in the 'idyllic rural ideal' of St. Mary Mead, sends her some modern novels which he hopes will introduce her to 'REAL LIFE.' They contain nothing of which she isn't already aware. Really, she muses, it is the would-be urban sophisticate Raymond who is the ignorant one. The 'facts of rural life' are only too well known to her: 'She had no urge to *talk* about them, far less to *write* about them – but she knew them. Plenty of sex, natural and unnatural. Rape, incest, perversions of all kinds.'

The strength of Miss Marple's response might seem to imply that she was about to be launched on a fearless exposé of squalid rural life along the 'realistic' lines urged by Raymond West. No such thought was in Christie's mind. From the very earliest short stories Miss Marple's views on village crime had been unequivocal. Again and again she insists that human life is much the same everywhere and that crimes committed in the country are no different in kind from those committed in towns. The human motives behind them are also the same. She knows full well that rural communities are small and their social range restricted, but for the keen observer like Miss Marple this is advantageous. It means that human nature can be known and studied more closely, more intimately than in the large impersonal society of large towns and cities. How an individual novelist might portray rural crime was an entirely separate, personal matter and did not affect the nature of crime itself.

As these views of Miss Marple's had always been there and were never to change in any substantial way, it is particularly worth noting that it is in the later novels they come to be restated so forcefully, and defensively. After years of silence, Christie was beginning to develop a strategy by which she could express indirectly some of the strongly held values and principles she had long denied herself the right of advancing in public. The exchange between Miss Marple and Raymond in *Caribbean* is in one sense characteristic of the banter between them that had been part of their relationship since the beginning. It is still the younger generation mocking its Victorian elders, but the once precocious young man is now a successful, middle-aged and controversial novelist, and the issues at stake between them are more combative and decisively literary. Beneath Raymond's attempt to persuade his old-fashioned aunt to become more adventurous in her reading habits, Christie is now actively employing Miss Marple as a cover for her own opinions, using her as a way of replying, indirectly as always, to the dismissive criticisms of her work that by 1964 when *A Caribbean Mystery* was published had become pretty well standard.

Raymond West's mocking description of St. Mary Mead as epitomizing 'idyllic rural life' which needs injecting with a strong dose of reality represents what was, and to a large extent still is, a general assumption that Christie's work portrays a 'cosy' unreal England that is focused overwhelmingly on village and country house life. The charge is particularly damaging because her novels do not claim to be in any sense gentle pastorals but centre on the terrible crime of murder which when presented in such an idealized environment lays itself damagingly open to the charge of being completely out of touch with the real world.

In pitching Raymond West against Miss Marple in this way, Christie would have had especially in mind Raymond Chandler's charge of dishonesty against British writers of what Chandler's fellow American Howard Haycraft had recently and enthusiastically, dubbed the 'Golden Age' of detective stories stretching from 1918 to 1930. In Haycraft's golden age, British writers, with Christie prominently among them, were regarded as being well ahead of the Americans. Chandler has two fundamental objections to these writers and, of course, to the whole idea of them constituting a golden age: they are 'too contrived and too little aware of what goes on in the world.' These are literary weaknesses, he announces, that 'really get me down.' As alternative models, Chandler offers himself and Dashiell Hammett, both of whom write detective stories which are realistic, or, in a phrase that would soon come to epitomize the American approach to detective fiction, 'hard-boiled.' For Chandler, Hammett was an inspirational writer, the man who took murder away from its customary artificial English setting and gave it back, in Chandler's striking words, 'to the kind of people that commit it for reasons, not just to provide a corpse.'[1]

It would be particularly neat to be able to suggest that Christie's use of the Christian name Raymond for Miss Marple's nephew was itself part of her response, but that's not possible: Raymond West was already well established as a character some years before Raymond Chandler made a name for himself with his crime novels. But there can be little doubt that Chandler is being referred to here and at a number of other similar moments. As early as *The Murder at the Vicarage* and without any hectoring from Raymond, Miss Marple herself had been reading 'a lot of American detective stories from the library' hoping they would help her track down Colonel Protheroe's murderer. And Miss Marple clearly followed her creator's example in keeping well up with American detective fiction. In Baghdad in the late 1940s, while Max was exploring ways for them to return to the Middle East, Agatha was reading 'thousands of American detective stories.'[2] Shortly after, in *A Murder is Announced* (1950) Miss

Marple is shown reading 'Mr Dashiell Hammett's stories,' this time with Raymond West's very specific recommendation in mind that Hammett was 'considered at the top of the tree in what is called the "tough" style of literature.' By now the polarization between British and American styles of detective fiction was firmly established, and the advantage was becoming set strongly in favour of American realism over faded British artificiality. Irritated by such assumptions and long since constitutionally incapable of answering them directly, it was characteristic of Christie that she should seize on the happy coincidence of her nephew's forename being shared with her hostile American critic and use it to reject the charges made against her.

She was certainly no more inclined to follow Chandler's self-promoting advice than Miss Marple was to adopt Raymond West's taste in modern novels. And why should she have done? After all, she had already pioneered and established a type of detective story that was entirely different from Chandler's, but just as original. By the 1940s when Chandler's criticisms were first published his dislike of the British detective story's reliance on elaborate plots and narrative trickery was understandable, but his claim to represent greater realism in his novels was less persuasive. The atmospheric urban settings and casual everyday violence of his novels made the case for a modernity that Britain couldn't easily match and was already influential on both sides of the Atlantic. But today Chandler's wisecracking dialogue and extreme moral idealism make his novels seem hardly less stylized than their golden-age equivalents.[3] The relevance of his advice to Christie, anyway, was slight. As Miss Marple says, it is crucially important that she should know about the darker aspects of life in St. Mary Mead, but she has 'no urge to *talk* about them, far less to write about them.'

This was Christie's own conviction as well. She doesn't go on to point out that she had long been committed to a very different way of writing about such matters, but she might well have done, for literary realism as a way of establishing, in Chandler's sense, a sociologically and artistically verifiable picture of life, never had been part of her intention or ambition. Indeed, almost from the beginning she had stood firmly against such an approach. Nevertheless, the criticism that her work is unrealistic in the sense that it is divorced from the 'real' world, has stuck. It is applied equally to the portrayal of murder itself, the social world in which murder occurs, and to Christie's literary style. Nor has this line of criticism declined over the years. It has, rather, become something of a general, readily accepted assumption that Christie is out of touch with the actual world and this has profoundly influenced her reputation. Though not, it has to be said with her huge and impressively varied readership. For some curious reason her readers appear not to take a critical line on these matters, or, perhaps, instinctively, they respond more positively. Traditionally it has been other writers of detective stories and professional literary critics who have led the way in denigrating Christie's remarkable talent.

In recent years a prominent spokesperson for this line of criticism has been P.D. James, herself a distinguished and popular English writer of detective stories. In her early work she was quite obviously very influenced by Christie. She acknowledges this in her autobiography, but ruefully and not as something to be proud of. About her early novel *Cover her Face* she says that it is 'very much a detective story in the mode of Agatha Christie, even if it aspires to probe more deeply into the minds and motives of its characters.' The qualification there is carefully judged. What, in James's view, was so unfortunate about Christie's influence was not only that it encouraged her to create shallow stock characters but also allowed her book to carry the air of a 'cosy, domestic, English village murder.'[4] Later James describes Christie as 'the arch-purveyor of cosy reassurance.' In her novels 'there is no real horror, no real blood or grief; indeed, even the murders are sanitized.' Once the murder mystery is solved, James concludes, 'normality will be restored to Mayhem Parva, the fly-in-amber village, which, despite its above-average homicide rate, never really loses its peace or innocence.'[5] These views were later considerably expanded in James's brief study of the genre *Talking about Detective Fiction* (2009) where the account of Christie is almost entirely negative.

As with Raymond Chandler before her, James is in part concerned to promote her own achievement and, more specifically, to bring the detective story firmly into the modern world. In short, to help rescue it from Christie's pernicious influence. In James's view, the post-Christie detective novel has moved positively on in every way. It is no longer isolated from reality; is more strongly aware of social, political, and psychological concerns; more intelligent; and more willing to face life by offering detailed and bloody descriptions of murder. It is also better written; less bound by generic restrictions; longer; less reliant on tricks and riddles to solve crimes. In short, generally closer to both the American hardboiled school of literary detection and the traditional literary novel. In short, it has abandoned or at least risen above, its limiting generic status. James even claims that 'because the detective story is usually set unambiguously in its own time and place, it often gives a clearer idea of contemporary life than does more prestigious literature.'[6]

It is clear from James's reference to 'Mayhem Parva, the fly-in-amber village' that she had read and highly approved Colin Watson's influential study of English detective fiction *Snobbery with Violence* first published in 1971 six years before Christie's death. Watson was responsible for coining the term Mayhem Parva to describe the smug village setting of characteristically British detective stories, and those of Agatha Christie in particular. The facetious tone of Watson's literary manner and his taste for smart derogatory phrases, cheerfully advanced whether what they express is true or not, found a ready following in all those who were eager to dismiss Christie's achievements as cheap and lacking intelligence. Watson, himself a writer of detective stories and an admirer of Chandler, used the name Mayhem Parva to represent a typical setting for a Christie murder, 'a cross between a village and a commuters' dormitory in the South of England, self-contained and largely self-sufficient.' The murders are fleeting, civilized, without violence or squalor, and once the whodunnit element has been resolved, the inhabitants, all instantly recognizable English stereotypes, return to their customary, quiet, snobbish innocence. The village atmosphere, according to Watson, is so 'picturesque' that it is capable of inspiring uninformed suburban dwellers' to hanker after retirement to 'the country.' What Christie creates is a 'mythical kingdom, a fly-in-amber land … a sort of museum of nostalgia.'[7]

It is obvious enough that Christie did choose to set most of her novels in relatively small or enclosed spaces, and notably towns and villages rather than large cities. This preference was shared generally with other writers of the time, many of them American as well as British, and was largely for reasons connected with the type of detective novel to which they were attracted rather than any social or class exclusivity. Nor has this narrative preference changed very much. Early and mid- nineteenth-century novelists had employed murder mystery as just one element in their large and more socially expansive work. Some – Dickens, Wilkie Collins, M.E. Braddon – had been quick to recognize the growth of the Victorian police force and especially the dramatic potential of the special Detective Department which had been established in 1842. But the two great founding fathers of the modern detective story, Edgar Allan Poe and Arthur Conan Doyle, were drawn to the short story rather than the Victorian novel. Within its confines they, and their thousands of imitators, found the concentration and intensity that were essential for their artistic purposes. Here they could establish a mystery, elaborate and solve it, with, ideally, the whole issue being settled, ingeniously and entertainingly, in the single reading which the booming late Victorian and early twentieth cetury periodical market encouraged. When writers like Christie began to expand into full length novels, they continued to aim for the tightness of form that the short story had favoured.

In this they were again following the example of Conan Doyle in such expanded Sherlock Holmes adventures as *The Hound of the Baskervilles* (1902). The modern detective novel quickly became restricted to a commercially viable length of about seventy or eighty thousand words. This allowed it to remain centred on one principal murder, with a larger amount of space now available to offer the reader greater variety than had been possible in the short story. According to the taste or ability of individual novelists there could be more than one murder, a larger range of suspects, more detailed setting and background, sharper social commentary, more red herrings, ever trickier plotting.

From the start the detective novel had had built into it the kinds of criticism that Chandler, Watson and James would later level at Christie, though it was generally agreed that too much expansion was a threat to the tightness and cohesion that the detective story required. Hence the eager search for enclosed spaces within which a mystery could take place and be contained. A village, a country house, or locked room were early favourites, but anywhere would do. A school, Oxbridge college, shop or office; a ship, plane or snow-bound cabin. There was surprisingly little disagreement, early and more recent, on the need for this kind of containment. Whatever the larger ambitions of her novels, this was a convention that P D James, just as much as Christie, relied on throughout the whole of her career. Where they parted company, and still do, was on the relationship between the detective story and the traditional novel. It was felt increasingly that by focusing on the solution of a murder mystery, the traditional detective novel had fatally restricted itself, becoming ever more removed from more serious literary fiction. It was the leading ambition of writers such as Chandler and James, and the focal point of their criticism, to restore this imbalance, to regain true literary status for the detective novel.

* * *

The recurrent charges against Christie of cosiness and village idealism, unimaginative writing and isolation from the real world, make it clear enough where she was to be placed in such a scale of fictional values. But Christie's portrayal of Miss Marple and St. Mary Mead had nothing to do with ignorance of the world or narrative sloppiness, or with any determined promotion of rural nostalgia.

It was, rather, the result of a conscious experimental policy on her part to develop a form of minimalism for the detective story in which the murder mystery is totally central, the focus of the reader's attention and the main means, even at times the sole means, of conveying whatever moral and social values are being explored, with nothing that could be considered extraneous.

At first this had been an instinctive response, brought about largely by the personal nature of of Miss Marple's creation, but Christie soon began to apply it more consciously to her other detective stories. The process was a mysterious one and remained so throughout her life, though its remarkable nature has not gone entirely unrecognized, most perceptively from a rather unlikely quarter.

Laura Thompson quotes P.D. James as saying of Christie: 'She has the ability to conjure a world without actually describing it.'[8] These words come from a recorded conversation and offer a far more perceptive view of Christie than is apparent in other comments published under James's own name. There is, understandably, an air of surprise about it, with James aware of describing a conjuring trick that has long fascinated, disturbed, and ultimately baffled her. And this may well be the case. After all, James's avowed ambition, along with that of many other detective-story writers of her generation, was, as we have seen, to bring back to detective fiction the kind of literary respectability that had been lost, largely under Christie's influence, and that meant expansion rather than reduction. And yet here is Christie being recognized as creating something of the longed-for effect in an entirely different, remarkable and unacknowledged way. It represents a literary achievement that clearly draws from James an unwilling admiration. Perhaps because of this ambivalence on James's part, her critical comment is spot on. Christie really does in some curious way of her own 'conjure a world without describing it.'

What needs to be further acknowledged, and appropriately so for a conjuring trick, is the extent to which it was the result of skill and application rather than luck. Also, how it was a technique pioneered only by Christie. The most admired of the other golden-age writers – Dorothy L. Sayers, Margery Allingham, Josephine Tey, Ngaio Marsh – whatever their separate abilities, had no interest in Christie's kind of extreme literary minimalism. They were all happy to employ whatever social detail and commentary were required to place the detective novel, to requote another one of P.D. James's telling phrases, 'unambiguously in its own time and place.' In their day the work of these novelists was often called upon by reviewers and critics to serve as a superior comparative example to that of Christie. The denigration was effective at the time, though it is now precisely the willingness of those novelists to engage so eagerly with the social world of their murder mysteries that has helped render their work dated in comparison with Christie's.

Christie herself had no wish to challenge the traditional or literary novel. She was certainly ambitious to write novels which were not detective stories and she did so with a certain amount of success. But her principal literary concern was to perfect a particular type of detective novel, and one of the main ways she did this was by stripping away all material that she regarded as irrelevant to the crime and its solution. There are, for example, very few descriptive or analytical passages of any kind in her novels, whether of places, buildings, environments, or character. The major exception to this generalisation is the detailed and comparatively lengthy exploration at the close of a novel, by Poirot or Miss Marple, of the personalities and motives of the various suspects in the murder being investigated. But physical descriptions of people are whittled down to essentials; sometimes to little more than whatever personal or physical qualities they need to have that will determine the part they are to play in the novel. Dates, together with historical and political information, in an historical or period sense, are also reduced to a minimum or omitted entirely.

In this she was not simply giving most of her energy to an over-ingenious riddle, another common criticism of her that is only ever half-true. Her aim was closer to that of a moral fable or fairy tale or Greek tragedy in that she is concerned that no part of her story should be extraneous to its central effect. Anything she does not wish to have placed before the reader is set carefully off-stage, as violent death is in Greek tragedy.[9] Every aspect of the story contributes to its understanding. She believed that too much detailed description – whether topographical or political or sociological – would result in a story becoming quickly out of date. This view did not lead, as it has done for other very different kinds of writers, to the creation of an alternative world or timeless land. Nor was it connected, other than very loosely, with the regionalism that was a prominent feature of English fiction of the late nineteenth and early twentieth centuries.[10]

In the nearby case of Wessex, for instance, Thomas Hardy employed a remarkable blend of fiction and topographical exactitude to create a very specific, locally identifiable part of the country. There is no uncertainty in his novels about where in England events are taking place even if most of the names of towns or localities he uses may not be found on a conventional map. Wessex was historically the name of a separate kingdom based on Hampshire and Dorset which has long ceased to exist. Hardy resurrected it, though he did not usually treat it historically. The heart of his Wessex is modern Dorset and areas immediately around it. Places in his novels are given a mix of real and invented names which are not difficult to link with their modern equivalents, while the extended atmospheric descriptions of the district's spectacular landscape are also easily recognized by the modern reader. The people and events of Hardy's novels are, in the main, contemporary, often aggressively so. Difficult as it may be to believe, much of Christie's fiction is set close to, even within, the same topographical areas as Hardy's. Christie's birthplace, Torquay, is in Devon, slightly west, in a strict sense, of Hardy's Wessex, and she, like Hardy moved easily around the south and southwest of England. But she possessed none of Hardy's desire to make any literary or regional claim to this part of the country. In a rather special sense she actually wanted to distance herself from it by emphasizing its general rather than its specific character.

Even so, a story needed to be of its time, and this she achieved not, as Hardy did, by the often startlingly modern nature of his themes, but through detail in action. It is one of the marked distinctions of a Christie novel that while it is often vague about where and when exactly it is set, the detailed aspects of the social relationships that have always been a mainstay of English realism – dress, speech, manners, food, drink, gardens and houses and a precise sense of topicality – are deployed with great skill and close observation. For her, extended description is inaction, and the speed and economy with which she is able to establish a scene can be quite remarkable. These effects are achieved by extremely brief descriptions of setting and characters bound together by totally convincing fast-moving dialogue. Descriptions of places and people are inserted effortlessly into the total cumulative pattern of her novels, a gradual yet apparently unstoppable moving forwards, leading eventually to an explanation or solution of everything that has taken place in the narrative. The combination of precisely realized social life and uncertain geographical and temporal settings makes a major contribution to the multi-levelled mystifying tone of Christie's novels.

That Christie didn't start out with these ideas fully formed or natural to her, is clear from the three full-length Poirot novels which were published before Miss Marple came on the scene. *The Murder on the Links* is a little outside of the main point being made here as it was an exercise in a type of French detective novel that was popular in Britain at the time.

Nevertheless, and naturally enough, Christie goes to a good deal of trouble to establish as effectively as possible an appropriately French atmosphere and mood. But the other two early novels, *The Mysterious Affair at Styles* and *The Murder of Roger Ackroyd* were set in contemporary England. In both she used the blend of fictional and real place names which was always to be her practice, though in her portrayal of the villages of Styles St. Mary and King's Abbott, Christie was consciously aiming to evoke a sense of typicality. Trying to 'give some idea of what I should describe as our local geography,' Roger Ackroyd says, 'King's Abbot, is, I imagine, very much like any other village.' However unobjectionably general that may seem to be, it was not the kind of claim that could later be made on behalf of Miss Marple. Although both of these early Poirot novels are set in 'typical' English villages, they are also embedded in a far more solidly realized social world than was ever to be considered for St. Mary Mead. With *Styles*, at the very start of her career, Christie turned naturally to the material that was most familiar to her. She was writing during the middle of the First World War and the impact of the war on every aspect of British society is made apparent in the book. In *Roger Ackroyd* as well the social structure of village life, the variety of its inhabitants, their particular tastes and pastimes are all portrayed with care and in detail.

None of this can be applied without severe qualification to Miss Marple. Her St. Mary Mead is astonishingly sparse in comparison with both Styles St. Mary and King's Abbott. It was obviously not only her personal life and family background that were to be kept hidden from the reader. Her 'local geography' was to remain something of a mystery as well. It's a subject that needs further consideration.

* * *

For a start, the key issue of village life, its prominence or not in Christie's fiction and especially her assumed determination to portray it as some kind of idyllic English existence, is singularly misguided. Any discussion of the issue must focus on Miss Marple, together with a handful of other non-Marple novels, because as we have seen, a village setting for Poirot was early discarded by Christie. Poirot is by nature a metropolitan, moving mainly in an urban, sophisticated society. For Miss Marple, though, the village is her home and her natural environment, and was to be so, at least as a base, throughout all of the novels, and a very special kind of village environment it turned out to be. Its portrayal was to help determine not only the distinctive tone of the Miss Marple novels but, more generally, to have a strong influence on the kind of detective story that Christie would go on to develop.

There is no reason whatever to believe that Christie was interested in promoting an idealized or 'picturesque' image of village life, for Miss Marple or anyone else to inhabit. Most of the Miss Marple novels don't actually take place in her home village, and in those that do Christie is so little concerned with presenting or promoting any kind of realistic or nostalgic image of rural life that for much of the time she might not be writing about the country at all. Any 'suburban dweller' who was sufficiently stirred by Christie's portrayal of St. Mary Mead to go and live in the country would need to be very 'ill-informed' indeed, and not just in ways mockingly invoked by Colin Watson. St. Mary Mead is obviously 'in the country' but it is difficult to know what kind of country it is or what purpose it serves.

There are virtually no topographical descriptions of any kind of the countryside around St. Mary Mead, or of the village itself: no sweeping downs, no winding lanes, no hills or valleys, no fragrant meadows, lonely moors, shady woods, rivers or streams. We are not even told what Miss Marple's celebrated cottage or her equally celebrated garden looks like. As we have seen, in 'The Tuesday Night Club,' the very first Miss Marple story, the atmosphere of the interior of her cottage was established by 'broad black beams' and 'good old furniture,' and that was it. The beams and the heavy furniture do not reappear in subsequent stories and novels. In the late novel *The Mirror Crack'd* we learn that at the 'old world core' of St. Mary Mead there is a 'little nest of Queen Anne and Georgian houses, of which [Miss Marple's] was one,' and in the much earlier *Vicarage* we are told that she likes making 'Japanese gardens.' Neither detail is developed here or elsewhere. Both are used purely for local narrative convenience. We are occasionally provided with details of the interior of the cottage and its rural setting, as with the nearby wood, for instance, in *The Murder at the Vicarage*, but not in any consistent manner.

Round and about St. Mary Mead, we are shown no working farms and therefore no farmers or agricultural labourers, and there are few animals anywhere, though in *Vicarage* there are poachers readily available for the tyrannical Colonel Protheroe, the local magistrate, to send to jail. It is rare to find anyone horse-riding or fox-hunting or bird-shooting or fishing. Indeed, apart from a very occasional acknowledgment, such activities are hardly mentioned. Among the Miss Marple short stories only 'The Case of the Caretaker' gives any sense of a larger or more prosperous 'county' society even existing. It is significant that this story was later expanded into a full-length novel, *Endless Night* (1967). As for the two final Miss Marple short stories, 'Sanctuary' (1954) and 'Greenshaw's Folly' (1956), both of which were written for special occasions, St. Mary Mead has no part to play in them at all.

In *Sleeping Murder* Colonel Bantry does go shooting, 'his spaniel at his heels,' and in *The Body in the Library* he talks about arranging for work to be done on one of 'the farms.' We are also told that when personally worried, as he has good cause to be in *Library*, he likes to visit the pigs. But the reader doesn't accompany him on these outings, though, significantly, the television viewer does. As Bantry himself is not a farmer, presumably the farms he mentions are run by tenants. But even this supposition is challenged in the later novels. After his death we learn from his widow Dolly in *The Mirror Crack'd* that their connection with the district has never been close. They had bought Gossington Hall as 'just a house with a nice bit of shooting and fishing attached' when the Colonel retired from the army.

This casual attitude of the Bantrys is particularly revealing because of the virtual absence in St. Mary Mead, along with farming, of the traditional social structures of country life. Although film and television adaptations of Christie's novels like to follow the idea of the aristocratic or gentrified Big House as an inevitable focal point, it is barely relevant at all to the Miss Marple's world.

* * *

Poirot is at ease with country houses, and they are central to some of those Christie novels which feature neither of her two star detectives. But apart from the occasions when St. Mary Mead is temporarily disrupted by colourful incomers, its social life is distinctly low-key and overwhelmingly middle-class. Neither of the two large houses in the district qualifies as what would generally be thought of as a 'Big House.' They are both owned by retired middle-ranking army officers who hold positions of authority in the district but who are without aristocratic or landed connections and provide no social lead or model. Even if they tried to do so, who is there to follow them?

Gossington Hall is eventually sold, with no regrets on Dolly's part, to a glamorous, mentally unstable Hollywood film star. Old Hall which is owned by Colonel Protheroe, the man who is murdered at the vicarage, suffers a similar, though less glamorous, modernizing fate. In the short story 'The Case of the Perfect Maid' it is described simply as 'a big Victorian house' which 'an enterprising speculator has divided … into four flats with a central hot-water system, and the use of "the grounds" to be held in common by the tenants.' These are a retired Indian judge, a rich eccentric old lady and her maid, a young married couple, and two maiden ladies. All of these would fit perfectly into St. Mary Mead, the social life of which seems to be curiously self-sufficient. At times it is reminiscent of Elizabeth Gaskell's *Cranford* (1853), though notably purged of the Victorian characters' obsession with all things aristocratic.

The retired army officers and Indian judges, together with a handful of local professionals, especially lawyers and doctors, set the social tone of St. Mary Mead. The vicar belongs in their company as well, though he is placed slightly apart because of his responsibility for maintaining moral standards, a task in which he is aided, or more usually hindered, by a large number of elderly spinsters and widows. Some of the professional men appear to have wives and children but they play no part in the novels. In *The Murder at the Vicarage* Griselda, an incomer married to the vicar, provides the reader with a glimpse of the social world she has left behind her in moving to St. Mary Mead. Teasing her elderly devoted husband, she lists the men she might have married as 'a Cabinet Minister, a Baronet, a rich Company Promoter, three subalterns, and a ne'er-do-weel with attractive manners.' The attractive ne'er-do-weel is the only one of Griselda's suitors who would have been a familiar social type to the inhabitants of this village. Poirot mixes naturally with such people in other social settings, but not Miss Marple or her neighbours in St. Mary Mead.

Domestic servants, though, are everywhere visible in Christie's novels, the earlier ones especially. Poirot is, naturally enough, always kind and considerate whenever he comes across them, but they are not part of his own daily life. Comfortably set up in his modern appartment, he employs professional helpers and occasionally uses Hastings as a personal assistant. Servants, however, are very much a daily reality for Miss Marple and, furthermore, a constant cause of her solicitude. She herself always has one maid, usually a very young and inexperienced trainee who comes to her from from a local charitable orphanage. Miss Marple actually sits on the orphanage's committee. She obtains her maid servants in this way because she feels it her duty to help them to obtain better positions than she herself can offer. It needs to be remembered that this was a time when employment as a domestic was often the only kind of work many young girls and women were able to obtain. They were often not even qualified for that, which is why Miss Marple sets about so conscientiously to train them. Her responsibility, though, extends far beyond making sure the girls know how to dust ornaments and air the beds. She watches over them in a kindly manner, allowing for the occasional moments of irritation at their lack of intelligence and the anaemia and adenoids from which they tend to suffer.

Here is one of those topics that have brought charges of condescension upon Christie, and not always fairly so. Most of these girls would have been very young, very poor and barely educated. They would also have suffered from a variety of physical complaints, ailments, and minor illnesses, of which adenoids can be taken as the type. Until the National Health Service was up and running in the late 1940s, treatment for most non life-threatening conditions like adenoids had to be paid for which was impossible for these girls, and, indeed, the majority of the poor and working classes. They were therefore expected to put up with the unpleasant symptoms of blocked nasal passages, blurred speech and and runny noses. These would have been very common conditions and are noted as such by Christie.

Whether she, or her characters, can be fairly charged with describing them in a condescending way is a different issue. It is certainly assumed by several characters in the novels that servants of the poorest class will not only be adenoidal but generally dim as well. The attitude is typified by Mary Dove (not herself a particularly prepossessing character) in *A Pocket Full of Rye*. Gladys, she says, is 'quite a decent sort of girl but very nearly half-witted. The adenoidal type.' On receipt of this description Inspector Neele nods understandingly. He doesn't much care for Mary Dove, but he knows perfectly well what she means about Gladys. On one occasion Miss Marple seems to place herself in this company. In *The Mirror Crack'd* she recalls the girls that used to be sent to her for training: 'Rather simple, some of them had been, and frequently adenoidal, and Amy distinctly moronic.' This, though, is from a novel published as late as 1962 and Miss Marple is looking back on a time long before the National Health Service was established. It is worth noting, very much in Christie's favour, that a central concern of this novel is not only to acknowledge, but to praise the changes that have taken place both in the health of those poor girls and, more generally, in the standard of domestic service.

It also has to be said that if there was very little Miss Marple could do about her maidservants' adenoids, she is always deeply concerned about their general welfare, and wherever possible helps them to live healthier and more hygienic lives. She is also a sympathetic listener to their personal problems. In 'The Case of the Perfect Maid' and *A Pocket Full of Rye* her finest skills as a detective, fuelled by fierce moral indignation that such vulnerable girls should be treated so unfairly or 'wickedly,' are unleashed on their behalf.

In addition to the work done by domestic servants, the everyday needs of St Mary Mead's principal inhabitants are met by an unrealistically large number of shop-keepers, tradesmen and delivery boys. In fact, the size of the village itself can vary according to the demands of whatever plot is in operation. At different times, it is shown to have its own church, taxi service, Post Office, railway station (branch line only), a police station (with just one policeman on duty), and a pub called the Blue Boar. Just beyond the pub there is a group of houses, the inhabitants of which rarely play any part in the various dramas that take place in the village. These houses are not to be confused with the Development which has a special significance in the post-war novels and will be discussed in its proper context in a later chapter.

But in no way can St. Mary Mead be said to possess the facilities or services crucial to the existence of the commuters' dormitory invoked by Colin Watson. For these it relies on the neighbouring town of Much Benham. Only two miles away, it is clearly of local importance. Without it St. Mary Mead would be even more isolated. Here at Much Benham is a hospital, a mainline railway station with a direct connection to London, and larger shops which provide not only a greater range of goods than St. Mary Mead but also some much-needed privacy. When in *Vicarage* Griselda Clement learns she is pregnant she goes to a bookshop in Much Benham to gather some information about motherhood. Unfortunately for Griselda, and unseen by her, Miss Marple is in the bookshop at the same time. It's not clear whether Miss Marple buys anything, but she takes careful note of the books that Griselda is consulting. Colonel Bantry goes to Much Benham for meetings of the Conservative Society, while for Miss Marple, when she's not snooping in its bookshop, it is of importance primarily as the headquarters of the county police. Here, in addition to cells and a mortuary, are the offices of Colonel Melchett and Inspector Slack, men of significance in Miss Marple's detective activities.

None of this can be sensibly described as idealized or nostalgic. On the contrary, it represents a perfectly recognizable and carefully evoked structure of rural towns, of varying sizes, serving slightly different functions, and purposefully interacting with each other. St. Mary Mead is one tiny part of this. It is true that Christie's literary method can occasionally render the topography of her novels mystifying in not quite the desired ways. But for much of the time it works exceptionally well. Featured towns tend to be given fictional names which make them sound vaguely rural, like St. Mary Mead and Much Benham. The same method is used for the counties. St. Mary Mead is in Downshire. Nearby are Glenshire and Radfordshire. Milchester is a large town somewhere towards the south west that has a university and a teaching hospital. Danemouth is a 'large and fashionable watering place' on the coast 'about eighteen miles from Gossington Hall' which would place St. Mary Mead itself a little nearer to the sea than the usual approximation of twenty-five miles. Some real names are retained, either because they are essential points of reference or they are introduced to indicate what kind of town Christie has in mind, and then replaced by a fictional equivalent once the connection has been made.

This technique is put to comprehensive use in *Sleeping Murder*. Gwenda Reed disembarks from New Zealand at Plymouth. Set on buying a house in the 'South of England' she hires a car and drives across Devonshire but finds nothing suitable. She then tours the south and stumbles across the 'charming seaside resort' of Dillmouth. In ways she can't be expected to understand immediately, here is exactly the house she has been looking for. A little later in the novel, Miss Marple, now deeply involved in the case, asks Dr Haydock to prescribe for her some recuperative 'fresh seaside air.' Haydock, an old friend and admirer, is always willing to connive at Miss Marple's little ploys, and he asks where she has in mind. Eastbourne, perhaps? Bournemouth? The Isle of Wight? In return, Miss Marple asks whether he wouldn't agree that Dillmouth would be more beneficial to her health? 'More likely to be the end of you,' Dr Haydock responds sardonically. Still, he agrees to play along, and with the approximate topography established for the reader, the plot moves on not to real-life Eastbourne, Bournemouth or the Isle of Wight, but to fictional Dillmouth. At the close of the novel, the mystery solved, Miss Marple, Gwenda and her husband Giles drive over to the Imperial Hotel at Torquay in Devon for a celebratory 'change of scene.'

If a line is drawn across the middle of this large stretch of southern England, roughly halfway between London and the south coast, then somewhere on that line is where St. Mary Mead is to be found. Where exactly is never revealed. Anne Hart suggests 'about twenty-five miles south of London' and a little less than that from the nearby seaside towns that appear regularly in the novels, and this sounds about right.[11] Whether it is possible to place St. Mary Mead more accurately must be put to one side for the moment. For now, it can be said that Hart's approximation will do. Even so, when a particular plot demands it St. Mary Mead does tend to move about the map. Its county is usually given as Downshire, but not always. Sometimes it seems to be nearer to Kent, where the original

St. Mary Mead in *The Blue Train* placed it, sometimes it seems to be in the Home Counties and very close to London, at other times it moves further West towards Dorset.

St. Mary Mead's slippery geographical nature would matter a little more if it had a distinctive character of its own (which it doesn't) or was a standard and regular locality for the Miss Marple mysteries (which it isn't). In fact, *The Murder at the Vicarage* and *The Mirror Crack'd* are the only two of the twelve novels that take place entirely within what has come to be regarded as the murder capital of rural England. Several other of Miss Marple's cases begin or end in St. Mary Mead, but are set mainly in other villages or towns in the south of England or elsewhere.

As most of the murder cases Miss Marple investigates take place outside of St. Mary Mead, it needed to be somewhere she could get in and out of, quickly when necessary. Not being a car owner, she relies on trains to move about and is very well-informed on timetables and the availability of cheap-day return tickets. By using the junction at Much Benham, it is easy for her to get to London, and once there she can move in any direction she chooses. Some of the journeys she makes are quite complicated and involve several changes of trains, mainline and London underground. Only on special occasions, does she choose to use the local taxi service which she insists, ignoring its many changes of ownership, on calling Inch's.

Although it is tempting to try to fix these fictional places with some kind of real-life identity, it matters little to the enjoyment of the novels if we don't know in which county St. Mary Mead is to be found. Nor is it of any more importance that in terms of the sociology of English village life St. Mary Mead is a non-starter. The blurring of this kind of information was fully intentional. Christie knew perfectly well what she was up to.

As Anne Hart observes, it is impossible 'to imagine St. Mary Mead without Miss Marple or Miss Marple without St. Mary Mead; it was the archetypal English village created just for her.'[12] This is very much to the point. The only significance of St. Mary Mead is that for years it was Miss Marple's training ground. The village has no reliable existence, topographical or sociological, apart from her relationship with it. St. Mary Mead is a good example of Christie's preference for fictional rather than real place names making excellent sense. It is also a perfect illustration of her use of non-realistic means to create an illusion of reality. Not only was St. Mary Mead created for Miss Marple, it still exists for her alone. It is, in effect, a one-woman village. All its other inhabitants are specimens and samples, preserved and observed, ticketed and classified. St. Mary Mead is Miss Marple's university, her library and, most of all, her laboratory where she studies human nature and formulates the theories that are tested on her regular forays beyond the village.

Chapter 5

Interregnum:
Life without Miss Marple

For Miss Marple, the years from *The Thirteen Problems* (1932) to *The Body in the Library* (1942) were an inexplicable interregnum. At the start of this period her character, personality, and credentials as a detective were all strongly established, with a handful of local puzzles and one full-scale murder mystery triumphantly solved. Looking ahead to 1942, there, ready and waiting for her, were most of the cases that would make her famous world-wide. In between, ten years of virtual banishment. In all that time, she was presented with just one further problem from the past, its nature and solution narrated in a rather creaky short story. For its oddity, if little else, that story deserves some consideration.

In 1934 Christie was commissioned by BBC radio to write a story which she herself was to read on what was then called the National Programme. The event took place on 11 May of that same year and the story was published in *The Home Journal* just over one year later. It was then called 'Behind Closed Doors' though always subsequently 'Miss Marple tells a Story' and did not appear in volume form until *The Regatta Mystery* (1939), a miscellaneous collection of Christie short stories published only in America. In the UK, 'Miss Marple tells a Story' was not collected until it was included, misleadingly, in the posthumous volume called *Miss Marple's Final Cases* (1979). We know little about how or why this particular story was commissioned, but even at this early date Christie did have close connections with broadcasting. Some years earlier she had been one of the six members of the Detection Club who joined together in an experiment to produce serial detective stories for the BBC. J.R. Ackerley, who at this time worked for the BBC was an admirer of

Christie's work and would have liked her to write original stories for him. She consulted her agent and they turned Ackerley down because of the relatively low pay the BBC was able to offer in comparison with that readily on hand from newspaper and periodical editors.[1] So, it is possible that it was Ackerley who finally persuaded Christie to broadcast a short story. The mysteries, though, remain. Why at this time? Why Miss Marple? Why this particular story?

As we have seen, Christie had gone to a good deal of trouble to close *The Thirteen Problems* with 'Death by Drowning,' a story which reaffirmed the image of Miss Marple as she had appeared in the second batch of short stories and *The Murder at the Vicarage*. Yet here, two years later, Christie seemed to ignore or overthrow all of that by turning back to the very earliest Miss Marple stories. She did not go so far as to recreate the original cottage atmosphere or to garb Miss Marple in Victorian lace, but nor is it entirely up to date. The story is told to Raymond and 'Joan' West. That is her revised Christian name, though the couple had only appeared in the very first meetings of the Tuesday Night Club, as also had Mr Petherick who brings the mystery to Miss Marple now. Christie makes it clear that she is not simply using up old material by having Miss Marple point out that Mr Petherick had died 'two years ago.' That is, two years before she narrates this latest story to Raymond and Joan. Therefore 'Miss Marple tells a Story' probably can't simply be regarded as a leftover piece of work. But nor can it be taken as a sudden decision on Christie's part to set Miss Marple going again. If that had been the case she would have wanted to continue to emphasise the makeover she had given Miss Marple in the later stories and *Vicarage* rather than toying with an earlier image. It could simply be sloppiness on Christie's part. Otherwise, the story is best taken as an indication, together with the fleeting thought three years further on that *Death on the Nile* might possibly be a suitable feature for Miss Marple, that the village detective hadn't slipped entirely from Christie's mind.

Whether Christie herself was unwilling to take up the personal challenge that writing about Miss Marple might well have caused her, or whether she was waiting for suitable new material to present itself, Miss Marple's removal from the scene was certainly not due to a general slowdown in Christie's activity. Nor was there any kind of decline in her creativity. Throughout the whole of this decade from which Miss Marple was so noticeably absent Christie's productivity was impressive even by her own extraordinary standards.

During these years she published, and largely wrote, more than twenty books, and for once this hyperactivity could not be attributed to one of her depression-provoked writing frenzies. On the contrary, it was a time of personal calm and steady achievement, the result, one assumes, of the happiness and security that came to Christie following her marriage to Max Mallowan and celebrated, perhaps, in the book which featured one of her lesser-known detectives *Parker Pyne Investigates* (1934). The mysteries that Pyne explores are of a rather special kind. He advertises his business with the slogan: 'Are you happy? If not, consult Mr Parker Pyne.' Although he readily acknowledges that relatively few people are happy in life, he is also convinced that the reasons for their unhappiness are limited in number. He therefore sets out to identify the cause of someone's unhappiness and to correct it. Christie said she much enjoyed writing about Parker Pyne and that personal enjoyment carries to the reader.

At the beginning of this period she collected together a volume of previously published short stories *The Hound of Death and other Stories* (1933). The work was of uneven quality and unsurprisingly so, dating back as some of it did to 1924. It seems to have been something of a clearing-up operation, because virtually everything else Christie wrote in these years was, like the Parker Pyne book, new. It was also characteristically miscellaneous, ranging from work for magazines, theatre, radio (including 'Miss Marple tells a Story'), and a little later even infant TV. She also published a new Mary Westmacott novel.

But it was the detective novel that absorbed most of her attention, and here newness and experimentation ruled as never before. They included several outstanding mystery novels which were unconnected with any of her named detectives, notably *Murder is Easy* and *Ten Little Niggers* (later to be renamed, *And Then There Were None*). It was, though, Hercule Poirot who dominated her imagination. The central role that Miss Marple had occupied in Christie's life for five years was now reclaimed by Poirot in the most flamboyant manner. In the eight years between 1933 and 1941, and on top of all of her other writing, Christie published fourteen new books devoted to Poirot, thirteen of which were full-length novels and one of which consisted of four substantial novellas. The quantity of the work was amazing enough, but the quality even more so. This was the time that Christie's high and, as it was to prove, unshakeable reputation as a writer of detective stories was established. Here are to be found many of Poirot's most celebrated cases, including *Lord Edgware Dies*, *Murder on the Orient Express*, *Death on the Nile*, *Cards on the Table*, *The ABC Murders*, *Murder in Mesopotamia*, *Murder in the Mews*, *Dead Man's Mirror*, *Appointment with Death* and *Hercule Poirot's Christmas*. One classic murder mystery after another, coming at the rate of more than two a year.

The minimalist narrative technique that Christie had begun instinctively with Miss Marple was now extended more consciously to Poirot. His image was already too well established to have been affected by the personal stress that had driven Christie to obliterate whatever she could of Miss Marple's past private life. But although Poirot himself stayed much as he had always been, he also became the main beneficiary of Christie's refined literary methods. The narrative line of his novels was further trimmed to give full attention to a book's central mystery; character and action were conveyed largely through dialogue; and all descriptive and analytical writing that might be considered digressive or extraneous, was rigorously pruned or omitted. The method was now strongly enough established to survive even a radical change in Christie's way of life.

Until the early 1930s, her detective fiction had been set largely in England, whether Poirot's London or Miss Marple's St. Mary Mead. When her thrillers required more glamorous settings she had drawn for atmosphere on either vague literary backgrounds or the experiences she had shared with Archie on their ten-month long world tour to promote the British Empire Exhibition in 1922.[2] But following her impulsive decision to visit Baghdad and her subsequent marriage to Max Mallowan there was a marked change in Christie's way of life. She was determined not to repeat the mistake she felt she had made by leaving Archie too much alone. This time she would stay close to her husband, travel with him, and as far as she could share in his work. There was no thought of her neglecting her own writing: it would be carefully integrated into the new marriage.

As Max was a practising archaeologist and often away from England on a dig, Christie committed herself to living for long periods of time in the Middle East and getting on with her writing wherever she and Max happened to be. It was fortunate that she never had been the kind of writer who was easily put off by changes of place and circumstances. The new arrangement seemed hardly to bother her at all. She set up a writing desk in what for many other writers would have been the most inhospitable of places and wrote, prolifically.

And, not only was she able to write in these unfamiliar circumstances, she wrote about them as well, the Middle East providing her with experience of foreign settings that she enjoyed and quickly got to know at first hand. Some of Poirot's new adventures still took place in England (whether written there or not), but others were placed in the Middle East, creating in effect a kind of sub-genre of detective stories. In some of her novels the archaeological excavations were used as settings. At other times, the atmosphere of the Middle East served very different narrative purposes: it became a natural, accepted part of her life.

As she moved backwards and forwards between England and the Middle East throughout the 1930s Christie would have been unavoidably conscious not only of the new and strange environments that thrilled her, but also of a less welcome air of European crisis, in Spain, Germany and the Soviet Union especially. Events in these countries were followed passionately and divisively in Britain, ensuring that the literary scene at home was dominated by political concerns and conflicting ideologies as never before. The Middle East itself was not immune from the political crises in Europe. Many of the areas where Max and Agatha lived and worked were under the imperial control of European countries, Britain and France mainly, with Italy more recently involved. Very soon the whole of North Africa and the Mediterranean was to become a major area of conflict in the 1939-45 war. The archaeological digs were affected not only by political reverberations from Europe, but by local disturbances as well, while the financial backers – who, no doubt, often included Christie herself – were becoming increasingly concerned at the growing instability of the whole area. Even so, it wasn't until very close to the actual outbreak of war that Max and Agatha finally decided they could no longer continue to stay in the Middle East and returned permanently to England.

For most of the 1930s these political issues, whether international or local, were rigorously excluded from Christie's novels. Her links with the Middle East had introduced a new element into her work that she valued, used to good effect, and succeeded in turning into something distinctively her own. But she did not let it affect her developing ideas about the kind of detective story she wanted to write. If she was tempted to introduce the political preoccupations of Europe and Britain into the novels that were now set in the Middle East, as many novelists one imagines would quite naturally have done, she firmly resisted the temptation because, along with her unwillingness to use dates and historical events or circumstances to fix the the action of a novel, it would have weakened the element of timelessness she was trying to achieve.

She also continued to avoid employing any form of extended local description for dramatic effect, a policy that was applied as strictly to the Middle East as it was to Dorset or Devon, and she resisted any temptation there might have been to turn the foreign settings of these novels into romantic or mythical places. Her approach was perfectly businesslike. Egypt is Egypt, Syria is Syria, the Nile the Nile. Life is dominated by the desert and heat. The special social conditions and the distinctive ways of living and working in such places continued to be recreated in detail, skilfully and with firm control. The atmosphere had to feel right, and it does. To reuse the striking words of P.D. James, Christie was more than ever, in some curious unrecognized way, managing to conjure up a world, and a very new and different one for detective fiction, without describing it.

She herself drew attention to this aspect of her method in *Murder in Mesopotamia* (1936). The novel's narrator is Amy Leatheran, a nurse who is brought out to Iraq to care for a patient. There she is caught up in the murder mystery and eventually persuaded that she is the best person to write an 'unvarnished plain account' of events. She is not keen to do so but accepts the task, protesting that she doesn't 'pretend to be an author or to know anything about writing.' Later she adds: 'I think I'd better make it clear right away that there isn't going to be any local colour in this story.'

She even claims that she 'doesn't know anything about archaeology and I don't know that I very much want to.' It wasn't the first time Christie had had a narrator of a novel make this kind of disclaimer. Many years earlier Anne Beddingfield in *The Man in the Brown Suit* had done so when the action shifted to South Africa: 'I guarantee no genuine local colour – you know the sort of thing – half a dozen words in italics on every page. I admire it very much, but I can't do it.' Not that it was then an issue for Christie. Anne Beddingfield was narrating a loosely structured thriller, one of Christie's very best, and was allowed to comment on anything that drew her attention or that the plot demanded.

Amy Leatheran, though, was part of a more focused experiment and under far tighter authorial control than Anne Beddingfield had been. Although there is no 'local colour,' as either of them understands the term, and Amy Letheran has little professional interest in the activities going on around her, this doesn't exclude close attention being given to the work of the archaeologists, their way of life, surroundings and the objects on which their efforts are so intently focused. Perhaps she succeeds in evoking local colour all the more effectively because everything she describes is new and strange to her, as it was to Christie herself. These details, after all, provide all that is needed to make effective the very particular kind of mystery that *Murder in Mesopotamia* is, and that, for Christie, was the important thing.

Amy Leatheran's comments on the amateurish nature of her writing efforts were clearly being used by Christie to answer or forestall anticipated criticism. Probably both. While Christie was now keener to introduce her own feelings and opinions on matters into the novels, this was still still not being done in her own voice. Instead, it was achieved either indirectly by use of an appointed narrator (as here) or sometimes very indirectly, even cryptically, by rather obscure, seemingly unconnected allusions and references. This kind of playful, self-referential qualitity, would even be embedded in the novels so neatly that Christie would very shortly succeed in bringing about major changes in the nature of her work that were barely noticed by her contemporary reviewers and critics.

For the moment though, she was committed to the tight narrative control of her detective novels and that meant not allowing any distracting attention to be given to either the exotic nature of her new surroundings or the growing signs of political turmoil. It is a mark of her very real success that even today her Middle Eastern novels are generally accepted not only as exciting mysteries but as exotic tales as well, with very little attention ever given to what exactly this means and even less attention to the indirection and subtlety of the effects she employs to create such an impression. As so often with Christie, many aspects of her work have been taken over by non-literary forces, the effects she strove for being radically displaced, though without necessarily destroying the tone or nature of the original work. One specific example must do for many.

* * *

For Christie the romance of this whole phase of her life was epitomized above all by the Orient Express.[3] The transcontinental train had first carried her to Baghdad, introduced her to ways of travel she fell for immediately, brought her a closely shared life with Max Mallowan, and provided new settings for her detective stories. The Orient Express was the visible pulsating, international link between old and new experiences and between the two very different settings she was now using in her novels. How could the murder mystery she created in 1934 especially to celebrate that wonderful train be anything other than the epitome of heightened romance and exoticism? It had simply everything.

There was the hideous child murder that had been committed in America, fixed by the single stark date 1930; the essential information about it communicated by evocative New York and New Jersey newspaper headlines, photographs and journalistic frenzy. Then an abrupt change to 'five years later,' the past crime making way for the present solution. There's Poirot preparing to cross the gloomy Bosphorus on a dank winter morning, leaving behind him one successfully solved mystery and totally unaware that he is to be immediately forced into another. He is on is way to join the Orient Express in Istanbul, the gateway between Europe and the East. For this first part of his journey he is escorted by a rather dim British army officer. In Istanbul, there is the bustle, colour, hissing steam and screaming whistle of the train as it prepares for the next stage of its journey; the luggage, along with mounds of food and drink being loaded on board, everything that is needed for the luxury journey; the mingling of people of different races, ages and social status, appearing from all angles as either travellers or merchants serving the travellers. And then, with the train barely started on its journey into the Balkans, it is trapped in gigantic snowdrifts, pulled to a halt, with the passengers locked on board while one of them is stabbed to death.

Isn't it all there, the brutal unneccessary child-murder; Christie's own ingenious take on it; a story of high drama set within an inexpressibly romantic atmosphere?

And yes it is, except that most of the details given here come neither from the novel nor from Christie herself. They are virtually all taken from two fine adaptations of the novel; first, the enormously successful 1974 EMI film of *Murder on the Orient Express* starring Albert Finney as Poirot; and, more recently, the ITV version in 2010 with David Suchet as Poirot. Neither of these screen versions is glaringly unfaithful to the spirit of the book, as has so often been the case with Christie adaptations. There were, inevitably, a few changes made to ease the transition from novel to film, but the murder, the mystery, the principal characters, and the solution are all presented largely as Christie devised them. This fidelity, though, is achieved by developing for filmic effect what is barely there in the original, or not there at all. It is generally accepted that in writing the *Murder on the Orient Express* Christie had in mind the real and recent case of the kidnap and murder of the Lindbergh baby in America. But Christie herself doesn't make the connection, nor does she fix the date of 1930 to the child murder of her novel, or the date of 1935 to the murder's solution (or to 1938 in the case of ITV). Nor does she make any use of sensational newspaper headlines and reports – as she was well capable of doing – to evoke the American background atmosphere.

All of the details of the fictional Daisy Armstrong's kidnap and murder come from Poirot's own reminiscences of the case, carefully prompted by the director of the rail company who is also travelling on the train. The case is recalled plainly and with little elaboration, in barely two pages of the novel. The gathering of the passengers and their boarding the train are treated in the same subdued manner. The novel opens in Aleppo.

Mary Debenham is already on the Taurus Express where she is joined by Colonel Arbuthnot and Poirot. They are all travelling to Istanbul to catch the Orient Express. Here is Mary Debenham's view from the train window in the station at Aleppo: 'Nothing to see. Of course. Just a long poor-lighted platform with furious altercations in Arabic going on somewhere.' At one of the stations on the way to the Bosphorus, Poirot simply watches 'the teeming activity … through a window pane.' The crossing of the Bosphorus itself is dealt with in the same subdued manner: 'The Bosphorus was rough and M. Poirot did not enjoy the crossing.' The bustle surrounding the departure of the Orient Express in Istanbul Christie barely describes at all. Instead she gives full attention to the subtle manoeuvring that takes place to find Poirot a berth on the crowded train: 'A whistle blew, there was a long melancholy cry from the engine … "We're off," said Macqueen.'

While the passengers are making their way to the train, the ITV adaptation introduces a violent scene of a local woman being stoned to death for adultery. Although this does not appear at all in the novel, it can still be regarded, from the point of view of the film, as not quite the irrelevant sensationalism it might have been. It is justified as a comparative illustration of how difficult it is to accept any single, all-embracing concept of justice. ITV also focuses on Poirot's devout Catholicism which includes him praying and frantically fingering a rosary while he tries to decide what to do. The EMI film has no such soul-searching by Poirot. This challenging of Poirot's absolute notion of justice is certainly the personal dilemma which he must face at the close of the novel, but Christie does not introduce his Catholicism as an element in it. The equivalent event she sets up to serve as a measure of how firmly Poirot is willing to adminster justice is the case he has just completed at the start of the novel which involves the French *not* the British Army. Both film adaptations retain the incident, but handle it in very different ways and attach less significance to it than Christie herself.

Throughout the novel, Christie's descriptions of places, people and the actual murder itself are precise, effective, underplayed. Even the spectacular scenery of the Balkans and the mountainous snowdrifts that bring the train to a halt and are used so dramatically in both film and television adaptations to isolate the murder scene while Poirot pursues his investigation, are given no special attention in the novel. They take place all right, but are simply there, glimpsed occasionally by the passengers through the train windows.

Christie's own stress is on the murder as it takes place on the train, its gradual unravelling, and the moral issues raised by it. The opening chapters of the novel are masterfully ambiguous, setting the scene while at the same time leaving open the question of just how much conscious collective manipulation is involved in getting Poirot on board at just the right moment. Something that he, of course, mustn't be allowed to suspect. Nor, in characteristic Christie manner, would most first-time readers be aware of how they are being misled along with Poirot. What follows consists largely of Poirot's interviews with the twelve passengers in the coach, the men and women, all connected in one way or another with the Armstrong family who have formed themselves into a self-appointed jury, judge and executioner as well. It is only as these details gradually come together from the separate interviews that full information about the Daisy Armstrong murder emerges. For Poirot it means a severe challenge to his own usually inflexible moral code on such matters, leaving him, at the muted ending of the novel, to announce to his fellow passengers that he has 'the honour to retire from the case.'

* * *

As the 1930s drew to a close the political pressures in Europe and the Middle East could no longer be ignored or avoided. The Mallowans were driven out of the area, and, whether connected or not but certainly at about the same time, Christie began, cautiously and privately as was her manner, to rethink her policy of making no references to public or political events in her novels. In *Orient Express* she had shown Poirot compromising his high sense of moral probity, giving way to the example of the other passengers who have themselves acted in ways they would normally have considered as alien to their own moral standards. A related kind of pressure was much in Christie's own mind. War was now very near, a new kind of war which would cover many parts of the world and involve civilians as well as combatants, and Christie had to decide how she was going to respond, both personally and as a writer, when it did eventually start. It could no longer be dismissed as a distraction, and it was clear that any compromise would necessarily oblige her to reconsider the minimalist literary methods she had developed so successfully.

That success had been largely commercial and personal. In the literary world it was undermined by a good deal of misunderstanding, even hostility. Instead of Christie being celebrated for her experimentation and daring, she had become regarded as someone aloof, indifferent, socially and politically unconcerned. As always, Christie herself contributed to that adverse image by stubbornly refusing to explain what she was trying to do. She treated it entirely as a literary problem, apparently leaving the books to speak for themselves. But what must have been especially galling to her was the assumption that she was somehow indifferent to or ignorant of the personal torment and suffering caused by the conflict that was now swiftly involving the whole world. Here, the discrepancy between outward image and inner experience, between her life and writing, was particularly extreme.

Every stage of Christie's life had, in fact, been profoundly influenced by war. Her troublesome brother Monty had served in the Boer war and later in the regular army. She herself had married Archie Christie early in the First World War so suddenly that even her mother wasn't able to attend the wedding and while he was serving in France she had joined the VAD (Voluntary Aid Detachment) and worked in a Torquay hospital, at first as a ward maid, cleaning and scrubbing floors, and then, after some basic training, helping to nurse the wounded troops who were soon being transported back home in horrifying numbers. It was hard, distressing work and Christie kept at it for eighteen months. She then worked as an assistant in the hospital dispensary, at the same time studying to become a qualified dispenser, and obtaining on the way the familiarity with poisons that was to serve her so well as a writer of detective stories. Her grim experiences as a nurse she used in one of the first of the Mary Westmacott novels.

In the Second World war, Max Mallowan insisted on serving in some capacity even though he could have claimed exemption. The result was that he and Agatha were separated for much of the war as she had earlier been from Archie. Greenway, her house in Devon was requisitioned for use by the American navy. In 1940, her daughter Rosalind, in an echo of her own marriage to Archie that Agatha must have found especially painful, suddenly announced that she was going to marry Hubert Prichard, a serving officer in the Royal Welch Fusiliers and a son, Matthew, was born to them in 1943. Major Prichard was killed on active service the following year. Once again desperate to do whatever she could, Agatha brushed up her dispensing qualifications in Torquay and later took a part-time job at University College Hospital in London.

War came to her in so many different ways. Her personal experiences of it – as sister, bride, wife, mother, nurse, civilian – were deep and seemingly never-ending. Like so many other people of her generation, apart from a few years in the late 1920s and early 1930s, there was really no time when she would have been entirely free from the ubiquitous pressures of twentieth-century warfare. At the start of the 1939-45 war Graham Greene, one of the contemporary writers Christie most admired and who in turn recognized the influence her great popularity as a writer could have, tried to persuade her to contribute to government propaganda. She turned down the invitation, deciding instead to continue entertaining readers in her own special way. Her compulsive, dedicated wartime writing was done in central London, much of it during the air-raids.

By the time of Greene's approach she had already begun to make changes to her work, and as always she kept what she was up to entirely to herself. There were no manifestos or declarations announcing changes of policy or practice. No publicity at all. The changes she was engaged in were tentative and held carefully within the frame of the kind of murder mystery which was now established as very distinctively her own. This was so much the case that her experiments seemed to have been carried out without any public recognition that she was trying to do anything different from before. Yet significant changes there were.

* * *

They began to take shape with a Poirot novel *Appointment with Death* which was published in May 1938, a time of intense national crisis. For something like two years, the British government had been ostensibly placating Hitler's Germany while at the same time desperately trying to catch up on the rearmament it had neglected for so long. While assuring the public that armed conflict could be avoided, it was also preparing for the war that was expected to start at any time. *Appointment with Death* appeared in the middle of this highly fraught period, just a few months before the prime minister Neville Chamberlain was to return from his latest negotiations with Hitler to announce that he had achieved 'peace for our time.' War would be declared almost exactly one year later.

Before appearing in volume form in May 1938 *Appointment with Death* was serialised in the *Daily Mail* under its temporary title *A Date with Death*. To advertise the serialization Christie took the unusual step of providing the *Mail* with a specially written introductory article. In it Christie said nothing directly about the political situation and not much about the forthcoming novel which she declared was 'sub judice.' Instead, it was here that she chose to make public her love-hate relationship with Hercule Poirot. Then, towards the close of the article, suddenly remembering, as it were, *Appointment with Death*, she listed three reasons for Poirot's interest in this particular case. First, because he is asked to look into the murder by 'a man whose passion for the truth was equal to his own'; Secondly, the technical difficulty of the investigation which involves 'reaching the truth in 24 hours without the help of any expert evidence of any kind'; and thirdly, 'the peculiarly psychological interest of the case, and particularly ... the strong malign personality of the dead woman.'[4] All three points carried meanings for Christie that would not have been apparent to the general reader then, or indeed ever have been. They are not really about how Poirot is to solve the murder but about the larger, unstated implications of *Appointment with Death*.

No specific reason is given in the novel why Poirot is travelling abroad at this time, but he carries with him a letter of introduction from his old friend Colonel Race to a Colonel Carbury who in spite of his general air of disarray possesses an exceptionally well-ordered mind, is a noted 'disciplinarian' and 'a power in Transjordania.' He is, presumably, the unidentified 'man' referrred to in Christie's *Daily Mail* article. Race, who had already appeared in a couple of Poirot novels, and most recently in

Death on the Nile a year earlier, is a highly placed member of the British Secret Service who operates undercover in various parts of the British Empire. Carbury is obviously in the same business. The murder case which he urges Poirot to look into is not said to carry any national or diplomatic significance. Even so, Carbury is particularly concerned that it should be investigated, and his views are treated with great respect throughout. He is even asked to take the chair 'in an official position' when Poirot delivers his final summary of the case. This has to be because he, or rather the country he represents, must show itself to be as keen as Poirot himself to settle the case of this 'malign' woman. As far as points two and three are concerned, it would seem quite unnecessary for Christie to say that in solving the case Poirot needed to draw on no 'expert evidence of any kind' because he never does: his 'little grey cells' as he has asserted in novel after novel are usually quite enough. But not here. As Poirot readily acknowledges, special areas of expertise are very much needed to explain the true psychological nature of the dead woman's 'malign personality' and its wider significance.

Appointment with Death centres on a group of American tourists in the Middle East. They make up a family group ruled over with calculated cruelty and horrifying insensitivity by their widowed mother Mrs Boynton. She qualifies as probably the nastiest character in all of Christie's work, someone who is unaccountably wicked. As usual, the dating of the novel's action is vaguely contemporary. If the world is in crisis this has no effect on the travellers' sightseeing or their personal problems. Although the imminence of war is never mentioned, Christie probably intended it to be the main theme of the novel, for *Appointment with Death* has one dominant informing idea. It is a detective story that conveys its meaning allegorically, with the murder victim being presented as a paradigm of totalitarian evil.

The ghastly Mrs Boynton's personality is discussed early in the novel by Dr Theodore Gerard, a world-renowned authority on schizophrenia, and Sarah King, a newly qualified doctor with a special interest in psychology. According to Gerard and, incidentally, to everyone else in the novel, Mrs Boynton is a 'sadist' who 'loves tyranny' and 'rejoices in the infliction of mental pain.' He explains: 'There are such strange things buried down in the unconscious. A lust for power – a lust for cruelty – a savage desire to tear and rend – all the inheritance of our past racial memories.' When Sarah agrees with him, Gerard makes the crucial extrapolation from the Boynton family to the wider world in terms which had never before appeared in a Christie novel:

> We see it all round us to-day – in political creeds, in the conduct of nations. A reaction from humanitarianism – from pity – from brotherly good-will. The creeds sound well sometimes – a wise régime – a beneficent government – but imposed by *force* – resting on a basis of cruelty and fear. They are opening the door, these apostles of violence, they are letting up the old savagery, the old delight in cruelty *for its own sake*!

A little later Gerard turns to Ecclesiastes (4:1-3) for reinforcement of his view, drawing attention to all of those who are 'oppressed' and have 'no comfort' because 'with their oppressors there was power, so that no one came to comfort them.'

Evil in its theological sense had long been of special interest to Christie, but the force it carries here is something new. The central conflict of the novel is between Mrs Boynton's harsh authoritarianism and the unwillingness or inability of her pathetically cowed children to stand up to her. At stake are all the virtues associated with both Christianity and humanism. If something is not done to help them they are in danger of being wiped out entirely. As the opening words of the book announce – with rather too much typographical emphasis – action against Mrs Boynton, any action, will be morally justifiable: 'YOU DO SEE, *don't you, that she's got to be killed?*'

The moral arguments regarding the Boyntons in the book are the same as those being used in Britain to decide how the country had to respond to the worsening international situation. Against the view that Nazism should be tolerated, was the argument that it was an evil and should be opposed whatever the cost and without compromise. For the supporters of all-out military action against Germany, their opponents' policy of 'appeasement' meant enduring the type of degrading subservience that the Boynton family have lived under for years. Each and every one of them is responsible for doing something about it, and the only solution is for Mrs Boynton, the epitome of evil, to be confronted and destroyed.

Christie had a second Poirot novel ready for 1938, this time linked specifically to the lucrative Christmas market. *Hercule Poirot's Christmas*, though, is surprisingly unseasonal in mood and pursues a similar political message to *Appointment with Death*. Simeon Lee is another tyrannical parent whose condition is presented as not simply peculiar to him but objectively and frighteningly at work in modern society. Lydia Lee explains the position to her husband: 'Evil is not only in one's mind. Evil exists! *You* seem to have no consciousness of the evil of the world. I have. I can feel it. I've always felt it – here in this house.' A political context for this novel is provided, quite explicitly, by references to the Spanish Civil War which had broken out in 1936 and was widely regarded as a forerunner of a larger war soon to come. The surest indication of Christie's political purpose in *Hercule Poirot's Christmas* lies in the unusual violence of the novel's central crime which seems too gruesome to be solely a matter of family revenge. As Poirot points out, it is the 'insistence' on blood that is shocking. There is blood everywhere: 'too much blood … sacrificial blood?' What has taken place is a 'blood ritual.' There are several references in the novel to *Macbeth*, always one of Christie's favourite Shakespeare plays, and, of course, the story of a brutal blood-soaked political murder.

Christie's most extraordinary experiment in this vein was still to come. *And Then There Were None*, was published originally as *Ten Little Niggers* in November 1939, two months after the war with Germany had started. It is one of her most ingenious fictional puzzles, based on Christie's deeply held conviction that in modern civilized society large numbers of people do, literally, get away with murder. Here, a group of ten men and women, who have all in their individual lives been directly or indirectly responsible for somebody's death, are brought together on an isolated island. One by one, they are called to account and executed. None of them survives. Why should they? How could they? Should anyone be allowed to live if all are equally guilty? Everyone is either a murderer or a victim. Together, they constitute, as Vera Claythorne slowly comes to understand, a kind of zoo where they are 'hardly human any more' and on whom a bizarre experiment is being carried out.

The man in control of the zoo is an official representative of British law, and, like Mrs Boynton and Simeon Lee a sadist, who has always experienced 'exquisite pleasure' watching accused people 'squirming in the dock, suffering the tortures of the damned.' On the island he is still able to indulge that kind of enjoyment, but with the added pleasure of catching up on some of those who managed to escape the law first time round. This may be perverted justice, but much of the world itself is now perverted in the same way. Where is a worthy judge to be found, or a jury come to that? At the close of the novel the island is empty of human beings, wiped clean, apparently beyond redemption. Evil is triumphant. Is there any way it can be effectively confronted? If some means is not found it will sweep to total victory, annihilating all democratic and humanitarian values.

Too fanciful an interpretation of a book that has always been accepted as an ingenious clever detective story, just that and nothing more? Well, Poirot claimed to despise conventional clues, but Christie loved them, and she was now increasingly using and concealing them to indicate some of her own insufficiently appreciated artistry. One such clue is used in *And Then There Were None*. Who is the perpetrator of this hideous campaign of semi-official murder, the crazed dictator who thinks he can do whatever he likes, and who, without opposition, leaves dead bodies scatttered over a small bleak occupied island off the coast of southern England? The adopted name of the mass murderer is U.N. Owen. It can belong to either gender and, by means of a pun, is informing his intended victims that they are, anyway, dealing with and at the mercy of the unknown. His given name, which opens and closes the book, also has meaningful puns built into it. Mr Justice Wargrave/Lawrence Wargrave. Is Justice or the Law going to act to prevent such terrible things happening in its name, or is it going to stand by and allow the Western world to be once again covered with war graves?

Within their defining detective-story frames these three novels published just before at the start of the war, are all, on one of their several levels, allegories of European society in the late 1930s, conveying their political warnings in extremely oblique, even obscure ways. Christie had no wish to remove the mystery element from them, or to make them in outward appearance strikingly different from what had gone before. Nor did she want to convert herself into a 'literary' or a 'political' novelist. Her aim was more subtle. She was asserting in the face of the criticism flung so easily at her that she was fully aware of the totalitarian threat to Europe and that she herself had considered views about it. The novels stayed as famously entertaining as ever, but they now contained clues and allusions that could be picked up or not as the reader wished. Of course there was no public statement about what she was doing. Instead, she allowed the point to be made by other novels, written or published at roughly the same time which seemed to go entirely against these new developments, and in a variety of different ways as well.

One of the oddest of Christie's attempts to introduce a political element into her work has only recently come to light through John Curran's work on Christie's notebooks. From November 1939 the *Strand* serialised the *Labours of Hercules* in what should have been twelve monthly instalments. However, only eleven instalments were published as the twelfth, 'The Capture of Cerberus,' was rejected by the magazine. This must have been because it was a remarkably crude satirical sketch featuring August Hertzlein, 'the dictator of dictators.' Some years later, the story was replaced by the infinitely superior version of 'The Capture of Cerberus' which is still familiar from *The Labours of Hercules* (1947). Hertzlein was quite obviously a portrait of Hitler and Curran says that although 'there is little evidence elsewhere in her work that she was particularly political' this whole story was unlike anything Christie had written before in being 'blatantly political from the first page.'[5]

Although Christie may not have been 'particularly political' in the past, she was, as we have seen, becoming increasingly so at just this time. Nevertheless, 'The Capture of Cerberus' in being so 'blatantly political from the first page' is strikingly different from the indirect and far more subtle ways, being explored here. It could, however, be particularly significant that the original version of 'The Capture of Cerberus' was due to be serialized late in 1940. This would have been just when her interest in testing out political themes was at its most intense. It therefore seems reasonable to assume that Christie considered the story another of those experiments and that the *Strand* did her a favour in forcing her to realize that she had so far been quite right to hold back on a direct approach. Never again did she try anything so gauche as the original version of 'The Capture of Cerberus.' But nor did she give up trying. With *N or M?* published in 1941, she almost mockingly demonstrated that after having tried with some success to convey her views on the war obliquely, she could, if she wished, write about it in the most traditional or 'realistic' manner.

N or M? portrays a middle-aged Tommy and Tuppence Beresford determined to contribute to the war effort much as Agatha and Max were. Here the minimalist techniques of the classic detective stories of the 1930s were dispensed with entirely and replaced by the more precise social, historical and political details of a traditional novel. It is set in the spring of 1940, the period of the 'phoney war' as the people of Britain waited tensely for the anticipated air and sea invasions by Germany. The political context of the novel is established by the German army's advance on Paris, the British evacuation from Dunkirk, and at home, the establishment of a fifth column by German spies and their British supporters. Although the climax of *N or M?* is somewhat over-dramatized, the wartime atmosphere in England is convincingly handled. In fact, Christie became so caught up in the contemporary nature of the book that she regretted not being able to incorporate some of her own wartime experiences into it. She wrote: 'I think that I could do a better last chapter up-to-date – taking place in a shelter when Tommy and Tuppence had just had their flat bombed.'[6] Nevertheless, she had demonstrated the larger point she wanted to make with *N or M?* by actually writing it, and, once it was done, she was not interested in repeating the experiment.

Instead, having absorbed the varying narrative techniques developed over the previous few years and shown that she could use them as and when she wished, she was prepared to move on yet again. And, as far as her own feelings were concerned, more confidently as well. At long last, she felt she was ready to bring Miss Marple back out of her long retirement.

* * *

The signs that this was a distinct possibility had been there for a while, though they would hardly have been apparent at the time. It's only in retrospect, once we can observe at a distance the way that Christie moved so swiftly, spontaneously, even arbitrarily, as it often seems, between seemingly very different kinds of novels on her way to fixing where exactly she wanted to be next, that a meaningful pattern can be observed.

In 1939 she decided to revive the short story 'Miss Marple tells a Story' which, as we have seen, had been written for the BBC five years earlier. It was the only Miss Marple item included in a collection devoted largely to Poirot and Parker Pyne which was published in America as *The Regatta Mystery and other stories*. Perhaps prompted by the republication of this story, she went on to publish the four new Miss Marple short stories which were published in *The Strand* during the war years. They were current, as it were, but old-fashioned when considered in relation to the extraordinary Miss Marple novels Christie was about to embark on. Here once again, we find very different types of writing published alongside each other in the most peculiar manner, as though demonstrating her ability to change or develop at will.

Nor was this all, for strong memories of Miss Marple were already being reawakened in a new novel that Christie had ready for publication in May 1939. It was called *Murder is Easy* and with it Christie moved sharply away from the Poirot dominated mysteries of the previous decade and back to traditional Miss Marple territory. The action of *Murder is Easy* takes place in the 'little country town' of Wychwood-under-Ashe, a close-knit community of the kind where Miss Marple would have been fully at home. Although she doesn't appear in the novel, her presence is strongly felt in the portrayal of two village spinsters Lavinia Pinkerton and Honoria Waynflete. Both of them are bright and alert, one of them disturbingly so. They are also notably 'shrewd' and recognized locally as such. 'Most of these rambling old dears,' says one of the other principal characters, 'are as sharp as nails in some ways.' The image is precisely that established for Miss Marple ten years earlier, the fluffy exterior not only hiding her inner shrewdness but also being used as an active means to conceal reality, though in this particular case of a very different kind.

Murder is Easy prepared the way for Miss Marple's return in much the same way as *The Blue Train* had done for her debut eleven years earlier. Both novels provide evidence of ideas being formulated in Christie's mind some time before they were ready to be given definite form. *Murder is Easy* contains no direct references to the war, though the opening of the novel, before it switches to small town life, evokes something of what might have been a wartime atmosphere. The protagonist Luke Fitzwilliam is coming back to England after some years serving as a police officer in the Far East. He is shocked to find dreary weather, crowds of people, 'all with grey faces … anxious worried faces.' As in other novels of this time, it is not simply murder that Luke has to confront, but, as the widow of one of the victims tells him, a deep conviction of Evil. There is, she tells him, '*so much wickedness* – that is the thought that is always with me – wickedness here in Wychwood.'

Was Christie thinking of a wartime role for her village detective? The idea is not impossible. After all, *The Body in the Library* published in 1942 was to be the first of three Miss Marple novels written closely together during the Second World War. It had also been published immediately after *N or M?* in which Christie had displayed her ability to deal in a socially realistic manner with wartime conditions. Given that for several years past Christie's writings had been quite clearly concerned, both directly and allusively, with thoughts of rampant irrational evil, totalitarianism and all-out war, her recent determination to incorporate a political element into her work, and remembering that this was an author who had been deeply affected by war at every stage of her life, why shouldn't she turn to Miss Marple at a new moment of crisis, just as she had done all those years earlier, in order to explore deeply internal thoughts and feelings of her own?

And this is what she did, though the form of Miss Marple's involvement could never have been predicted by an outsider. In the earlier years of personal trauma Christie had emloyed Miss Marple's mid-Victorian confidence to help bolster her own insecurity. This time it was to be Christie's own greater understanding of what she wanted of her spinster heroine, prepared for by the experimental novels of the late 1930s and early 1940s, that paved the way for Miss Marple's return. Now, Christie was not trying to work out a personal dilemma that she had been unexpectedly plunged into, but trying to understand an age of world-wide violence in which everyone, the innocent as much as the guilty, was involved whether they wanted to be or not.

Chapter 6

Psychology, Psychoanalysis and Shakespeare

So, what did Miss Marple do in the war, or in either of the world wars come to that? In terms of national effort, and in comparison with Christie, the answer has to be nothing at all. She didn't join the VAD, scrub hospital floors, work in a hospital dispensary, tend the hideously wounded being shipped back from France, or care for foreign refugees. Nor did she have her St. Mary Mead cottage requisitioned for war purposes, or take in evacuees, or do any other useful wartime work. And, most certainly, she was not caught up in a heartbreaking, doomed love affair with a married serving soldier in the 1914-18 war as has been suggested by a recent television series. As far as her own awareness of the world around her was concerned, she seems hardly to have known that a second world war was going on. But as a detective her skills and technique made large and unexpected advances.

It seems that sometime during the late 1930s Miss Marple must have begun a serious study of psychoanalysis. She never admits to this any more than she acknowledges that a war is in progress. But at least Freud is mentioned several times in the novels of this period devoted to her, which is more than can be said for the wartime leaders. Hitler, Stalin, Mussolini, Churchill, and Roosevelt are never referred to at all.[1] Of course it is Christie rather than Miss Marple whose interest in Freudianism needs to be considered. But it is reasonable to assume there was some kind of transference, to use an appropriate if tricky psychoanalytical term, of this acquired knowledge from author to subject, with Christie quite consciously reserving her interest in psychoanalysis for Miss Marple's long-delayed return.

The subject of psychoanalysis doesn't go entirely unmentioned in previous studies of Christie, but it tends to appear in them for very specific biographical reasons and not, as it could well do, for its relevance to her methods as a writer. Even its place in the biographies is contentious. This is because it is connected with the massive controversy of the disappearance and her biographers disagree fundamentally on how much attention it should be given, as they do on virtually everything else concerning those notorious missing days.

According to Janet Morgan, shortly after the actual disappearance was resolved, Christie consulted a Harley Street psychiatrist in in an attempt to try to understand what had happened to her.[2] This fits with the explanation at the time from a united Christie family that Agatha was a victim of amnesia. In Archie's words: 'She has suffered from the most complete loss of memory and I do not think she knows who she is.'[3] Morgan also says that Christie's personal determination to understand what had happened to her continued for many years and that even 'after the War' she consulted a psychoanalyst at Oxford to try to 'reconstruct the events of that dreadful time.'[4] Jared Cade, however, insists that no evidence exists for any of this ever having taken place and suggests that the 'immediate family allowed' Morgan to 'infer' that Christie had undergone psychiatric treatment, the assumption being that it was all part of the family's continuing cover-up.[5] Laura Thompson appears to refute Cade on this point by stating unequivocally: 'In early 1927 Christie had gone, at her sister's suggestion, to a psychiatrist in Harley Street.'[6] However, this does not mean that Thompson supports the amnesia diagnosis. Instead, taking a line that is highly fanciful she argues that as an artist Christie lived life differently from other people. To artists 'everything is a story. That is their escape, their freedom.'[7] So, at her sister's suggestion, Christie went to a psychiatrist 'to maintain the fiction that she had lost her memory and needed to recover it: in other words, she was lying about herself to find out the truth about herself.'[8]

Christie makes no mention in the *Autobiography* of seeing a psychiatrist, though writing much closer to the actual events she did perhaps hint that it might have taken place through her alternative writing self Mary Westmacott. In *Giant's Bread*, published in 1930, Vernon Deyre is shown undergoing hypnosis to recover his lost memory, and a number of commentators, including Janet Morgan, accept that these scenes were based on Christie's own experience.[9] And, of course, they may have been, but how can we know? The follow-up Westmacott novel, *Unfinished Portrait*, published four years later details the marriage failure, includes a nervous breakdown and an attempted suicide but makes no mention of any psychoanalytical treatment. There is quite obviously a great deal in both novels that is drawn, directly, from Christie's own life, but as far as this particular issue is concerned, why should we accept one of these two fictional accounts as true rather than the other when there is no external supporting evidence for either?

Whether or not, and in spite of this dispute, there is no doubt at all that Christie had a genuine interest in both the theory and practice of psychoanalysis. Furthermore, it was a long-standing and developing interest which existed well before her disappearance and increased steadily throughout the 1930s. It may well be that the disappearance and its immediate aftermath encouraged Christie to take a deeper interest in psychoanalysis, on both a general a personal level, but the disappearance was not the source of that interest.

The same is true of her fascination with dreams which was lifelong and, as with psychoanalysis, is everywhere apparent in her novels. In the *Autobiography* she acknowledged her admiration for J.W. Dunne's once-fashionable *An Experiment with Time* (1927) which she read while on her first visit to Baghdad. Dunne gives a good deal of attention to dreams as well as time, and Christie claimed that reading him made her see 'things more in proportion; myself less large.' She never makes a similarly enthusiastic claim of having been influenced by Freud, but there was no need for her to do so. By the time she came to read Dunne, Freud was already for her a regular point of reference. He is alluded to several times in the *Autobiography*, while in the novels she uses the language of psychoanalysis constantly and knowledgeably from *Styles* onwards. At the close of *The Man in the Brown Suit* (1924) she is confident enough about what she is saying to have Suzanne Blair who 'goes in rather for psychoanalysis' attribute Sir Eustace Pedler's amoral behaviour to a 'fear complex.' Subsequently, there are similar references to psychoanalysis in many of her novels long before she took up the subect more substantially and with a new kind of centrality, as we have seen, in *Appointment with Death* and other related pre-war novels. Poirot alone offers solid evidence that Christie hadn't needed to undergo a nervous breakdown to learn about psychology or any of its various branches as it was an essential element in his much-vaunted methodical approach to detection.

* * *

Even before Poirot himself makes an appearance in *Styles* he is described by Hastings as someone who believes that all good detective work is 'a mere matter of method.' Poirot himself later explains that this method depends on mind or intelligence, an activity far removed from the hunting for visible clues that so impresses the less sophisticated Hastings: 'This affair must be unravelled from within.' He tapped his forehead. 'These little grey cells. It is up to them.' He also talks of reaching one particular deduction by 'looking at the matter psychologically.' The basic elements are therefore present right at the start but they are not linked decisively together until Poirot's second full-scale case, *The Murder on the Links* (1923). While 'Order and Method' remain 'his Gods,' a crucial additional factor is introduced. 'There is such a thing as the individual touch,' Poirot suddenly announces to a scornful French detective. 'I am speaking to you now of the psychology of crime.' However methodical the approach, it must eventually confront the 'brain' behind the crime, and this means that the 'true clue' has to be 'a psychological clue.' So, Poirot's fundamental approach, as outlined in these very early works, is a logical sense of order and method placed at the service of a deep personal insight into criminal psychology, and it is this that sets him apart from everyone else involved in a case. As he later asserts dogmatically in *Lord Edgware Dies* (1933): 'One cannot be interested in crime without being interested in psychology.'

In some respects he was doing little more than follow the example set by his two great literary predecessors, Conan Doyle's Sherlock Holmes and Edgar Allan Poe's Auguste Dupin, both of whom relied overwhelmingly on the power of their minds to unravel mysterious, seemingly inexplicable events. The original element in Poirot rests on the the importance he attaches to the psychology of a particular crime or criminal. Holmes and Dupin wouldn't have been particularly surprised by this either, but while understanding what Poirot meant they wouldn't have used his kind of emphasis. He is strongly conscious that he is taking a twentieth-century line, that the boundaries surrounding what had once been known as psychology had shifted decisively since the time of his great predecessors.

There's a neat illustration of the changes that have taken place in another early novel, *The Murder of Roger Ackroyd* (1926). During a discussion between Poirot and Inspector Raglan, Poirot asks how Raglan sets about his work. 'Method' he replies. Poirot is delighted. That, he exclaims, is what he believes in as well: 'Method, order, and the little grey cells.' Raglan doesn't see anything surprising in this: 'Well, we all use them, I suppose.' That doesn't suit Poirot. He raises the stakes by suggesting that the quality of the little grey cells being employed needs to be taken into account and so does 'the psychology of a crime. One must study that.' This is going quite a bit too far for Raglan. 'Ah!' he sighs, 'you've been bitten with all this psycho-analysis stuff? Now I'm a plain man.'

It is notable that Poirot hasn't mentioned psychoanalysis. It is simply that his reference to psychology has triggered thoughts of it in Raglan's mind. Nor does Poirot take up the challenge. He elegantly deflects the discussion away from the whole topic. What is clear is that Raglan sees no difference between psychology (meaning the science of the mind in general or, and increasingly so as far as Poirot was concerned, of human behaviour), and psychoanalysis (meaning specifically the method of treating mental illnesses or neuroses associated with Sigmund Freud). By this time in the mid-1920s psychoanalysis was well established as a medical procedure and many of its basic terms had become widely popularized and were being used by imaginative writers, Christie among them. But it was still controversial and often distrusted as dealing in an overly intellectual or rarified manner with rather daring, largely sexual, subjects that had hitherto been taboo as far as any kind of public discussion was concerned. By backing away and declaring himself a 'plain man' Raglan is telling Poirot that he doesn't want to be dragged into any dangerous or cranky activities that a sensible policeman would do well to stay clear of.

Even so, it is a little surprising, that Poirot himself doesn't take up the challenge. Nor does he ever announce his personal adherence to psychoanalysis rather than psychology. Strictly speaking, that is true of Christie as well. Sometimes she refers to psychiatry instead of psychoanalysis, meaning the branch of medicine that deals generally with mental illnesses rather than that specifically formulated by Freud, but she tends to prefer to use the older, blanket term of psychology to cover all such mental activity. Not that that stops Poirot or Christie from using some of the key terms and concepts of psychoanalysis whenever they feel the need to do so. As part of Christie's own growing interest she sets Poirot increasingly in working harmony with professional psychoanalysts, strikingly so in *Appointment with Death*, but also to give just a few other examples at this same kind of time in *Death on the Nile*, *The Labours of Hercules*, *Death in the Clouds*. Poirot is never surprised by the views he hears expressed: nor does he actively dispute them or, indeed, appear to be converted. As he explains in *Five Little Pigs* (1943): 'I had to ... examine the facts and to satisfy myself that the psychology of the case accorded itself with them.' There are even several indications, notably in *Death in the Clouds*, that Poirot's technique of encouraging suspects to talk without constraint is a way of encouraging them to 'tell you what you want to know' is very close to the Freudian technique of free association, or 'the talking cure' as it was often known, something that he himself appears to be aware of.

But overall, he remains content with his own idiosyncratic form of behavioural psychology, a structured, rational approach which enables him to fit the right person to a particular crime. There is an extended demonstration of this operating in *Cards on the Table* (1936). Poirot's reasoning is based on his observation of how the different characters play bridge. This convinces him of two things. First, that the murder of Mr Shaitana must have been premeditated, and secondly, that of the four players only Mrs Lorrimer had the necessary mental ability to plan such a crime in advance and then carry it out. Mrs Lorrimer seems to confirm Poirot's analysis of her when she owns up to being the murderer. Initially he believes her. But he later concludes that the act of murder she describes could only have been the result of a spontaneous act, and this he rejects as impossible for her as a person and a bridge player. She continues to insist she is guilty, but he no longer believes her. His confidence in his own judgment is unshakeable because 'no one can do a thing that is not *dans son caractère.*' This is also one of the novels in which Poirot is so certain he is right that although he has no reliable evidence he is willing to resort to a very dubious trick, and some specious reasoning as well, in order to obtain a conviction. Circumstances take over leaving psychological certainty to one side.

Apart from the knowledgeable use of appropriate terms, most of this has little direct connetion with the functioning world of psychoanalysis. There, a methodical approach rigorous enough to satisfy even Poirot is certainly called for but the material it handles is not strikingly prone to reason or order. On the contrary, it is often fundamentally unsystematic and irrational, taking its inspiration from dreams, verbal errors, and sudden slips rather than the stern logic Poirot admires. It demands a willingness to act upon totally unexpected leaps of thought, making imaginative and often mysteriously apt connections between apparently unrelated things. All of this Christie fully understood and when necessary she allowed Poirot to share the benefits of her knowledge without ever passing on the credit directly to him. She could not, however, get away with the same casual approach when it came to Miss Marple.

* * *

Things might have been different if, from the beginning, Miss Marple had not been an unavoidable victim of Poirot's dedication to criminal psychology. As this was already fixed as his very own province it was impossible for Miss Marple to take it up as well. To do so would have seriously compromised her independent image and status as a detective. There was no such difficulty with other essential qualities. She is allowed a sharpness of mind and an ability to marshall facts and information clearly and logically that equal those of Poirot. These abilities, though, are not boastfully flaunted by her as they are by him. Instead, her sharp mind is carefully hidden behind the fluttery old-maid facade. Nor, again for fear of repetition, could she be allowed any professional expertise in the field of professional criminology in any way comparable to that possessed by Poirot, whether intellectually or careerwise. Instead, she was allotted the much homelier field of 'human nature' as her special province, along with village parallels, snooping on neighbours, gossiping cronies, and all the other spinster accessories.

There was, though, from the very beginning more than just this kind of domestic amateurism to Miss Marple. In *Vicarage* we are told, almost in passing, that she has been discussing Colonel Protheroe's murder enthusiastically and at length with her visiting nephew Raymond West, and, as we learn later in the novel, his views are aggressively up-to-date and entirely psychoanalytical in their nature and terminology. Is it possible that this far back Christie had some kind of inkling of how Miss Marple might eventually develop as a detective? Perhaps not at the time, but it is worth noting that when she was writing *Vicarage* in 1930 Christie herself already understood how psychoanalysis might function in these circumstances and retained that understanding until Miss Marple's return twelve years later.

And not just 'retained.' Christie's interest in pychoanalysis grew steadily in the years that followed, reaching a peak in the late 1930s and extending through to the end of the war in 1945. During that period there was a good deal of heightened public interest in Freud, with London ceasing to be merely an outpost of his theories. Terminally ill, he had been moved by friends in 1938 from Nazi Austria to London where he died on 23 September the following year, barely three weeks after war had been formally declared. Following his death the professional psychoanalytical community in Britain became fiercely divided over the future of Freudianism with London establishing itself as a centre for the controversial development of child psychoanalysis.[10] Christie could well have followed these controversies. They coincide very neatly with her eagerness to use Freudian ideas in her work. And, it is not impossible that the wartime debates on child psychoanalysis were to be influential, a few years further on, in encouraging Christie's own controversial introduction of children more actively in her murder mysteries beginning with *Crooked House* (1949). That must be a matter of conjecture, but like many other people at the time, she did quite clearly recognize a new value in the previously distrusted theory and technique of psychoanalysis as a means of comprehending the shocking levels of human brutality uncovered by the war. Freud left behind him not only a battle to take possession of his heritage, but also a world seemingly at the mercy of the kind of amoral human violence he had long warned was only precariously contained by civilized societies.

Of great significance in opening up to Christie new ideas and theories was the influence of her marriage to Max Mallowan and the regular contact she now enjoyed with his professional friends and colleagues. Suddenly there were different subjects, and more importantly, intellectual and academic approaches to them, open to her that would not have been so naturally available before. Archaeology and the art and culture of the Middle East most obviously, but much else besides. Ancient and modern history, national and international politics, and new systematic approaches to literary criticism and art history as well as psychoanalysis. These would all have been subjects of daily discussion among her new friends and acquaintances and, inevitably, they began to enter more substantially into her fiction.[11]

It was not that such subjects needed to be introduced to Christie. Far from it. Her approach to any knowledge was never systematic or academic. She responded to fresh ideas and approaches instinctively as a dedicated novelist, using them as and when and to whatever degree suited her. One of the scholarly acquaintances she made through Max and with whom she was in regular contact later in her life was the well-known historian A.L. Rowse. He said that what he found most striking in Christie was the number of different things she knew about, 'the sheer range of her experience.'[12] This is surely something that will have been recognized by every unprejudiced reader of her books. And it had always been there. What Max and his scholarly colleagues provided was a sharpness to Christie's natural curiosity, a context within which she felt able to explore new ideas and where appropriate to attempt to incorporate them into her work.

* * *

It was within this pervasive intellectual climate that Christie began to develop the special interest in Shakespeare that some years later would so impress Rowse and even lead her to make a public statement on the subject. Rowse, who was not someone easily impressed, happily acknowledged the depth of Christie's appreciation of Shakespeare's work, an area of expertise that he usually liked to claim very much for himself. He had made his academic reputation as an historian, but in the 1960s he became obsessed with theories about Shakespeare's life which he surmised from the poems and plays, especially the sonnets. Rowse produced many books and editions in support of his literary passion which culminated in the early 1970s with the claim, announced in articles in *The Times* and then subsequently in a full-length book, that he had identified the 'dark lady' of Shakespeare's sonnets. It was a controversial stance and derided by some, but not by Christie. She published a signed letter in *The Times*, 3 February 1973, in which she supported Rowse and added some lively, similar theories of her own, relating key moments in *Antony and Cleopatra* to possible events in Shakespeare's own life. [13]

When she wrote her letter to *The Times* Christie already knew Rowse personally and had discussed these matters with him. It was during their home and college discussions, that she had revealed the intimate knowledge of Shakespeare's plays that so impressed Rowse. Nor was the relationship one of an amateur being strongly influenced by a professional: it was very much a shared approach. Rowse was full of self-promoting publicity about his Shakespearean discoveries while Christie had no public reputation for any knowledge of Shakespeare at all. But by the time of that moment very late in her life when she offered a public endorsement of Rowse, Christie was speaking from many years experience of reading and thinking about Shakeseare. References and allusions to a large number of his plays and poems had appeared in her work from the earliest days and he was always a favourite source for the titles of her novels. It was, though, in the late 1930s that she began to consider Shakespeare's work in different and deeper ways. Literary interpretation quickly became a passion.

During the war years, separated from Max, she went frequently to the London theatre, taking in whatever performances of Shakespeare were being put on and discussing her ideas endlessly with theatrical and academic friends. As she observes in her autobiography, in wartime she found it 'wonderfully refreshing' to be with actors because it was so much their job to create alternative worlds to the currently nightmarish real one. To Max, she sent full descriptions of these theatrical experiences which contained personal interpretations of individual plays of exactly the kind she would later exchange with Rowse. Max was sufficiently impressed to suggest that she might write 'a short and simple book on Shakespeare the Man,' offering, with a touch of academic superiority, to help her out on 'the scholarship side.'[14] Understandably, Christie wasn't drawn to this offer, and why should she have been? Her main focus was, as always, on her murder mysteries. But Max was right to pick up his wife's main interest as being on the man rather than, say, his poetry.

It was above all the psychological complexity of Shakeseare's characters that fascinated her, a depth of portraiture that allowed particular characters to be interpreted or produced on stage in contrasting, even contradictory, ways. Christie enjoyed speculating on the different versions of the plays she saw as well as trying to relate her own interpretations back to possible sources in Shakespeare's own life. She did not share Rowse's historical interest in trying to fix a definite identity for biographical purposes, but was, rather, toying with the more fleeting or floating imaginative ways of a kind that she herself understood perfectly. 'I think, perhaps, as writers do,' she observes in the Rowse letter to *The Times*, 'he pondered and planned a play to be written some day in the future.'[15] Something, of course, that Christie herself had done all of her life. It was precisely the indeterminate time lapse between an experience and its transformation into a work of art that fascinated Christie, in both Shakespeare and her own practice. Now she found, Shakespeare's plays were beginning to affect the way she thought about her work, not just as a source book for apt quotations and the titles of novels, but in more subtle psychological and structural ways.

The nature of Shakespeare's influence was extremely complicated, not least because it was linked inextricably with that of Freud. At times it is almost impossible to separate the two, but it does seem reasonable to assume that Christie's lifelong familiarity with Shakespeare was enhanced, transformed even, by her growing admiration of Freud. The debt of influence must really run in that direction, so consistently psychological or 'Freudian' are the detailed interpretations that Christie advances of Shakespeare's plays. Indeed, as Laura Thompson has so rightly noted,

Christie's approach to Shakespeare can be described as being close 'to the Freudian school of literary criticism.'[16] At the same time, Christie was too restless a writer, too changeable and unpredictable to give herself over completely to any single, dominant influence. What she was beginning to see in both Shakespeare and Freud were ways of expanding the significance of her murder mysteries, adding new levels of meaning to them without substantially altering the basic detective story format. It provided one of several acceptable ways for her to start moving cautiously beyond the minimalist techniques she had developed in the earlier 1930s.

It was Freud who led the way. Shakespeare was never to inform Christie's work as comprehensively as Freud was to do in the three wartime Miss Marple novels. But nor was he ever far away. If Freudianism offered to explain certain psychological insights, Shakespeare provided the dramatic illustrations. Freud himself had always openly admitted that the great poets and dramatists of the past had understood and formulated memorable ways to express his theories long before he himself had appeared on the scene. Christie seemed to have grasped this relationship between Freudianism and imaginative literature instinctively and quickly began to put it to her own, highly original, uses.

Although Shakespearean quotations and allusions appear in many of Christie's novels, and increasingly so from the late 1930s onwards, they have rarely been given any but passing attention by her critics and biographers, Laura Thompson excepted. Presumably this is because the references to Shakespeare are usually taken as little more than ornamentation, a convenient form of local window dressing as used by many novelists. And they can be this, but they are often very much more. Christie possessed a knowledge of a large number of different plays, with, perhaps, *Macbeth* and *Othello* her personal favourites. Her use of the plays is extremely flexible and difficult to generalize about. In fact, so varied is her use of Shakespeare that it is wise never to take any particular example for granted but rather to consider each one within its own context. Christie's celebrated subtlety in the laying of clues that may mean one thing or another or all sorts of possible things, applies in this case as well. Here are a few of many possible examples.

* * *

When Inspector Craddock, in *A Murder is Announced*, observes that Phillipa Haymes would 'make a good Rosalind' the reference to *As You Like It* is appropriate and entirely local. He has been searching for the young good-looking Phillipa who is thought to be a war widow and is temporarily working as a gardener. Craddock finds her 'sliding easily down the trunk of a tree,' her 'nice legs encased in breeches.' He is, we are told, a 'a Shakespeare enthusiast' who has played the part of Jacques with great success in a performance of the play for the Police Orphanage. In addition to recalling this experience with pleasure, he is also no doubt remembering the rural setting of *As You Like it*; that Rosalind would have been played by a boy in Shakespeare's day; and noting how sexually attractive (in a Tom-boyish way) Phillipa would be in a modern performance of the play. These are echoes that the reader may enjoy picking up on, but the occasion adds nothing of substance to the main narrative. Nor is there any need for Craddock's links with Shakespeare to be taken up later in the novel.

The situation is very different in *The Moving Finger* when Megan Hunter, in an early meeting with Jerry Burton, tells him bluntly that she doesn't like Shakespeare, and then instantly changes this to, well, perhaps, *some* Shakespeare. Jerry's initial response to the scruffy and socially awkward young girl is sarcastic and patronizing. Megan, who doesn't recognize the sarcasm, goes on to explain that she *does* like Goneril and Regan in *King Lear*. This is because 'they're *satisfactory*, somehow.' It's a totally unexpected word for her to use, though delivered without any affectation on her part, and it shuts Jerry up. When Megan, who sees no reason to challenge Jerry's superiority in such matters, asks him why Goneril and Regan were 'like they were,' he promises to think about it. Immediately, though, he is slightly shaken and forced to admit to himself that he had 'always accepted Lear's elder daughters as two nasty bits of goods and let it go as that.' When the conversation is picked up later in the novel, he still has nothing to add. It is Megan who has been doing the thinking. She has now decided that the characters of Goneril and Regan were clearly formed by 'that awful old father of theirs.' His insistence that they should 'suck up to him' all the time was bound to make them 'go a bit rotten and queer inside.' For much the same reason, Megan says, he deserved Cordelia's 'snub.'

Whether or not Megan is right about *King Lear* is beside the point. What does matter is that different meanings can be read into the exchange between Megan and Jerry, as they can into the relationship between Lear and his daughters. What this exchange anticipates and what the novel confirms subsequently, is that Jerry suffers from a debilitating lack of self-confidence and, although attractive and likeable, is a far from trustworthy narrator. Megan, on the other hand, in spite of her shabby outward appearance and her local reputation for being something of a nitwit, has the strength of character to survive her own distressing family background and emerge as someone who has plenty of intelligence, independence and courage. Miss Marple, it should be said, without calling on help from *King Lear,* reaches similar judgments about both Megan and Jerry.

These two examples, one straightforward, the other more expansive, show Christie using Shakespearean references to heighten the reader's understanding of particular characters. At other times they function in ways that are far from local but intended to illuminate entire novels, as in *Hercule Poirot's Christmas* where the references to *Macbeth* are sustained in their dramatic force. The starting-point, the quotation 'Who would have thought the old man to have had so much blood in him?' is Lydia Lee's initial response on seeing Simeon Lee's body lying in 'a great pool of blood,' with blood 'splashed all around' making the comfortable sitting room 'like a shambles.' In *Macbeth* these words are used, not as here, to express early horror at a brutal murder. They come late in the play, in the celebrated 'Out, damned spot' scene and mark Lady Macbeth's recognition that there is no escape from the personal taint of the blood she has encouraged her husband to shed. She is evoking not blood splashed all over the place as Lydia Lee is, but the lingering pervasiveness of Duncan's shed blood and her realization that the guilt and horror will never be washed away. Christie uses the same technique in *Hercule Poirot's Christmas,* making the whole murder mystery truly explicable only by understanding the full implication, in context, of Lydia's early response.

Poirot begins his exploration by carefully changing the words 'so much blood' in the original to '*too much blood*' (italics used in the text*).* For him the extreme violence and the 'insistence on blood,' which would surely be unnecessary if the task were simply to get Simeon Lee out of the way, are the key to the mystery. There is something 'sacrificial' or 'ritualistic' about the murder of this frail shrunken old man that has produced, and Poirot now returns wonderingly to the original quotation, '*so much blood.*' Both the 'too' and the 'so' he will later decide, are relevant to the situation: together they confirm that the explanation of the murder lies in 'the character of the victim.' This, of course, is a key tenet of Poirot's psychological method and when it is challenged he calls Shakespeare to his aid again, this time *Othello*, claiming that 'the frank and unsuspicious mind of Desdemona was the direct cause of her death.' This reference is not pursued. It is supporting evidence. The central *Macbeth* connection is then taken up again. If there is too much blood splashed around the murder room for it all to have belonged to Simeon Lee, or indeed to any one human being (as, indeed, is the case), it still, metaphorically speaking, came from him. It is his blood (in the sense of his character, progeny or past actions) that has brought murder upon him and created the blood-soaked room. It must also, therefore, be the reason for the ritualistic manner of the murder. Nor is his the only source of the blood that appears to be spreading, so unnaturally and frighteningly, everywhere. Pilar carries it with her from war-torn Spain. While trying to get to England her car had been hit by a bomb 'and the chauffeur he was killed – where his head had been there was all blood.' The ongoing nature of that blood shedding is not going to be neatly settled by Poirot. Nor will the threatened blood of the wider world conflict that is implied here, and unavoidably so in 1938, the year in which *Hercule Poirot's Christmas* was first published.

Although *Othello* appeared in *Hercule Poirot's Christmas* only in passing, it was given a far more central role in several other works. It was obviously a play that fascinated Christie, for both the depth of its psychological insights and the different interpretations it is capable of inspiring. Christie herself employed several different interpretations of the play. In *Hercule Poirot's Christmas,* as just noted, Desdemona is described as someone whose 'frank and unsuspicious mind … was the direct cause of her death.' This theme of the unconscious power of certain exceptionally beautiful women was one that Christie used more than once in her career. A remarkable, expanded vsersion of it is to be found in *The Mystery of the Spanish Chest*, one of Christie's novellas that has received very little notice of any kind, but which, in this context especially, is of some significance.

The *Mystery of the Spanish Chest* was first published in volume form in 1960 as one of six stories collected under the fancy title of *The Adventure of the Christmas Pudding and a selection of entrées*. It was a reworked version of a short story called 'The Mystery of the Baghdad Chest' which first appeared in the *Strand* magazine way back in 1932 and had only been reprinted in the miscellanous American collection *The Regatta Mystery and other stories* (1939) which, as noted earlier, also contained 'Miss Marple tells a Story.' The basic story of 'The Mystery of the Baghdad Chest' and *The Spanish Chest* is essentially the same, but important changes of detail were made to the later version. The setting was altered, with Hastings being replaced by Miss Lemon, and some of the other characters renamed. The most striking development was that in the earlier story there were no references at all to Shakespeare but by the time of *The Spanish Chest* his presence had become dominant. The emphasis, as in *Hercule Poirot's Christmas* is once again on Desdemona's 'frank and unsuspicious mind' though no longer does this render her the innocent cause of her own murder. It works in quite another way.

In both 'The Baghdad Chest' and 'The Spanish Chest' the central character is a Mrs Clayton whose Christian name, Marguerita/Margharita is spelt a little differently in the two stories. Her husband is the victim. He is mysteriously stabbed and his dead body concealed in a large chest. In both stories Mrs Clayton is extremely beautiful with a power over men of which she is totally unaware. This has been the cause of several unprovoked incidents in her past and is now responsible, indirectly, for her husband's baseless jealousy and murder. In 'The Baghdad Chest' Mrs Clayton is presented very basically as a 'simple childlike woman' who is 'born to trouble the souls of men.' The narrative is too undeveloped for the strength of the story and the conclusion, especially the identity of the murderer, is strained. These weaknesses are all transformed in *The Spanish Chest*. The fatal attractiveness of Mrs Clayton remains mysterious, even to Poirot until he talks with one of her gossipy women friends.

She feels that given Mrs Clayton's 'extraordinary effect on men' her husband might well have been 'insanely jealous,' but was probably not. After all, if he had been, wouldn't he have 'done her in'? You know, she adds, 'Othello – that sort of thing.' It's the idea Poirot has been searching for and soon he is urging everyone (including the bewildered Mrs Clayton herself) that if they want to understand Clayton's murder they should read *Othello* and properly consider the character they have overlooked. The innocent Desdemona may have an extraordinary effect on men, but so does Iago, and his brilliant manipulations are concious and direct, unlike Desdemona's and Mrs Clayton's. Once revealed, these interpretations of Shakespeare's play are seen, in retrospect, to pervade the reader's understanding of the whole of *The Spanish Chest*, making it not only a highly effective Christie murder mystery, but also an imaginative literary interpretation of a key aspect of *Othello*.

Much the same can be said of *Curtain*: *Poirot's Last Case* (1975). *The Spanish Chest* was probably adapted from 'The Baghdad Chest' in the late 1950s at a time when the attraction of Freudianism was fading for Christie, though that of Shakespeare remained strong. *Curtain* belongs firmly with Christie's psychoanalytical experiments of the Second World War and shows the influence of both Freud and Shakespeare in something like equal measure, though *The Spanish Chest* contains no mention of Freud and focuses entirely on Shakespeare. However, the technique employed in both works is very similar. As in *The Spanish Chest* the Shakespearean theme in *Curtain* is introduced relatively late in the novel but once grasped resonates back through all of the earlier action. The realization by the reader that *Othello* is the key to understanding what has gone before runs parallel with the more customary business of having the identity of the murderer revealed and then understanding for the first time all that had been unclear before. This technique is heightened in *Curtain* by closing the novel with a written postscript which the now dead Poirot has arranged to have delivered to Hastings. It places Hastings, who seems as blind as ever to what exactly Poirot is up to, in the same position as the reader.

Stephen Norton, the suspect Poirot is tracking in *Curtain* has gradually mastered a way of commiting murder by proxy. This is achieved by suggestion and insinuation. He functions by instilling doubts in the mind of a susceptible victim who is driven to commit murder or to contribute decisively to a murder on Norton's behalf.

Poirot recognizes in him, here at the end of his own career, the 'perfect criminal' who can 'never be convicted of a crime.' And, the protoype, as Poirot comes to understand, is Iago who is also 'the perfect murderer' whose crimes are committed by others while he himself remains 'outside the circle, untouched by suspicion – or could have done so.' In his postscript Poirot not only links Norton and Iago together, but also offers a full psychoanalytical case study of his life, detailing Norton's family, upbringing and emotional background in order to explain how the feeble insecure boy came to develop 'a morbid taste for violence at second-hand.'

Although written some time in the early 1940s and, it may be assumed, modified or added to in relatively minor ways subsequently, *Curtain* was not to be published for another thirty years. By then it would come to be seen as something of an oddity, a rather curious way for Christie to tidy up Poirot's career in advance.[17] And perhaps it was, but it can also be seen more positively as being strongly connected with Christie's wartime fascination with Freudianism. That it was to be put to one side for an indefinite period may not have mattered very much to Christie. For the first time since the late 1920s she was allowing Poirot to take second place to Miss Marple, and there was no thought of killing her off in advance. Far from it. Thanks mainly to Freud, and with strong support from Shakespeare, Miss Marple's new career was about to take off.

Chapter 7

Miss Marple's Wartime Case Book:
The Body in the Library, The Moving Finger, Sleeping Murder

In 1965, in one her rare newspaper interviews Christie was reported to have told G.C. Ramsey that she considered the first chapter of *The Body in the Library* to be her 'best beginning.' She did not explain why and Ramsey didn't press her to do so. He did, however, go on immediately to report her as saying, and with no further explanation from her or himself: 'So … an elderly crippled man became the pivot of the story.'[1] Christie, as we have seen, always loathed interviews. In the few she did give, she comes over as edgy and defensive, with the views expressed being either entirely innocuous or not to be trusted. Sometimes, as she no doubt feared, she was caught off-guard and provided her interviewer with some unexpected pieces of genuine information, as may have happened in this case. Whether or not she was accidentally revealing some hidden feelings to Ramsey, the beginning of *The Body in the Library* really can be taken not only as one Christie's best, but much more than simply that. She might well have regarded it, and justifiably so, with a characteristic element of secret pride.

The novel opens in Dolly and Arthur Bantry's bedroom at Gossington Hall. Dolly is waking from a dream. She would normally expect to be gently roused by the maid with her usual cup of tea, but this morning is different. Christie gives a careful, detailed account of the dream itself and Dolly's waking responses to it. The experience is treated quite explicitly as an exercise in Freudianism in which the contrast between what Freud calls the 'manifest' and 'latent' elements of a dream are used not only to give a dramatic start to a murder mystery but also to establish an important subordinate theme as well.

Here is Dolly's dream, the dream she is enjoying so much that she doesn't want to leave it. In Freudian terms, we are given it in its manifest form; that is, the dream she is able to remember on waking:

> Her sweet peas had just taken a First at the flower
> show. The vicar, dressed in cassock and surplice,
> was giving out the prizes in church. His wife wandered
> past, dressed in a bathing-suit, but as is the blessed habit
> of dreams this fact did not arouse the disapproval of the
> parish in the way it would assuredly have done in real life.

Fundamentally it is what Freud claimed all dreams to be – a distorted wish-fulfilment. As gardening is virtually the only thing Dolly ever thinks of, her longing to star in the village flower show could well be about to become a reality. But this perfectly ordinary desire is complicated by extraordinary elements. The venue for the show is all wrong. It is not impossible that the vicar could be handing out the prizes, but the ceremony would hardly be held in the church. Nor would Griselda, the vicar's wife, be taking the opportunity to turn the church flower show into a beauty contest, a competition which she might well be capable of winning while Dolly would have no chance at all. Instead of being outraged by these goings on, the congregation cheerfully accepts them which, as Dolly sleepily realizes, they would certainly not have done in real life, this being 'the blessed habit of dreams.'

The discrepancy in age between the vicar and his wife, together with the local comments the marriage has provoked about her unsuitability for such a role, will be remembered from *Vicarage*, though it is not something that is ever likely to have bothered Dolly. She is, after all, not a village gossip. She is one of the most decent, respectable people in St. Mary Mead. Yet it is her insecurities that are being revealed, her subconscious worries that are placed within a wider context of sexual frustration and repression. Before her dream comes to an end Dolly is hoping to 'extract as much pleasure as possible' from it. In the dream Dolly's skills as a gardener and Griselda's sexual attractiveness are both acknowledged and accepted without any concern. They exist in separate spheres with no competition between them, and the congregation is happy to approve that situation. All is harmonious in St. Mary Mead.

Gradually Dolly's 'inner consciousness' alerts her to the sounds of the house stirring. It is nearly time for her to take her familiar place in the daily world. Half awake, she listens 'unconsciously' for the arrival of her morning cup of tea, but this time there is good reason for her to want her strange dream to continue and for it not to give way to reality. What she hears is a knock on the door and the maid's hysterical voice telling her that lying on the hearthrug in her husband's library is the dead body of a young girl. And it is not the body of someone enjoyably sexy like Griselda, but a young blonde in a 'backless evening dress of white spangled satin … the face … heavily made up, the powder standing our grotesquely on its blue swollen surface ... a cheap, tawdry, flamboyant figure.'

As a detective story, *The Body in the Library* functions at a fairly straightforward whodunnit level which is how it is usually read. A murderer is at large, clues are left, Miss Marple is called in, and eventually she tracks down the guilty party. There is, though, another major theme in the novel that has been ignored by commentators, though it is patently present, heralded by Dolly's dream and central to the larger concerns of the book. It deals with relationships between young women and older men.

The most obvious murder suspect in the novel is Arthur Bantry, peacefully asleep beside Dolly when the news breaks. After all, the dead girl is in his library, and he must be considered the person most likely to know how she got there. That's what the villagers quickly decide, and Colonel Melchett, the Chief Constable, also feels compelled, in a civilized man-to-man exchange, to ask Arthur quite frankly whether or not he was involved in any way with the girl. All of this is understandable enough. It is Dolly's response that is unexpected. 'He isn't like that,' she assures Miss Marple, 'He *really* isn't … He's just – sometimes – a little bit silly about pretty girls who come to tennis … There's no harm in it.' Then, growing more defensive, she adds sadly: 'And why shouldn't he? After all, I've got the garden.'

Here is the 'latent' element of the dream, the underlying concerns, feelings or experiences that have provoked it in the first place and which sleep, serving what Freud regarded as its protective function, has transformed into the harmless version which is all the dreamer remembers. It is the psychoanalyst's task to help the patient to reach back beyond the distortion to find the truth. This is what Christie now has Dolly doing. She obviously is worried by her husband's silliness about pretty young girls, and, whether she likes to acknowledge it or not, it does involve her in a competition. Her dream has made her face up to this fact by setting her gardening skills against the physical attractions of someone like Griselda.

Miss Marple, living up to her reputation for believing the worst about people until they can be eliminated from an enquiry, smiles at Dolly's cryptic remarks and tells her not to worry. But of course she does. There is never any reason to believe that Arthur has been involved sexually with the unknown girl, let alone killed her, but an element of doubt remains in Dolly's mind on both of these possibilities. Although the reader of *The Body in the Library* is hardly expected to remember it, many years earlier at the large dinner party in 'The Herb of Death' Dolly had openly criticized Arthur for always 'maundering on about young girls.' It is, therefore, an established character trait and a long-standing worry to Dolly. Presumably she is right in *The Body in the Library* to say that Arthur never moves beyond simply being silly about the girls and she can live with that situation as long as her lingering insecurity is not revealed. But her private fear is now about to go public and she knows very well that she can expect no tolerance from the village congregation.

Miss Marple's erstwhile cronies are quick off the mark, with Miss Hartnell quite sure of what went wrong: 'She thought too much about her garden, and not enough about her husband,' which, after all, has much the same coded message as Dolly's: 'And why shouldn't he? After all, I've got the garden.' And this is the view that soon spreads through the village. Far from happily taking no notice of the bizarre events going on around them as they do in Dolly's dream, Arthur's neighbours cold-shoulder him, and Dolly enlists Miss Marple's help to sort things out which, of course, she eventually does. But the kind of interest that Colonel Bantry shows in young women does not fade away. Instead, it moves strongly elsewhere in the novel.

* * *

Placed at the centre of *The Body in the Library* is a most unusual family group. They are resident at the Majestic Hotel and presided over by wealthy businessman Conway Jefferson. He is confined as a 'helpless cripple' to a wheelchair after being involved in a plane crash in which his wife, son and daughter were all killed. Here, in Christie's mysterious quoted words to Ramsey, is the 'elderly crippled man' who becomes 'the pivot of the story.' His daughter-in-law and son-in-law who were not in the crash have long been treated by Jefferson as if they were his own children, though they are not in fact blood-relatives. The murder theme of the book is initiated when Jefferson develops an interest in Ruby Keene, a young professional dancer at the hotel. It is his plan to adopt Ruby that angers the surviving members of his 'family' and turns them all into potential murderers. As with Colonel Bantry, Jefferson is never seriously suspected of being a murderer. He is generally thought of as a good and generous man. He also has influential friends in the police who, with the exception of the abrasive Inspector Slack, are eager to clear him of any impropriety in his relationship with Ruby.

Miss Marple, though, threatens to take a different line on all of this and for doing so is rebuked by Sir Henry Clithering. Conway Jefferson, he tells her angrily 'isn't just a nasty old man.' Miss Marple goes 'quite pink' and insists she wasn't implying anything of the kind. But she was, and unwilling to admit it she tries to explain her attitude away by launching at Sir Henry a long bumbling series of village parallels.

Among them, there was Mr Harbottle who abruptly dismissed his devoted sister-housekeeper and replaced her by a bright young maidservant. And Mr Badger, the chemist who 'made a lot of fuss over the young lady who worked in his toilet section' and would only give her up when his wife was able to prove he was being tricked out of money. Miss Marple is observing, as diplomatically as possible, that everywhere older men are manipulating young women, or being manipulated by them. Why, she is implying, should Jefferson be any different? Or, perhaps, Colonel Bantry? It's a common fact of life that needs acknowledging. Why try to hide it? It is all there, she tells Sir Henry, in the story of King Cophetua and the Beggar Maid. Sir Henry is becoming increasingly annoyed and demands to know why his friend Conway Jefferson should suddenly have developed this 'Cophetua complex.' The psychoanalytical term is entirely his. The reason why Sir Henry is so defensive is because he fears that Miss Marple may be including him in her generalizations about the sexual fancies of older men, as is indicated by his touchy response to her introduction of Cophetua.

The reference, which Sir Henry clearly grasps, is to an anonymous ballad called 'King Cophetua and the Beggar Maid.' It was first printed in the early seventeenth century by which time it was already a popular favourite enough to be included in Thomas Percy's celebrated collection *Reliques of Ancient English Poetry* (1765). Shakespeare refers to it in several of his plays and so do other Elizabethan dramatists. Christie had known of it for a long time.[2] And so it seems had Miss Marple. The story would also have been known to her from her beloved Victorian poets and painters. There is a Tennyson poem and an Edward Burne-Jones painting on the subject. Freud does not refer to the ballad. It is Sir Henry who recognizes it as a particular kind of complex, and it is certainly a story that fits very well with the literary legends and dramas that Freud felt had a special ability to survive through time because of the way they embody fundamental truths about human behaviour. He draws on a large number of such stories, most famously, of course, *Oedipus Rex* and *Hamlet*.

As was often the case, Victorian artists sanitized the story they had inherited. Tennyson's brief poem 'The Beggar Maid' leaves out most of the narrative and concentrates on the King and his courtiers drooling over the unexpected beauty of the maid. Burne-Jones follows Tennyson in emphasising the beggar maid's beauty but he portrays it as distanced and dignified. He also symbolizes the relationship between the couple by elevating the maid to a throne-like position in the painting, with the hatless king seated reverentially at her feet. Neither of these interpretations face up to the element in the story from which it derives its lasting psychological interest. In this respect Miss Marple is more courageous than her Victorian heroes. She omits nothing.

Cophetua was an African king who, according to the balladeer, is regarded as unnatural because: 'He cared not for women-kind/ But did them all disdain.'[3] Cupid decides to intervene in this unacceptable situation and aims 'a dart' at the king. From his window, the transformed king sees a poor beggar maid 'all in grey' and of a 'degree so base' standing with other suppliants at the palace gate. He falls instantly and wildly in love with her. He orders that she prepare herself to marry him:

> "Come on," quoth he, "and follow me,
> Thou shalt go shift thee clean."

Once she has taken this advice and changed into new clothes, she marries the king and adjusts effortlessly to her elevated position. They live quietly together and when they die are mourned by their loving subjects. Nothing is ever said about her looks, and rightly so because it is not her beauty that draws the king to her. Presumably he is surrounded by beautiful and accessible women at court all the time, and it's his lack of interest in them that worries his people. Whether Cupid actually chooses the beggar maid as appropriate for this particular case or whether his action is arbitrary, the king's lack of interest in women is transformed into a sexual passion for a woman who is poor, raggedly dressed, and dirty.

Such relationships were not unknown to the Victorians, and certainly not to Christie and Miss Marple.[4] The 'Cophetua complex' has a continuing relevance in the Freudian manner because over the centuries it has been able to adapt itself to very different social circumstances. For the Medieval/or African Cophetua, the problem is one of 'degree.' In modern terms it becomes a matter of class. At first the courtiers are not happy with having the beggar maid elevated above them, but they are obliged to follow the king's wishes, and they are delighted to learn that his chosen wife plays her part well and is no threat to them.

Christie does not attempt to follow through consistently with any direct comparison between Jefferson and King Cophetua. It is clear throughout *The Body in the Library* that she is conducting an experiment, testing out her ability to introduce an additional Freudian theme to her murder mystery, as she had already done less substantially with international politics in *Appointment with Death* and *Hercule Poirot's Christmas*. Even so, the further connections she does make with the ballad (or allows Miss Marple to make) are pertinent.

Before his accident Conway Jefferson had been a successful businessman. He is still very wealthy, a modern king, surrounded by the surviving members of his family who are dependent on him and act accordingly much as courtiers would do. They are happy to continue like this, expecting him to die soon when they will inherit his money. Until Jefferson befriends Ruby Keene there is no suggestion that he has any interest in women: it is possible that his particular crippled state has rendered him impotent. One change in him is that since his accident he has become more interested in the young. The hotel manager's defensiveness on this point is surely meant to be revealing. He says: ' Mr Jefferson's very fond of young people … I don't want to have any misunderstanding … he's always keen on seeing young people enjoying themselves: watches the tennis and the bathing and all that.' This information is given to illustrate what a kind and generous man Jefferson is, though one can imagine that Miss Marple in her present cynical mood, might identify less honorable motives. And, of course, many other characters in the book come to share Miss Marple's views once Jefferson begins to pay attention to Ruby Keene.

It is at this point that the 'Cophetua complex' carries most force. Ruby comes from a working-class background and is described by the hotel manager as 'rather cheap in style, perhaps, for a place of this kind, but nice manners – quiet and well-behaved.' Edwards, Jefferson's manservant and one of the more disinterested characters in the novel, describes her as 'a common little piece.' Everyone accepts she is a gold-digger and that Jefferson is behaving like an old fool. Sir Henry voices the thought of many in the book: 'If she'd only been a girl in his own rank of life.' To which Miss Marple replies pointedly that that 'wouldn't have been nearly as satisfactory from his point of view.' And it's at this moment that she first introduces 'King Cophetua and the Beggar Maid.' Later, directly challenged on this same issue Jefferson himself defends his choice with reference not to the beggar maid but to the near equivalent Cinderella who was 'turned into a princess overnight.' Why shouldn't he act the part of a 'fairy-godfather' to Ruby Keene and transform her in the same way?

Within the novel as whole, the Cophetua parallels gradually fade away. Arthur Bantry is shown to have had nothing to do with the dead body in the library; Dolly's loyalty to her husband is vindicated; Ruby dies; and Jefferson comes to acknowledge that he has made a fool of himself over Ruby. He admits that he 'must be turning into a silly old man' which is generally a more acceptable adjective that Sir Henry's earlier 'nasty.' Having survived the murder attack, Jefferson decides to leave his money to his grandson who has hitherto been rather neglected. The main characters are thus exonerated. But still, and although no sexual motive is directly involved, it should be noted that the most unpleasant aspect of the whole novel and acknowledged as such by everyone involved, is the trickery and the dressing up in tawdry unsuitable clothing, and then murdering, an entirely respectable and innocent schoolgirl. 'I hope and pray she knew nothing about it' says Miss Marple in an act of benediction for this latest example of mankind's depravity.

Although the Cophetua theme was not fully developed in *The Body in the Library*, we can be quite sure that it wasn't just a passing fancy of Christie's. She had used it to demonstrate that she was able to establish an extended subsidiary theme for a novel, and to bind it so closely into the text that nothing of the murder mystery's usual suspense was lost. It is also clear that her experiment was not being dropped. It was to be further expanded, with Miss Marple once again being used as the focal point. As reluctant as ever to announce her artistic intentions in any direct way, Christie was becoming more and more committed to leaving hints, allusions as to her present and future aims, and, doing this in characteristically cryptic ways.

In *The Body in the Library*, looking quite consciously ahead to *The Moving Finger*, her next and Miss Marple's second wartime novel, she planned to present a full-scale working out of the same theme even though in that novel the ballad would not be mentioned at all. And Christie was confident enough of her plan to leave a clue to her intention in *The Body in the Library*. It comes in the list of the village parallels which Miss Marple throws at Sir Henry to illustrate her long experience of men behaving foolishly over much younger women. This one features 'Jessie Golden, the baker's daughter.' By the time Miss Marple gets to include her in the list of parallels Sir Henry has had enough. 'What happened to her?' he asks wearily. Miss Marple's reply has absolutely nothing to do with the case in hand but is an oblique though undeniable reference forward to a key character in *The Moving Finger*: 'She trained as a nursery governess and married the son of the house, who was home on leave from India. Made him a very good wife, I believe.'

* * *

The Moving Finger is Christie's updated and sustained version of the Cophetua complex. It is a fully detailed case study, and one in which station and class remain elements but are subordinated to a process of twentieth-century psychoanalytical theory. It is also a book in which little is to be accepted at face value. Country living, social respectability, sex and gender, all conventional images are confused and challenged. Even the crime, indicated by the title, isn't what most people assume it to be.

As Miss Marple plays a relatively small part in *The Moving Finger* it is sometimes suggested that the novel wasn't conceived of as a detective story at all and that Miss Marple was only introduced late in the day for marketing purposes. That is possible: it was something Christie did with several Poirot novels. The argument rests on the fact that Miss Marple does not appear at all until three-quarters of the way through the book and even then doesn't feature prominently until her dramatic intervention at the very close. Nevertheless, there is a good case to be made out that Miss Marple was used quite deliberately in this way so that she could act, late in the action, as a sympathetic spokeswoman for the psychoanalytical concerns being explored throughout the book. This kind of role would make good sense because the central story is not concerned primarily with Miss Marple or even with the writer of the poison-pen letters, but with Jerry Burton who has came to Lymstock, accompanied by his sister Joanna, to recuperate after a flying accident.

Jerry is the sole narrator of the book and therefore, like Roger Ackroyd, responsible for telling his own story. He is not involved in any criminal activity, though that doesn't make his account of events any more trustworthy. After all, King Cophetua is not called upon to explain his actions. Nor is he expected to understand them. How could he? He is the patient, not the analyst. The ballad allows Cupid to cure Cophetua by setting him on the sexual course most congenial to him. That is what happens in *The Moving Finger*.

Few details are given of Jerry's accident or the nature of his injuries, but he is unable to walk without a stick and there are concerns that he may be permanently crippled. His London doctor tells him there is no reason why he shouldn't get well again as long as he remembers that his problem is not just physical: 'When it's a question of healing nerves and muscles, the brain must help the body.' As soon as he and Joanna arrive, they become interested in the poison-pen affair. Jerry even begins to fancy himself as a detective. Like most other people, including the local doctor Owen Griffith and the police, Jerry regards the writing of poison-pen letters as a 'pathological' matter, the work almost certainly of a woman, someone probably unmarried and sexually repressed. When Joanna asks in amazement why anyone would write such things, he tells her blithely: 'You must read Freud and Jung and that lot to find out. Or ask our Dr Owen.' It is, actually, Jerry who could do with a course of such reading.

Between brother and sister there is a constant interchange of lively and very frank sexual banter. Most of it concerns Joanna's many love affairs, one of which is currently unresolved. For Jerry there seem to be no similar experiences to look back on. The only moment when Joanna has the chance to return her brother's jokes about lovers is very different in tone from his. She tells him she was worried that during his time recovering in hospital he had taken no notice of his 'remarkably pretty nurse ... An attractive minx, too – absolutely God's gift to a sick man.' When Jerry says he finds her conversation 'definitely low,' she lowers it further: 'So I was much relieved to see you've still got an eye for a nice bit of skirt. She *is* a good looker.' The more recent 'nice bit of skirt' who has given Joanna some hope that her brother's injury has not totally deadened his interest in women is Elsie Holland, the Symmington family's nursery governess. The tartness in Joanna's jokey tone is because she realises that Jerry has already failed the test with this particular woman.

The occasion referred to had taken place a couple of days earlier. Jerry had caught sight of Elsie walking along the street and been literally flattened by the experience. The scene is one of classic burlesque, with Jerry's initial experience of Elsie being suitably bathetic. Overcome by the beauty of the 'floating goddess' before him, by the 'curling golden hair' and the 'exquisitely shaped body,' Jerry, in his own words, is lifted into a state of such 'intense excitement' that 'something had to go.' He falls to the ground, and is rescued by the extraordinary vision who picks up his shopping and his stick and hands them to him. Then she speaks and the spell is broken. 'How strange,' Jerry reflects, 'that a girl could trouble your inmost soul so long as she kept her mouth shut.' He is referring to the voice as being a class give-away, with the woman's physical attractiveness being deflated or devalued the moment she speaks. Jerry draws easily on that kind of class condescension. For one moment Joanna seems to support her brother's view by claiming that in spite of Elsie being a 'good looker' she lacks S.A. (sex appeal), a judgment that is general rather than snobbish. Jerry, however, immediately re-asserts his own ingrained snobbery by replying that if Joanna is right then it's 'just as well' that Elsie is only a nursery governess.

The reason why Jerry's view of Elsie changes so abruptly has in fact little to do with the quality of her speaking voice. That's a quickly grasped excuse, and one not shared by everyone. It doesn't seem to bother Richard Symmington, or other men in the town, who find her so attractive. What Jerry can't accept is that unknowingly she has publicly humiliated him. Her beauty has reduced him to a state of collapse. She even has to pick up his stick and hand it to him, confirming his fear that the flying accident has rendered him permanently impotent. Christie didn't need Freud to write this scene, though she was no doubt familiar with his views on symbolism in *The Interpretation of Dreams* that 'all elongated objects, such as sticks ... may stand for the male organ.'[5] Nor did she need Freud to discover the special therapy that Jerry's condition requires. She had her very own 'Cophetua complex' for that.

Jerry is saved sexually by Megan Hunter. Their first meeting reverses the shame inflicted on him by Elsie, with Megan falling off her bicycle 'more or less ... at my feet.' She is a 'tall awkward girl,' twenty years old though looking 'more like a schoolgirlish sixteen.' That is the polite view of her. Some of the local people talk openly of her as 'half-witted.'

Her clothes are 'drab and unattractive' and she usually wears 'lisle thread stockings with holes in them.' Ignored by her mother and her stepfather, and unemployed, she has nothing to do but wander or cycle aimlessly about the town. Joanna is quick to understand the nature of Jerry's interest in her. 'I'd thought of taking her for a walk,' he says. Joanna replies: 'With a collar and lead, I suppose.'

The relationship between Jerry and Megan is brought to a head in a scene that is still capable of shocking the reader. Jerry describes it as the moment when he went 'mad' and well he might. While he is waiting to catch a train to London for a medical check-up, Megan joins him and, mooching aimlesslessly about, as scruffy and more childish than ever, she asks Jerry to lend her a penny to buy some chocolate from a machine. He gives 'baby' the money, and then as the train is about to depart, suddenly drags her into the carriage and carries her off to Joanna's London dressmaker. He doesn't actually strip Megan himself, but that's what he has in mind when he hands the job over to Mary Grey, telling her that Megan is 'a little cousin' of his: 'I want her turned out right in every particular from head to foot … stockings, shoes, undies, everything!' King Cophetua had said much the same, only more succinctly: 'Thou shalt go shift thee clean.' And, indeed, Megan, the modern beggar maid is transformed. All it has taken is a few hours of hard work by a fashion and beauty specialist.

While this transformation is taking place, Jerry's doctor, who knows nothing of Megan, is expressing his astonishment at the progress his patient has made. Searching around for an explanation he suggests that Jerry must have 'found a blonde' in Lymstock. That provokes 'guilty thoughts of Elsie Holland' and Jerry deflects the doctor's inquisitiveness. Whether he himself ever understands what has happened is doubtful. Probably not. Frightened by Elsie's beauty, temporarily incapacitated by it, and explaining away his collapse by switching attention to her flat voice, he recovers sexually by being able to dominate someone who looks like a clumsy, scruffy, awkward child but who can be transformed by him and him alone into a suitable partner. That domination is epitomized by his violent action is abducting – 'raping' was the common word for exactly this situation in earlier times – and taking total control. The town is understandably scandalized by his action but holds back judgment when Jerry makes it clear that he is in love with Megan and plans to marry her. As a wedding present Joanna gives Jerry and Megan an Old English sheepdog, and, separately, an 'extra collar and lead.' Megan is puzzled by the gift, but is assured by Jerry that it is just 'Joanna's little joke.' Perhaps!

Miss Marple is not around to influence the main stages of Jerry's sexual recovery, but she does quickly understand what it is all about. She is brought late into the case not only or even primarily to reveal the identity of the writer of the poison-pen letters, a mystery that she and Mrs Dane Calthrop settle between themselves quite effortlessly, but to act as a kind of consultant psychoanalyst for Jerry. Her interest in him functions on the two different levels of the story. She focuses on Jerry's amateurish atttempts at detection, but probes more tellingly elsewhere. She questions him about his views on the poison-pen affair and his dreams, and then pronounces in her most authoritative manner that although she can see he is 'a very clever young man' he doesn't have enough confidence in himself. 'You ought to have,' she tells him.' This is just before the abduction. It would be wrong to say that Jerry takes Miss Marple's advice: going 'mad' in the way he does is hardly gaining the kind of confidence she has in mind. Still, the abduction of Megan is his instinctive way of overcoming his personal insecurity and re-asserting his sexuality. Shifting easily between the roles of detective and analyst, Miss Marple is explaining that only by developing more self-confidence will Jerry be able to understand the various mysteries, whether sexual, psychological, social or criminal, that are deeply rooted both in himself and in a community like Lymstock.

* * *

Sleeping Murder marked a significant change of emphasis in Christie's use of psychoanalysis in that she moved her exploration of unorthodox sexual relationships away from the village or small town and into the family. Although Miss Marple continues to combine the roles of detective and analyst, she is aware that she still has much to learn and at the close of the novel she charges herself with stupidity for not having seen the truth earlier. This, of course, is in her usual self-deprecatory manner, but it is perfectly just here, for *Sleeping Murder* is a novel about processes rather than deduction. Anyone who knows John Webster's Jacobean play *The Duchess of Malfi* (as Miss Marple does) should be expected to guess early on who the murderer will turn out to be. Gwenda Reed hasn't come across the play before, but now as she sits watching this 'tragedy of a warped and perverted mentality' and hearing delivered the despairing expression of guilt 'Cover her face. Mine eyes dazzle, she died young,' she screams in horrified recognition (though not yet understanding) of the truth she is seeking. She, Miss Marple, and readers of the novel, have all been given one big obvious 'clue,' as Miss Marple herself calls it when the murder mystery is finally solved, for *The Duchess of Malfi* is a play about incest, and that also is the central theme of *Sleeping Murder*.

In the play, Ferdinand and the Duchess are not only brother and sister, but twins, a point emphasised by Webster in order to make Ferdinand's sexual feelings uambiguously plain. Christie lessens the immediate shock of this relationship by giving Dr James Kennedy and Helen different mothers, making them only half-brother-and-sister. He is also considerably older than her, and presented at times as a kind of father figure, though of a very significant kind. For Miss Marple, the Victorian father he calls to mind is the notorious Mr Barrett of Wimpole Street, someone whose feelings for his daughter were, as she points out, similarly 'possessive and unwholesome.' This slight watering down of Webster's Jacobean openness was inevitable. It would have taken a far more iconoclastic writer that Christie or indeed any other British novelist of the time to do otherwise. Indeed, it is quite possible that one of the reasons for her willingness to handle such a controversial subject at all was the awareness that *Sleeping Murder* was only going to be published after her death. Much the same is no doubt true of *Curtain* which was written at the same time as *Sleeping Murder*. In their exploration of the inner working of criminal minds (with Poirot's own included in this particular case) both novels show author and detectives at their most psychoanalytical.

Even so, in *Sleeping Murder* Christie's sexual daring is particularly notable, not least for the way that in many key areas she was willing to stay so close to Webster. Dr Kennedy may only be Helen's half-brother, but he usually refers to her as his sister and he clearly regards her as such. Webster's Ferdinand is obsessed with any suitors the Duchess may attract and does all he can to prevent her marrying, mentally torturing himself by imagining his sister 'in the shameful act of sin.' When the Duchess does marry, he torments and tortures her, tries to drive her mad, and finally has her murdered. Dr Kennedy is similarly obsessed with his 'sister's' boyfriends, doing everything he can to drive them away. He spreads completely false rumours that her perfectly normal behaviour as a young girl is really that of a 'nymphomaniac.' Miss Marple further suggests that he even uses his authority as a doctor to allow a foot infection of Helen's to remain untreated. His determination to stop her forming relationships through playing tennis is so extreme that 'one night' he secretly cuts the net 'to ribbons' to prevent her friends coming to the house. Throughout the whole of her brief life he has terrified her. Helen does grow to understand the situation but in the showdown she has with Kennedy her criticism of him is only overheard, not witnessed, so that nobody at the time realizes it is Helen speaking. Her words are italicised in the original: *'You're not normal. Go away and leave me alone. You* must *leave me alone. I'm frightened. I think, underneath, I've always been frightened of you.'* When she does eventually marry and Kennedy can no longer bear the torment of his sexual jealousy, he strangles her. Over her dead body, and watched from the stairs by the three-year old Gwenda, he now repeats, from the *Duchess of Malfi*, the tortured words that Ferdinand utters over the body of *his* murdered, incestuously desired sister: 'Cover her face. Mine eyes dazzle, she died young.'

While pretending to tell Gwenda and Giles all he can remember about his missing sister, Kennedy, a general practitioner, denies having any special knowledge of mental illness: 'I'm not a psychiatrist myself.' Not, perhaps in terms of professional qualifications, but he certainly knows enough to place himself in control of a plot that functions centrally on a psychoanalytical level. For years Kennedy manages to conceal all evidence of his sexual obsession. He also skilfully plants and nurtures in Halliday the delusion that he is a murderer. Although Dr Penrose, who *is* a trained psychiatrist and in charge of the sanatorium to which Halliday is sent, comes to believe that Halliday was 'emphatically not a killer,' he can offer no explanation for the depth of his 'obstinate fixation about Mrs Halliday's death.' Penrose, the professional, and Halliday, the victim, are both outwitted by Kennedy the self-proclaimed amateur. So completely are they manipulated by his version of events that while in Penrose's custody Halliday commits suicide, making it seem that the truth about the affair is now securely hidden.

In *The Moving Finger*, Miss Marple had played what appeared to be a surprisingly minor role in the investigation, emerging at the close as a kind of professional consultant or adviser. In *Sleeping Murder* this pattern is reversed, with Miss Marple active and purposeful throughout. She happens to be with Gwenda at the crucial performance of *The Duchess of Malfi* and seeks from her an explanation of why it upsets her so much ('Suppose you sit down here, dear, and just tell me all about it'). Gwenda explains that it is only one of a number of mysterious experiences she has had and that she is thinking of consulting a psychiatrist. Miss Marple agrees this is a possibility, there being 'excellent mental specialists in London,' but instead takes on the case herself. She becomes, in effect, the psychoanalyst who talks Gwenda and her husband Giles through to an understanding of their family troubles. In order to do this she establishes with them what is for her an exceptionally affectionate relationship, and a controlling one as well. She has something like a free hand in the investigation, initating action, advising, warning, and governing her young patients. There is no one else. The police are not involved until near the close of the book, and then only because of the current murder of Lily Kimble. They can do nothing about the much earlier death of Gwenda's mother until they have evidence that she was murdered. That responsibility rests entirely on Miss Marple's willingness and ability to demonstrate some very special skills.

The intended original title of the book *Cover her Face* carried the reader directly to its major source *The Duchess of Malfi*, but *Sleeping Murder*, the replacement which Christie was obliged to find years later, went beyond the immediate reference and drew attention to a book that functions on many different levels. The new title describes a murder committed some time ago and left unsolved: also a murder that has emerged from sleep like a dream and which may or may not have taken place. It further draws attention to the constant movement throughout the novel between conscious and unconscious acts. The search for the truth bursts through Gwenda's slumbering subconscious as half-formed memories or nightmares provoking fears that she herself is mentally ill. 'The things I know are all underneath' she admits in bewilderment. Only by analysing those dreams and bringing the experiences which have provoked them to light will the truth be established.

This method, and the main narrative pattern of the book, is what the young Freud in his studies of hysteria written with Joseph Breuer and first published in 1895 had called abreaction, the release of anxiety by reliving the experience that caused it. It's a dangerous course to pursue, and Miss Marple, with the proverbial advice about dogs in mind, urges Gwenda and Giles to let sleeping murders lie. They refuse. Full of admiration for their youthful courage, Miss Marple helps them to a solution and a cure. She is reluctant to act because she realizes they will be moving into a family's hidden past, its unconscious, an unknown, dark, and potentially terrifying place, as indeed it turns out to be.

Not for the first time, Miss Marple finds a gardening analogy to epitomize what is going on, and it parallels Gwenda's understanding that 'the things I know are all underneath.' As Miss Marple waits for the murderer to reveal himself she occupies her time clearing the garden of bindweed. 'Such nasty stuff', she explains to Inspector Primer who, of course, she is 'priming' in such matters: 'Its roots go down underground a long way … a very long way … and terribly harmful, Inspector, squeezing the life out of the pretty growing flowers.'

* * *

As if the hidden psychoanalytical nature of these three wartime novels and the concealed publication plans for one of them didn't create enough complications, Christie added to them a very different kind of puzzle. If it applied to just one of the novels, then it might be dismissed as a local error, but it actually applies to all three, suggesting that she could hardly have been unaware of what she was doing.

As we have seen, Christie personally associated all three of these Miss Marple novels with the 1939-45 war, though only in terms of their composition. *The Body in the Library* was written and published in 1942 and *The Moving Finger* the following year. According to Christie's own account, *Sleeping Murder* and *Curtain* were also written in the early years of the war. They were then locked away with the intention of being published posthumously. Putting the special circumstances of their composition aside, all of these novels were written, in what by now had become the classic Christie manner, to give the impression that their action was taking place at some unspecified point in a mid twentieth-century England. In none of them does Christie convey any impression of a war taking place or of having recently taken place. Considered solely as an exercise in writing, this must have involved a good deal of thought and planning on Christie's part. This, of course, was what Christie excelled at, and she rarely took any easier options that may have been open to her. Here, for instance, if she had wanted to give to the novels a wartime relevance she could well have followed her own example of *N or M?* and have set the novels unequivocally during the war. That possibility was rejected in favour of sending Miss Marple off to explore the psychological nature of shocking, timelessly incomprehensible human violence. But this doesn't seem to have been enough for Christie. She took the process of mystification at least one step further by placing within each of the three Miss Marple wartime novels clues which indicate that, after all, the action of all three may have been actually taking place either during the war or shortly after. These clues are tucked away in order not to interfere with the otherwise total absence of wartime atmosphere, but they are undeniably there.

Throughout *The Body in the Library* Colonel Bantry has expressed his open contempt for the young film director Basil Blake. Towards the end of the novel when he hears that Blake is to be charged with murder, Bantry feels vindicated in his dislike and starts to be distinctly Blimpish. Miss Marple stops him with a touch of sarcasm unusual in her. Blake, she explains, joined the A.R.P. (Air Raid Precautions) which had been formed in 1938, when he was eighteen years old and had had his chest badly crushed while bringing four children out of a burning house.

Bantry is suitably embarrassed and mutters: 'I never knew that ... Always thought he'd shirked the war.' This information is presented to the reader suddenly and inexplicably. The only reasonable implication to be drawn from it seems to be that the novel is set shortly after the close of the Second World War in a Britain which in all all other respects shows no after-effects of war of any kind.

The equivalent moments in *The Moving Finger* are more obscure. The starting point of the novel is Jerry's flying accident. We are not told what kind of accident it was, though Jerry is treated with sympathy by his new neighbours, and Miss Emily Barton's response is: 'A flying accident? So brave, these young men.' That would normally be taken to refer to wartime conditions, though not, of course, inevitably so. Later, Jerry discusses a dream with Miss Marple that has been prompted by the phrase 'No smoke without fire.' This phrase is used repeatedly by the villagers to suggest that the various accusations set going by the poison-pen letters may not be entirely unjustified, but Jerry, for no reason the reader or anyone involved can be expected to understand, mixes it up with 'war terms.' He then abruptly dismisses the connection with, 'No, that was another dream.'

In *Sleeping Murder* the wartime clue is offered even more indirectly, though once interpreted it does appear to attach a date to the novel that is unusually precise for Christie. We are told that the performance of *The Duchess of Malfi* which Gwenda attends takes place at His Majesty's Theatre in the Haymarket, starring John Gielgud. As Charles Osborne has noted, this 'can only have been' a specific performance of *The Duchess of Malfi* which featured John Gielgud as Ferdinand and Peggy Ashcroft as the Duchess.[6] Osborne's general point was right, though he seems to have made a slight mistake in fixing the date of the performance as being in 1944. It was, actually, part of an extended Gielgud season held at the Theatre Royal, Haymarket which opened with Somerset Maugham's *The Circle* in October 1944 and closed with *The Duchess of Malfi* in April 1945. This was the only occasion Gielgud ever played the role, and the very slight change Christie makes to the name of the theatre is hardly even an attempted disguise. Although the actual play was well received, it was regarded by some, including members of the cast, as too shocking to put on at this time. This criticism was turned upside down when reviews of the play appeared in the same newspapers that carried reports of the horrors being revealed daily as Allied troops liberated German concentration camps.[7] This has to be the performance and the wartime setting that Gwenda disprupts by screaming out in subconscious recognition of the hidden horror in her own life.

It is impossible to know what Christie hoped to achieve by inserting these specific wartime references into novels that otherwise had nothing to do with the war. It is, surely, inconceivable that they were all due to carelessness. Perhaps, like so much else in Christie's later work they carried some unknown personal meaning for her which she failed to integrate fully or meaningfully into the larger narratives in which they appear. Nevertheless the present examples are very clearly *not* integrated, and linger in the mind as unsolved puzzles. That in itself makes it worth drawing attention to them, but they also connect with a larger puzzle concerning one of these particular novels.

John Curran has recently challenged the truth of Christie's account of the composition of *Sleeping Murder*.[8] It will be remembered that she claimed to have written *Sleeping Murder* and *Curtain* early in the war and had placed both manuscripts in safe keeping with a view to having them published after her death whenever that might be. This plan was first made known to the general public in Francis Wyndham's 1966 interview with Christie, and confirmed in the *Autobiography* which was published posthumously in 1977. Curran argues that *Sleeping Murder* was actually written some years later than Christie had claimed. He suggests moving 'the writing of it nearer to 1950, i.e. almost ten years later than the supposed early 1940s date.' No explanation is offered as to why Christie should have entered into this curious kind of cover-up of what was, after all, in itself a form of subterfuge, and much of Curran's case, especially his speculations regarding Miss Marple, is circumstantial. The strongest part of his evidence is taken from the notebooks which, as Curran more than anyone else has made us so aware, were used by Christie in a random, unsystematic manner which often makes them unreliable as any kind of chronological guide to the composition of the novels. More substance, though, is provided by two entries quoted from the notebooks which carry specific dates regarding 'plans' for *Sleeping Murder*. These dates are 1947 and 1948.

It has to be said that Curran has a case, or perhaps part of a case, that is worth making. Furthermore, it is one that is strongly supported by the puzzling wartime reference in *Sleeping Murder* that I have been discussing here. If it is right to identify the performance of *The Duchess of Malfi* in *Sleeping Murder* as having taken place in April 1945, then the novel could not have been written and locked away several years earlier in the way that Christie describes. It must be the case that at least this part of the novel which describes a key psychological moment in the plot would have had to be written towards the close of the war or at some time afterwards and therefore adds credence to Curran's argument that Christie was still making 'plans' for *Sleeping Murder* after the date she put aside the completed the manuscript. Even so, it remains the case that we have no way of knowing the nature or extent of those plans. In typical Christie manner the details offered in the notebooks are either brief or uncertain. As always, the planning would have been taking place almost entirely in her mind, not on paper.

It is, however, possible that there is a sensible solution to this particular problem. The argument I have offered throughout the present chapter supports the view that *Sleeping Murder* was originally written just as Christie claimed. All three Miss Marple wartime novels, together with the one Poirot novel *Curtain*, are powerfully united by Christie's intense, and relatively fleeting, interest in pschoanalysis. They were obviously all written at about the same time. There are no similar Miss Marple or Poirot novels written earlier or later that function in the same way as these three works. At the very least, it makes good sense to accept that *Sleeping Murder* and *Curtain* were substantially written now. But there are also good reasons to believe that they didn't remain hidden away until their publication many years later. Christie was pre-eminently an impulsive, spontaneous writer. Much of the celebrated planning was not even entered in the notebooks but took place in her mind. She didn't usually have the manuscript of a novel by her for long enough to revise or alter it and must have found it a pleasant experience to be able to return occasionally to *Sleeping Murder* and *Curtain* to add a passage, change a detail, or modify the plot in line with her later thoughts.

And this, surely, is what happened. In fact, Janet Morgan describes Christie in 1950 as dusting off what would become *Sleeping Murder* in order, as Christie herself wrote, to go 'over it thoroughly, as a lot of it seems to date.' She added 'on rereading it I think it's a good one.'[9] The 'plans' for *Sleeping Murder* in the Notebooks could well refer to specific alterations or changes, or even to structural developments that in 1947 or 1948, she had in mind or had suddenly thought of. Given her generally disorganized approach to the notebook entries, it is far more likely to refer to something like this than to be a personal declaration that she was about to start work on a new novel or new version of *Sleeping Murder*.

Chapter 8

Crime in the Welfare State:
A Murder is Announced, They Do It With Mirrors

Victory in Europe was declared and celebrated throughout Britain on 8 May 1945. In the Far East the war continued for a further three months. It ended only when the American Air Force dropped an atomic bomb on the Japanese city of Hiroshima on 6 August and another on Nagasaki three days later. In between the close of the war in Europe and the close of the war in the Far East a general election was held in Britain. In purely constitutional terms it was long overdue but with wartime conditions still in operation and large numbers of British troops actively engaged overseas there was a strong case to be made for a further delay. When the political parties disagreed on this, the wartime coalition was discontinued and a general election took place on 5 July.[1] It was in many respects an extraordinary thing to do. The result of the election was extraordinary as well.

Although led by Winston Churchill, the revered leader of the wartime coalition, the Conservative Party was beaten decisively by Clement Attlee's Labour Party. The principal reason for the victory was the broad and brilliantly calculated appeal of Labour's election campaign. Both parties were faced with the urgent need to repair a seriously war-damaged country, but Labour looked much further ahead, offering a futuristic vision of a social and political reconstruction of the entire nation. The aim was to create a new kind of democratic egalitarian society, one that was fitting for the people who had made such huge sacrifices over the previous five years. The failure of British politicians to respond in a similarly grateful manner after the First World War was very much in the minds of both politicians and electorate. Those mistakes were not to be repeated. Nor were the mass poverty and unemployment of the inter-war years to be allowed to return. With a parliamentary majority of more than one hundred and forty over all other political parties, the Labour government committed itself to the nationalization of key private industries, a massive programme of public housing, the creation of a free health service, and a fairer education system.

'New' was the word of the moment. There was much talk at the time of the building of a New Jerusalem, and a few years later in 1952, following the death of Britain's wartime monarch George VI and the accession to the throne of his daughter Elizabeth, of the birth of a New Elizabethan Age. Neither label survived for long. The ideals and dreams of the immediate post-war years quickly faded. For years to come Britain was to remain inextricably involved with large areas of the world, but there was little of the exhilarating, buccaneering spirit associated with the first Elizabethans. At home the image of a radically reformed Britain as a shining spiritual centre of inspiration was gradually transformed into a more mundane patchwork of social experiments that came to be known collectively as the Welfare State.

After five years in which the Labour government had pushed stubbornly on with its programme of social reforms in spite of being constantly deflected by massive international, financial and domestic crises, the voters began to show signs of weariness. In the general election of February 1950, Attlee's overall majority was cut to five, making it just possible for Labour to hold on until October 1951 when a second election returned the Conservative Party, still led by Winston Churchill, to power. There were some voices calling for Socialism to be overthrown as forcefully as Conservatism had been six years earlier, but not many. Although the Labour Party had been rejected by the electorate, its radical social reforms survived, strongly approved by both Labour and Conservative supporters. For the most part the Welfare State was continued, even enhanced, with its slogans and aspirations now painted blue rather than red. It was the start of a period of consensus politics in Britain that was to last for some thirty years.

* * *

After the publication of *The Moving Finger* in 1943, the third of her wartime cases to be written though only the second to be published at the time, Miss Marple had been sent on another of her periodic rests. This time it was for seven years. She was not reintroduced to the reading public until June 1950 when *A Murder is Announced* was published, and she was slightly though significantly different from before. Her mind was as fresh as ever though it was no longer guided by a Freudian passion. Nor was she any longer untouched by passing time. What looks like her carefully calculated reappearance took place between the 1950 election, which saw the Conservatives overhauling the Labour government's huge post-war majority, and their return to full power in 1951. To use those popular terms of the time, Miss Marple had missed out on the early attempt to build a New Jerusalem, but was fresh and ready to play an active part in the New Elizabethan Age. As usual, the reader was given no reliable news about what she had been doing during the years of post-war austerity, though she is shown to be more generally aware of the massive changes that had been taking place around her during Britain's traumatic period of post-war austerity and reconstruction. She even refers occasionally to wartime experiences, other people's mainly, but now and then her own as well.

The return of Miss Marple was not the only event in 1950 of personal significance for Christie. It marked her sixtieth birthday and *A Murder is Announced* was her fiftieth published title. In the same year she began writing her autobiography in which she would quite consciously, skilfully, deviously even, set about trying to lay down the pattern of her life as she would like it to be remembered after her death.

It was clearly intended that Miss Marple was to play a positive role in this phase of reminiscence and reassessment. After all her fitful comings and goings she was back to stay and being prepared to share whatever future as a writer remained to Christie. Poirot was still about of course, as unchangeable and impossibly ancient as ever, but Miss Marple was ready to have her age manipulated as and when that should prove necessary. Christie had been thirty-seven years old when she created a Miss Marple approximately twice her age and over the years she had occasionally modulated Miss Marple's image and sharpened up her looks. Now, as

Christie moved self-consciously into her sixties, grateful she had survived the war and prepared to continue her active writing life, it was once again time for Miss Marple to be given a new kind of flexibility. Not in order to become basically any different or younger, but to follow Christie herself in being more adaptable. In terms of age, Christie was beginning to catch up with Miss Marple and in the curious way of fiction, that meant that the age gap between them now seemed less important than it once had. From now on the two women would move steadily closer together with their views and opinions often becoming interchangeable. This was the kind of bonding, referred to in the Preface, that struck Julian Symons so forcefully when he interviewed Agatha Christie in 1961. He found himself talking with someone who seemed to 'radiate' the very personality of Miss Marple. As for her preference for Miss Marple to Hercule Poirot, he felt that was so obvious there was no need even to ask her about it. [2]

For Christie the changed attitude towards Miss Marple was a form of artistic as well as personal relaxation which she was to make good use of. For some time she had been conscious of critical charges that her work had become old-fashioned. That kind of criticism was never totally fair: the best of her books had always exuded an impressive air of timelessness, an effect consciously worked at, as we have seen. But there was a real issue at stake and it had less to do with the format of her work than with its content. Change was being forced upon her. Five years of world war and then a further five of a reformist Labour Government had all but wiped out the social settings she had relied on for the classic detective novels of the 1920s and 1930s. In welfare-state Britain they were beginning to look decidedly historic.

Poirot and Miss Marple couldn't just be left as survivals of a bygone age. In one way or another their relationship with the welfare state needed to be adapted if the two great detectives were not to seem absurdly out of place. Christie had already demonstrated her willingness to relax the stark minimalism of her detective stories of the 1930s by introducing into them political and psychoanalytical elements. That had been during a time of international upheaval and change. Now, with a fundamentally different kind of society established at home, more subtle concessions had to be made. There would be some uneasy moments, especially with Poirot confronting the new teenage culture of the 1950s and 1960s, but Miss Marple now felt more manageable to Christie as the two women moved ever closer together.

During the war, Miss Marple had acted as a surrogate for Christie in examining cases which were as appropriate for a psychoanalyst as a detective. Now, with that phase largely over, she was to be used in the same kind of manner to explore a radically transformed social world. In some respects it is similar to the way in which, twenty years earlier, Christie had gradually released Miss Marple from the confines of the Tuesday Night Club so that she could observe the flapper generation of *The Murder at the Vicarage*. Now, with her mid-Victorian image retained and her age and energy lightly readjusted, Miss Marple became an active member of welfare-state Britain. In another of Christie's conjuring tricks, Miss Marple is made to seem both further removed from and notably closer to the social world of the novels in which she appears. The old narrative ingenuity was to be refreshed by adapting itself to a much altered social order.

In June 1950 wartime austerity was beginning to ease a little and life was feeling slightly less constrained. A Conservative government was on its way back and a New Elizabethan Age in the offing, as Christie prepared to 'announce' Miss Marple's return. It was an occasion, and one that deserved to be marked in a suitably high, celebratory manner.

* * *

A Murder is Announced has all the verve of a classic Christie murder mystery. Much of the dialogue is written in her best light romantic comedy style. At the same time it is one of her most theatrical novels, and one of the most artificial, strongly influenced by the successsful secondary career as a dramatist in which Christie was currently engaged. 'Well, here we are, all set,' Miss Blacklock murmurs as she carefully appraises the 'double drawing-room' at Little Paddocks, her house in the 'large sprawling picturesque village' of Chipping Cleghorn. Although they have not been invited in any formal sense, guests are expected, and Miss Blacklock is making sure everything is ready for them. It might have been a stage set for one of the synthetic drawing-room comedies that had long provided staple theatrical fare for the West End and repertory theatres throughout Britain before John Osborne ridiculed them out of existence with *Look Back in Anger* a few years further on in 1956.

Gradually the guests assemble, their curiosity aroused by an advertisement in the local *Gazette*: 'A Murder is announced and will take place on Friday, October 29th at Little Paddocks at 6.30 p.m.' Surely it must be a joke! Or a party game, perhaps? Yet, as predicted, when the mantlepiece clock chimes half-past six, the drawing-room is plunged into darkness, the door crashes open, a powerful flashlight moves round the room, and 'a man's hoarse nasal voice, reminiscent to all of pleasant afternoons at the cinema' orders: 'Stick 'em up!' While the guests gasp and giggle at this unexpected treat, three shots are fired. When the lights are switched on, the body of a young man is lying dead in the doorway and blood is dripping from Miss Blacklock's ear.

Miss Marple isn't one of the guests, but she is soon called to play her part in the drama. She is receiving treatment for her rheumatism ('Very bad of late') in nearby Medenham Wells, paid for, of course, by Raymond West, and is described as looking 'very old' with 'snow white hair and a pink crinkled face and very soft innocent blue eyes.' She is also 'heavily enmeshed in fleecy wool.' When she reads of the shooting in the paper, she realizes she has information that might be of use to the police. Sir Henry Clithering, who happens to be visiting the local force, encourages his colleagues to seek her help, and introduces her in a suitably histrionic manner: 'Once more a murder is announced – for the benefit and enjoyment of Miss Marple.'

It is a world in which the identities of virtually all of the principal characters are blurred and uncertain. They may seem to be familiar from earlier Christie novels, serving well-defined social or domestic roles in this small community, but that itself is an illusion. Here no one is to be trusted; no one plays a clear socially defined role. Not necessarily vicious or murderous by intent, they are merely pretending to be people they aren't, adopting fake personalities. In this they are representative of the whole community, perhaps, in some ways, of the entire nation. Are they covering up shady pasts or guilty secrets, or are they simply on the make or in hiding or innocently shielding a loved one or planning murder?

Epitomizing this kind of uncertainty, and something of a new and not entirely happy departure for Christie, is Mitzi, Miss Blacklock's stroppy maid, a European refugee. There is never any real doubt that she has suffered from Nazi persecution, but her constant complaints and shrill neurotic manner provoke little sympathy in the people she lives with. The tricks played on her by the younger members of the house, who are visibly bored with talk of the recent war, are unthinkingly cruel. Patrick Simmons, a cousin of Miss Blacklock's who lodges with her, might be forgiven for making Mitzi an apple-pie bed, but hardly for sending her an anonymous postcard warning that the Gestapo are on her track. Understandably Mitzi doesn't regard that or the opening murder announcement as funny. Nor is she amused when the wonderful chocolate cake she makes when she can obtain the ingredients is dubbed by Patrick 'Delicious Death.' For someone of Mitzi's background death can be neither funny nor delicious. Nevertheless, the cake she is persuaded to make for Dora Bunner's birthday becomes the means of an extremely heartless murder.

Could Mitzi be guilty? How is it possible to know whether or not she is a genuine refugee? As a loud, comic foreigner, always complaining that her life is in danger, isn't she an obvious suspect, someone likely to commit a murder rather than be murdered? Why shouldn't she be an active participant in the delicious death joke? After all, it is Christie herself who is the main cook, the compiler of irresistible concoctions, the story-teller with the remarkable ability to allow the reader to experience death not as terrifying or shocking or frightening but as pleasurable. The jokes and tricks in *A Murder is Announced* have multiple meanings just as the characters carry more than one identity and various plays within plays are acted out. In one of these Mitzi herself is called upon to make a virtue of her complaining nature by acting the part of an hysterically terrified refugee. Miss Marple too is temporarily transformed, shedding the rheumatism and old age that brought her here in order to play a very active part in Miss Blacklock's final unveiling. And there's one more surprise to come. It has always been obvious that Miss Marple is a good actor: we now learn, with no warning at all, that she is a first-class mimic as well.

Christie's narrative skills in *A Murder is Announced* are employed not only to create a mystifying whodunnit but also to raise general issues of great seriousness which are in themselves mystifying. Miss Marple should be perfectly at home with the village setting of Chipping Cleghorn which, as she herself says is not unlike St. Mary Mead. But she isn't. In part her uncertainty comes from the lingering effects of the war with which everyone in the novel is still trying to come to terms and which Christie conveys neatly and precisely. Her skill in this respect has not gone entirely unremarked by commentators.[3] Here, within what should be a typical comfortably off Christie village everything has become slightly shabby: the gardens are neglected, houses unpainted, housework is shared among everyone rather than done by servants, rationing is in operation and standards of life are kept up only by a highly developed system of barter. Nor is any of this seen as a temporary phase, soon if ever to be corrected. Once removed from St. Mary Mead, Miss Marple comes to understand that the type of village community in which she learned her trade is changing beyond recognition. Whether human nature has changed with it is something she has yet to settle in her own mind.

Before the war, she tells Inspector Craddock, her own village had been a network of familiar relationships. Not ideal or perfect or anything like that but understood by all involved, and therefore manageable. But no longer. Nowadays 'people just come – and all you know about them is what they say of themselves.' Craddock needs no persuading. The problems being outlined by Miss Marple concern him as well. In his world, ostensibly much larger than hers, he also can no longer 'know' people with any certainty:

> They were just faces and personalities and they were backed
> up by ration books and identity cards – nice neat identity
> cards with numbers on them, without photographs or
> fingerprints. Anybody who took the trouble could have
> a suitable identity card.

They agree that 'the subtler links that had held together English social rural life' have fallen apart. The multiple suspects and false trails of *A Murder is Announced* are no longer founded on deviations from clearly identifiable social norms. They have been replaced by alienation which has now become the necessary concern of Miss Marple and Inspector Craddock.

The ways in which people are murdered – shooting, poison, strangulation – have not, of course, changed; and financial gain remains here the prime murder motive. But the source of money has become worryingly impersonal and the society in which it operates increasingly difficult to comprehend. The earlier crimes which Miss Marple had been called upon to solve had usually been driven by personal greed or sexual passion. Identifying the perpetrators of those crimes was achieved by separating them off from other members of their group, the guilty being those who are left after the innocence of everyone else has been established. In comparison, the murders in *A Murder is Announced* are cold-blooded and committed in a fraudulent attempt to lay claim to a fortune amassed by a pre-war financier Randall Goedler, a man of 'daring speculations and rather theatrical publicity.' After his death his wife Belle had retreated to an isolated Scottish castle. She herself is now dying, totally innocent and ignorant of the murderous activities unknowingly inspired by her late husband's financial wizardry.

The distancing of Belle Goedler is an extremely clever plot device that serves to cheapen still further the falseness of many of the individual poses struck in the novel. Goedler himself had treated the accumulation of money as an exciting game, an end in itself, in which questions of morality and ultimate purpose were never really considered. Miss Marple is up to solving the murders that take place in Chipping Cleghorn because they involve recognizable forms of human wickedness, but what ultimately lies behind them is far less clear. Perhaps, after all, people haven't really changed, but the times have, and drastically so. For the moment, the vast impersonal Goedler fortune together with the criminal trickery it provokes are beyond Miss Marple's comprehension. They seem to her to be frighteningly symbolic of a modern world in which pervasive impersonal forces are rapidly displacing the intimate human relationships she had always prided herself on understanding.

All of the seven Miss Marple novels that followed *A Murder is Announced* were to continue, in a variety of different ways, to explore the changing nature of post-war Britain. This meant, inevitably, that the air of detachment Christie had so carefully developed for her pre-war detective stories was no longer relevant. She could not write about and comment on this new world without to some extent making her own feelings clear. Miss Marple may have unconsciously initiated Christie's narrative refinement of the 1930s, but she had not been involved in its later experimentation. Poirot had been principally concerned then and he was now more difficult to adapt. In contrast, Miss Marple, having been left alone by Christie for so long, was more flexible, more capable of serving Christie's new purposes.

The critical response to the change this led to in Christie's novels has been largely negative. It has often been argued that what was taking place was a decline in Christie's skill, with the great murder mysteries of the 1930s representing an ahievement she could no longer attain. As Miss Marple was to receive so much more attention in the post-war period, she has tended to be seen as the principal victim of this supposed decline, with her novels representing a falling away from the standard set by the earlier masterpieces. For John Curran, *A Murder is Announced* 'is easily the best of the Marple titles … the last of the ingeniously constructed, daringly clued and perfectly paced detective novels.' But the subsequent Miss Marple novels are then all seen as failing in one way or another because they do not conform to that ideal pattern of the perfectly constructed detective story. [4]

What tends to be ignored in such accounts, as so often in discussions of Christie, is the conscious element of change in her work. *A Murder is Announced* meant that Miss Marple was back and flamboyantly so, but in her own right and not as a shadow of Poirot. The post-war Miss Marple novels move sharply away from the now firmly established Poirot model by giving less centrality to a murder mystery and more consideration to the social nature of crime. In the process they allow Christie herself and Miss Marple as her surrogate much more prominent roles. In this respect, *A Murder is Announced* is an important transitional work. It is still a first-rate murder mystery, but also a social and literary exploration of why things couldn't continue as they once were. Christie's powers were not in decline at this point, as it has often been claimed. They were changing so that she could write significantly different detective stories for the character she felt personally closer to than had ever been possible with Poirot. And this meant surrendering the sleek minimalist techniques of the 1930s in favour of a broader social and political context which was more suitable for a transformed post-war Britain. It was a new type of challenge, and at first worryingly and testingly so.

* * *

Thematically, *They Do It With Mirrors* (1952) has important elements in common with its immediate predecessor *A Murder is Announced*. Once again Christie was working to establish a mood of high theatricality. The title itself refers to the way in which a conjurer uses mirrors to create a fake atmosphere in order to distract the attention of the audience from what is actually taking place. But whereas the theatricality of *A Murder is Announced* is allowed to play allusively throughout the story, creating an air of sustained illusion that makes it one of the best Miss Marple novels, in *They Do It With Mirrors* the theatricality is placed too apparently as a plot device at the very heart of the action, turning the novel, arguably, into the weakest of them all.

For the moment Christie's narrative confidence seemed to have been thrown out. She was reasonably clear on what she wanted to do with Miss Marple after *A Murder is Announced* and that purpose would not change for the rest of the detective's career, but the change was difficult to manage. The murder itself in *Mirrors* is handled cleverly enough: the wider criminal setting, though, feels overloaded and lacking in focus. That the main action takes place in what would normally be considered unfamilar Christie territory adds to the sense of disharmony. Social issues are now given an unusual centrality. The imbalance this creates works against the effectiveness of *Mirrors* as a novel, but it also reveals in the clearest possible way just what it was that was beginning to worry Christie about post-war Britain, and that had to be clarified before her work could move forward.

The novel opens with Miss Marple being reunited in London with Ruth Van Rydock, one of two American sisters she had first met as a young girl on an educational visit to Florence. Over the years Miss Marple has kept in touch regularly with Ruth, though only on a Christmas-card basis with the other sister Carrie Louise Serrocold. Both women are now married and rich, with entirely different attitudes to money. Ruth's interest is personal, a means to keep her looking young. In the opening scene with Miss Marple, which is offered in a rather unlikely manner as being typical of their meetings over the years – 'in Claridges, or the Savoy, or the Berkeley or the Dorchester' – the English spinster sits demurely in the expensive London hotel room while her American friend tries on fashionable gowns, consciously displaying her 'still shapely legs' and 'exquisitely corseted' figure. The Miss Marple observing this display is 'white-haired, with a soft pink and white wrinkled face and innocent blue eyes.' She is 'dressed in rather dowdy black,' carries 'a large shopping bag,' and appears 'every inch a lady.'

Unlike her sister, Carrie Louise is an idealist with no personal interest in money. It is there solely to help fund the aspirations of others. Her current project is Stoneygates, a rehabilitation centre for juvenile delinquents run by her husband Lewis Serrocold. As Ruth Van Rydock performs her individual fashion show, she explains her concern that Carrie Louise is in some kind of personal trouble and urges Miss Marple to visit Stoneygates to see if Carrie can be helped in any way.

Here, as in *A Murder is Announced*, we have the the power of vast wealth to control events, except that in *Mirrors* the money in operation is a notably international, philanthropic affair and has not one source, but three. These are the phenomenal wealth of America; the Gulbrandsen Trust, established by a Scandinavian businessman who had 'built up a fortune so colossal that really philanthropy had been the only solution to the disposal of it'; and, in post-war Britain, the fledgling Socialist State. The exact status of Stoneygates as a reform institution for juvenile deliquents is never convincingly explained by Christie. Nor is the manner in which it relies for its existence on all three sources of wealth. Carrie Louise's American money finances the dreams of her husband Lewis; the Gulbrandsen Trust provides the money to run Stoneygates; and the British government is somehow responsible for approving or authorizing the treatment of the more than two hundred juvenile delinquents housed by the instititution.

Britain's desperate financial plight, especially in comparison with modern America, is conveyed by Ruth Van Rydock's patronizing attitude to Miss Marple. Her way of bringing Miss Marple and Carrie Louise together is to invoke the hardship being suffered by so many people in Brtain since the war. She suggests it would be kind of Carrie to invite Miss Marple to stay for a while because 'dear Jane' sometimes 'has hardly enough to eat' and is 'far too proud ever to appeal to old friends.' Miss Marple keeps her thoughts to herself, but she diplomatically agrees that 'going to Stoneygates as an object of charity – more or less under false pretences' is quite a good ploy. And, as unpleasant as in some respects Van Rydock's account is, Miss Marple is often shown in the post-war novels as having very little money to live on. Her constant need to make do becomes an increasingly important factor in her character and her work.

If *Mirrors* seems disturbingly unlike earlier Miss Marple novels, this is largely because the community on which it focuses is so commanding, impersonal and, in the way it operates, abstract. Miss Marple is obliged to confront not simply an old friend and whatever personal problems she may have, but a large-scale social experiment. Even village parallels are hard to find. When she does come up with one, it is relevant enough but seemingly trivial in this world of tricks and illusions. Institutional wealth and the idealism it funds are focused intently on the issue of juvenile delinquency. The delinquents themselves, though, do not commit the murders that take place at Stoneygates. Corrupt idealism must take the blame for them, and also the responsibility for betraying the young people it claims to be helping. It is the system that is wrong, wasting its huge resources on seemingly empty theories, making the social problems it claims to be solving worse rather than better. These are the concerns that were worrying Christie and which she sets out rather awkwardly to communicate in *They Do It With Mirrors*. They were worrying much of the British nation as well.

* * *

Crime was not one of the post-war Labour government's successes. In fact, it was something to which, in the early days at least, little serious attention had been given. The main reason for this was that mid-twentieth century Socialist ideology was still profoundly influenced by antiquated environmentalist beliefs whether of the Marxist or the John Ruskin and William Morris variety. Crime, the argument ran, is the product of social deprivation. Ensure that people have good health, housing, and education, and crime will take care of itself. It could be confidently assumed that once the Welfare State was fully operating criminal activity would rapidly decline. That was the theory. Unfortunately, it didn't seem to be working. There was already startling evidence on hand to suggest that high social ideals had no effect whatever on criminal behaviour.

During the Second World War, with the British nation widely exalted for its patriotic and idealistic sacrifices, it has been estimated that criminal activity, measured by indictable offences, rose by nearly 70 per cent.[5] It continued to grow in the immediate post-war period. In 1947, at a time of exceptionally severe financial hardship in Britain and heavy military commitment abroad, the prime minister Clement Attlee felt obliged to make a statement in parliament condemning the 'spivs and other drones' whose activities were so widespread that they were threatening to undermine the government's policy of social reconstruction. Emergency legislation was quickly introduced to try to control the situation.[6]

For the moment blame could be placed on poor social conditions and wartime disruption. When living and educational standards for all rose then crime rates would surely fall. That was the expectation. But they didn't. Nor did things markedly improve with the advent of a Conservative government. Political consensus reigned here as elsewhere. In 1951 the Conservatives inherited from Labour a record crime level, and for a few years seemed able to keep it under control. Then in the mid-1950s, with the Conservatives still in power, the crime rate began once again to accelerate, this time unstoppably. The statistics are extraordinary. In the period 1945 to 1955 the average yearly number of indictable offences hovered around half a million. In 1960 it shot up to three quarters of a million: by 1965 it had passed one million. Ten years further on and even that figure had more than doubled.[7]

Throughout these years it was common to speak of Britain as suffering from a crime wave and there was a permanent mood of public outrage at the visible amount of criminality, especially on the part of the young. To many it still felt right to argue that these were wartime children who had been deprived of normal parental control, though the high incidence of crime during the war itself sat uneasily with this theory, and anyway, as the years moved forward most young criminals could no longer claim any direct connection with either the war or poverty. The election campaign of 1958 was won by the Conservatives with the argument that the standard of living in Britain had never been higher, or, in Harold Macmillan's catchy words, that 'most of our people have never had it so good.'[8] The realization by older voters that this was clearly true, allied with their memories of wartime sacrifices, made the anti-social behaviour of their children and grandchildren all the more inexplicable. Professional criminal activity was now augmented by an youth culture that appeared to glorify the cosh, razor, flick-knife, and knuckle-duster; organized street gangs, casual burglary and violent assault. It announced its existence openly by boastful uniforms that quickly (and not always by any means fairly) became associated with criminal intent: Teddy Boys at first (and Teddy girls), followed by Mods and Rockers.

The principal item of legislation that the Labour government hoped would deal with these problems was the Criminal Justice Act of 1948. This did not represent new thinking on the part of the Labour Party, but consisted largely of pre-war liberal-progressive ideas carried forward for enactment in the new mood of post-war optimism. Far from doing anything to ease public disquiet, the Criminal Justice Act quickly became a further cause of outrage. Penal servitude (i.e. imprisonment with hard labour) was abolished, along with most forms of corporal punishment, notably 'judicial birching.' Rehabilitation centres of various kinds were set up to try to prevent young people from going to prison. These supplemented the Borstal system which was still, for a short while, to be regarded as effective and worth maintaining. The new sentences and institutions carried popular labels that caught on with the general public as well as crime novelists, Christie included. Among the new terms introduced were detention and attendance centres, corrective training, and, a concept that would prove both useful and highly adaptable over the coming years, the 'short, sharp shock.'

It had been intended that proposals for the abolition of capital punishment would also be contained in the 1948 Act, but the strength of the opposition made this impossible and the reformers were forced to back down for the moment and start again, moving forward slowly, step by step. Under the Homicide Act of 1957 restrictions were placed on the crimes for which capital punishment could be imposed. Also under this act, a long-standing anomaly in English criminal law was clarified and, incidentally, provided the general public, and Christie, with another favoured, and often ironically applied label. This time 'diminished responsibility.' In 1965, under a private member's bill introduced by Sidney Silverman, parliament agreed to suspend capital punishment for an experimental period. It was eventually abolished in 1969.

Even allowing that the issue of capital punishment was rather special and would always be controversial, many people still thought it outrageous that while crime rates were rising to ever higher levels the official way of dealing with them was to reduce or abolish entirely all forms of physical punishment. Gone were hard labour, birching, flogging, heavy prison sentences and, in many cases, incarceration of any kind. In their place were measures which showed little evidence of deterring, reforming, or rehabilitating young criminals.

These issues were fiercely debated throughout the 1950s and 1960s, with the political consensus staunchly resisting any move to modify the reformist trend. Christie's natural conservative instincts were largely against the reforms, and as she has sometimes been unthinkingly criticised for this, it should be stressed that her views were by no means exceptional. In this sharply divided campaign she was in very respectable company indeed. Her views were shared with large numbers of the public, often a clear majority. It is unlikely that very few of the new reforms would have survived a popular vote which, of course, they never had to face. Nor did the public seem willing to be converted. Donald Thomas records that in the late 1960s 'about two-thirds of the electorate' continued to support the reintroduction of flogging for violent criminals.[9] Popular opinion was voiced by influential figures. They included churchmen, police, journalists, judges, teachers, magistrates, politicians, peers, and ministers. In the early years, the Lord Chief Justice himself led the opposition to the reforms and in several notorious cases Home Secretaries (both Labour and Conservative) were unwilling to exercise clemency, as the law allowed them to do, and waive the death penalty. In taking this kind of stand their actions were opposed by many of their parliamentary colleagues, but not by the nation at large.

* * *

Here, in brief, is the complex nation-wide debate that underpins the portrait of Stoneygates in *They Do It With Mirrors*. Christie followed the public debate on crime with great interest, and its main elements and terminology are to be found everywhere in her post-war novels, those featuring Miss Marple especially. The care with which Christie now began to adapt her narrative methods to the new criminal climate is apparent from her treatment of the juvenile delinquents in *Mirrors*. They do not, surprisingly perhaps, provide a serious suspect for the murders that take place in the novel; nor are they condemned or excused for their past behaviour, which shows considerable fair-mindedness on Christie's part. Rather, the delinquents themselves are viewed as the victims of competing ideologues. In a narrative sense they are little more than essential background. Any personal accountability they might once have been expected to possess has been undermined by wealthy philanthropists, psychiatrists, idealistic politicians, and social theorists, many of whom are shown to be misguided, even corrupt.

In *Mirrors*, Miss Marple's wartime enthusiasm for psychoanalysis is now overshadowed by a strong element of cynicism. This is not shared by the administrators of Stoneygate. Their faith in it remains absolute. One resident doctor, the significantly named Dr Maverick, who Miss Marple thinks looks 'distinctly abnormal himself,' describes psychiatry as having 'come into its own during the war … the one positive good that did come out of it.' Miss Marple would clearly have agreed with the first part of that statement, but not the second. Her change of attitude is to be found in Gina Hudd's humorous warning to her about Stoneygates: 'You tumble over psychiatrists everywhere underfoot. Enjoying themselves madly. Rather like Scout-masters, only worse.' But although Miss Marple now seems to be so uninterested in the subject that at one point she admits to being unable to tell the difference between psychiatry and psychology,

Mirrors did not represent a permanent change of attitude on Christie's own part towards the true value of either. It was, rather, a temporary protest at the convenient way she felt that psychiatry was being used increasingly to explain away, even to excuse, anti-social behaviour.

Crime itself rather than any individual criminal act is now Christie's main subject and her treatment of it, in *Mirrors* at least, is highly schematic. The characters in the novel who suggest that the Stoneygates approach may not be the right way to deal with rising crime rates – Wally and Gina Hudd, Inspector Curry and Miss Marple – are regularly dismissed by those in charge of the institution as incapable of understanding what is truly at stake. Furthermore, Lewis Serrocold and Dr Maverick are shown to have no interest in helping the murder investigations or, indeed, of considering issues of crime and punishment in any terms other than the kind of 'corrective or constructional training' followed at Stoneygates. That the current Stoneygates regime is revealed ultimately to be involved in a ridiculously ambitious con-trick, does seriously weaken the emotional force of the novel, though Christie's/Miss Marple's general position remains perfectly clear. Never before had Miss Marple been so blatantly the spokeswoman for Christie.

There is one particularly revealing exchange between Lewis Serrocold and Miss Marple. Serrocold is about to suggest, quite unjustifiably, that Wally Hudd might be responsible for the attempted poisoning of Carrie Louise. After all, he has 'no interest in or sympathy for what we're trying to do ... He's young, crude, and he comes from a country where a man is esteemed by the success he makes of life.' Miss Marple replies sharply, and to Serrocold's astonishment, that there can be nothing wrong in that. In contrast to such a positive view of life, 'we are so very fond of failures.' What Britain needs, she goes on to explain, is precisely more of the American attitudes that Serrocord is deriding. Although she does not acknowledge the source of her ideas, Miss Marple has obviously been reading George Orwell. As her politics would usually have been very far removed from his, there could hardly be a stronger indication of her sudden and passionate interest in social issues. The point she is making about Britain being too fond of failure comes straight from Orwell's essay, 'England Your England.'[10] And so does the kind of supporting evidence she gives, notably Britain's symptomatic pride in the retreat from Dunkirk and its fondness for poems like 'The Charge of the light Brigade' and 'The Revenge,' all of them defeats and failures. The use, however, to which she puts Britain's curious fascination with failure is quite different from Orwell's. He instances it as one of many strange but lovable national characteristics that conceal the nation's fundamental decency and strength. But for Miss Marple it is a sign of a decadent Britain, slavishly following misguided social policies, and by that there can be no doubt she means the whole underlying theory of the Welfare State as represented by Stoneygates.

She offers a firm corrective as well. Instead of giving so much attention to juvenile delinquents, and applying to them policies which are patently unsuccessful, she argues that Britain needs to encourage 'young people with good heredity' who have been ' brought up wisely in a good home' and who have the ' grit and pluck and the ability to get on in life.' That the reference to 'heredity' there has nothing to do with class as such, and everything to do with misguided State policies, is made clear in her admiration for the working-class American Wally Hudd who is leaving Stoneygates ('the bughouse' as he calls it) to return to America with Gina so that they can build a future for themselves just as the old pioneers had done. There, still actively at work, is the true original Elizabethan spirit which has largely vanished from modern Britain.

And finally, to re-inforce her main point Miss Marple invokes Shakespeare. For much of the novel the reader has been teased with the possibility that Gina, the beautiful Italian, is about to leave her American husband for one of two other men both of whom Miss Marple has been quick to recognize are in love with her. Now Gina announces she has decided to stay with Wally. She promises him she will 'forget all about Stoneygates and Italy and all my girlish past and become a hundred percent American. Our son will be always addressed as Junior. I can't say fairer than that, can I, Wally?' Before Wally can answer Miss Marple intervenes with strong support of Gina's decision: 'You certainly cannot, Kate.' When Wally gently corrects the foolish old lady for getting his wife's name wrong, Gina assures him: 'She knows what she's saying! You see – she'll call *you* Petruchio in a moment' The reference is to the closing scene of *The Taming of the Shrew* when the hitherto rebellious man-hating Kate not only succumbs to her husband's authority but delivers a magisterial rebuke to two other disobedient wives. Today, it is easy enough to intrepret Kate's speech, like Gina's, as blatant anti-feminism. But placed in its original context, which is what Miss Marple is doing, it is a rejection of moral chaos and a defence of national orthodoxy. It is the kind of stance, Miss Marple is claiming, that is needed in post-war Britain.

Although *They Do It With Mirrors* was something of an oddity in Miss Marple's career, and hardly one of her more intriguing mysteries, it was an oddity with a purpose. There is an unmistakeable air about it of Christie for once being determined to have her say about political and social issues, or rather to allow Miss Marple and Gina via Shakespeare to express views that were clearly her own. Never again would Christie take on a State institution like Stoneygates. Nor did she immediately continue to pursue the theme of juvenile delinquency. Neither, though, disappears from her work.

Rather, they both point forward in subtle, often indirect ways, to important things to come. Juvenile delinquency would be confronted again by Christie some years further on, while on a broader plane she would continue to be no longer willing to accept crime in its classic murder mystery form as a spectacular but essentially separate and socially isolated act. She was now quite consciously trying to deal with crime in a national context; presenting in action, and, of course, within the detective story format, the new kind of post-war Britain she had identified in her discussions with Chief Inspector Craddock in *A Murder is Announced*. Immediately, in *Mirrors*, she had tackled head-on one central feature of that transformed world, and had done so quite a bit too brashly. That mistake would be corrected. As always, Christie was quick to learn from her mistakes and eager to move on.

Chapter 9

'Houses for the People':
A Pocket Full of Rye, 4.50 from Paddington,
The Mirror Crack'd from Side to Side

A t first sight *A Pocket Full of Rye* (1953), *4.50 from Paddington* (1957) and *The Mirror Crack'd from Side to Side* (1962), give the impression that Christie was putting the vagaries of *They Do It With Mirrors* firmly behind her and returning Miss Marple to traditional territory. There is much in all three novels that is familiar.

Rye is centred on a large family house in a prosperous commuter suburb in the Home Counties; *Paddington* on a Victorian mansion, also in the Home Counties, while *The Mirror Crack'd* takes as its focal point the Bantrys' modernized former home in St. Mary Mead. The principal murders are all family based with the main suspects coming either from within a narrow family circle or close to it. Admittedly the Hollywood element of *The Mirror Crack'd* means that some of the suspects are way beyond Miss Marple's usual experience, but even their alien ways are controlled by the main action of the novel being linked so firmly to St. Mary Mead. One valued connection with the past is provided by the return of Chief Inspector Craddock of Scotland Yard with whom Miss Marple had established such a sympathetic understanding in *A Murder is Announced*. The relationship between them is made special for Miss Marple because Craddock is the godson of Miss Marple's old friend and admirer Sir Henry Clithering, and that provides her with a sense of continuity as well as friendly support in both *4.50 from Paddington* and *The Mirror Crack'd*. For *A Pocket Full of Rye* Christie even applied to Miss Marple for the first time one of the narrative devices she had employed so many times before with Poirot, a plot sketched out along the lines laid down by a popular nursery rhyme.

Even so, in spite of these links with the past, the classic Christie detective story format is no longer what it had been, and the controls imposed by the family settings are to some extent illusory. In all three novels Christie is consciously using plot and character not simply to puzzle and entertain. They continue to do that all right, but they also draw attention to very specific changes in British society. No longer is Miss Marple driven to try to understand ways of life that are essentially alien to her, as Christie had had her misguidedly attempt to do in *Mirrors*. Instead, she is obliged to recognize that the effects of the social changes she has to confront are all around her, within families and environments with which she is pefectly familiar, even in St. Mary Mead itself.

Houses and housing, for instance, not only provide essential settings in these novels, as they had done from the very start of Christie's career, but are major themes in their own right. Both *A Pocket Full of Rye* and *4.50 to Paddington* focus on large family homes run by dysfunctional families. Rex Fortescue, the owner of Yewtree Lodge in *Rye*, is outwardly a successful City financier, but even before murder comes to him he is suspected by the police and Inland Revenue of being involved in shady business dealings, while the crime that brings Miss Marple into this seedy area of the stockbroker belt involves reawakened interest in an abandoned gold mine in West Africa, a surviving remnant of the Empire that by the 1950s Britain was hurriedly dismantling.

It is generally agreed there is little good to be said for any of the permanent inhabitants of Yewtree Lodge. When Inspector Neele first arrives at the house, the housekeeper Mary Dove informs him cheerfully that the Fortescue family are 'all quite odious.' He himself is quick to brand them as all 'very unpleasant people.' And so they are. No longer do we have a fundamentally decent community disrupted by murder, or even, as in *A Murder is Announced*, driven to adopt disguises by personal or social circumstances. Now, virtually everyone is on the make and capable if not of murder, at least of some kind of criminal or antisocial activity. In a revealing conversation, Miss Marple tries to assure Pat Fortescue, that 'there are not so many Yewtree Lodges' in England. But she sounds as though she is really trying to convince herself because it is clear that Yewtree Lodge in all its unattractiveness is being offered as a microcosm of post-war British society. The depressed mood is so pervasive that even Pat Fortescue, who is one of the few sympathetic characters in the book, is unable to escape its influence. Her own family background is one of 'crookedness in the racing world' and her attempts to escape its legacy has led her into a series of unhappy personal relationships, the latest of which is central to the murder plot of *Rye*.

The world Pat now belongs to is no better than the one she had hoped to escape from. It is made up of dishonest or incompetent businessmen, social climbers, gigolos, crooks, plunderers of what is left of the Empire, and 'aristocratic riff-raff.' Everything about the house itself is fake and pretentious. 'Call it a lodge, indeed,' muses Inspector Neele, pondering his own childhood: 'The affectation of these rich people!' And Neele 'knew what a lodge was. He'd been brought up in one.' This, he decides, is a 'mansion.' Pat, using one of Christie's own favourite indicators of a family's worth or otherwise, describes the garden as 'quite the nastiest' she has ever been in. This is no longer, as it had been in *A Murder is Announced*, a matter of wartime neglect or lack of money, but the complete absence of any kind of 'individual taste' or personal interest. Everywhere there is a disturbing lack of personal initiative and drive that is repeatedly explained away in terms of the inhibiting pressure of the modern bureaucratic state, a line employed as personal justification for their actions by both honest and dishonest characters. The unpleasantness of the children of the house is heightened by their all having Christian names that were chosen by their dreamy romantic mother from Tennyson's *Idylls of the King*. The chivalric code that might once, in Miss Marple's view especially, have been suitably matched with Victorian aspirations, now provides a rather pathetic ironic commentary on Britain's reduced national, financial, and moral ambitions.

Miss Mary Dove who watches over and skilfully manipulates Yewtree Lodge is a new kind of independent woman character for Christie, a modern up-to-date variation on the long familiar dishonest or morally unstable family servant, and quickly recognized as such by the police. She is also a corrupt version of the near-perfect Lucy Eyelesbarrow who will partner Miss Marple in her next case, *4.50 from Paddington*.

Although Mary Dove and Lucy Eyelesbarrow are strongly contrasting moral types, they are united by Christie's astute understanding of the changing status of domestic service in post-war Britain. As a child and young woman Christie had taken the presence of household servants for granted, and they feature prominently in both the *Autobiography* and her early novels. Today it is reasonable to assume that most readers think of domestic servants as a necessary component of Christie's fictional world, and so they are, but only pre-war. The same was not true after 1945. In fact, Christie was greatly concerned to record, with something like sociological exactitude, major changes that had taken place.

In 1931 more than 5% of households in England and Wales still employed at least one resident domestic servant. That meant a total of more than 700,000 servants, mainly women. These were employed primarily by the middling but not necessarily prosperous class that Christie often wrote about. By 1951 the number of households containing any kind of residential servant had dropped below 1% to a total of 178,000 servants, and was continuing to fall sharply.[1] The changes embraced fundamental attitudes as well as circumstances. In both the war and the early idealistic years of Welfare State egalitarianism, domestic service had become widely stigmatized as a form of unacceptable dependency. Women who had once had few employment prospects other than domestic service were being actively encouraged to look after their own families, aided by greatly improved, and free, health, medical and educational opportunities. Or, as an attractive alternative, they could take higher paid employment in the new light industries that seemed, for a few years after the war, to represent Britain's economic future.

The changed nature of post-war domestic service had already been well explored by Christie in *A Murder is Announced* where Miss Blacklock's house Little Paddock is in effect a much extended family, consisting all but entirely of women. The only servant as such is Mitzi the refugee, with all of the other women assuming they must help out, in one way or another, in running the household. The thriving and extensive local barter system in goods and services which this highly respectable community supports is actually a form of wartime black market which, along with rationing, continued to operate for some years after the end of the war. The visiting police are astonished when they discover this highly efficient, technically illegal set-up, though Miss Marple knows all about it. She actually explains some of its intricacies to Inspector Craddock who 'in a kind of despair' delivers a statutory warning to the inhabitants of Little Paddock that what they are doing is against the law. He then diplomatically drops the subject.

Self-help or making do, usually in less communal ways than those in *A Murder is Announced*, are regarded as middle-class necessities in all of Christie's post-war novels. In *4.50 from Paddington* responsibility for maintaining Rutherford Hall falls to the sympathetically portrayed, emotionally depressed figure of Emma Crackenthorpe, who slaves thanklessly for her father and brothers; while in the later *Nemesis* the three Bradbury-Scott sisters struggle to keep their large family home going with the help of 'a very nice woman who comes in' but only 'in the morning.' Miss Marple herself has difficulties with domestic service which are solved for her, as we shall see, in a manner that is rather unorthodox, at least as far as transformed assumptions in the welfare state were concerned.

Not only is Christie calm and realistic about the changing nature of domestic service, on one particular aspect of it she is remarkably forward-looking. First-rate domestic service, she points out, will always be readily available but only to those who are able and willing to pay for it, the social status of this new class of domestics being largely irrelevant. The old relationship between employer and employee has not disappeared, though it is now barely recognizable. Inspector Neele, for one, doesn't understand it at all. When he suggests to Mary Dove that he would have thought she had the 'brains and education' to have a better job, she replies: 'My dear Inspector Neele, this is the perfect racket. People will pay anything – *anything*- to be spared domestic worries.' Mary is secretly enjoying herself by making a pun on 'racket.' Lucy Eyelesbarrow's motives are more respectable than Mary Dove's, and her portrayal far more idealized. Nevertheless, they are based on exactly the same realization that in a world where there are no longer enough servants to match the reduced demand, domestic service is a wonderful career opportunity. Lucy has a degree from Oxford and rejects a possible academic career to enter the more lucrative 'field of domestic labour.' Cedric Crackenthorpe expresses astonishment at Lucy being 'a skivvy,' and she laughingly puts him in his place: 'You're out of date. Skivvy, indeed! I'm a Household Help, a Professional Domestician, or an Answer to Prayer.'

She is a whole universe removed from the maidservants and cooks who tend for the families in Christie's early novels. Before the war they had regarded it as absolutely essential that they should have at least one live-in servant who would usually have been poorly paid and not always very good at her job. Lucy Eyelesbarrow and Mary Dove are highly skilled specialists who can be employed only by the rich or well-off. Even the Crackenthorpe family in *Paddington* wouldn't be able to find the fees that Lucy demands if, in order to get the case moving forward, Miss Marple hadn't offered to subsidize Lucy's drop in earnings. In context, with Miss Marple presented throughout these novels are relatively hard-up, that sounds a rather unlikely tactic, probably introduced by Christie to make the larger point about modern domestic service. Mary Dove is a live-in housekeeper, but Lucy is a freelance and aggressively independent. She picks and chooses jobs as she pleases, limits the time spent on any one of them, restricts her hours of work so that she can take regular holidays abroad, and is a member of a London Club where she arranges to meet Miss Marple in order to discuss the possibility of helping her look into the railway murder.

The portrayal of Lucy Eyelesbarrow and Mary Dove is sometimes assumed to be the product of wish-fulfilment or nostalgia on Christie's part, but it was nothing of the sort. She was being accurately predictive about long-term trends. She was also picking up on contemporary feelings. Post-war governments weren't over-pleased by what was widely and unflatteringly regarded as the decline of domestic skills in Britain and came under pressure to counteract the trend. Some of the policies urgently introduced to fill the domestic gap, included the setting up of training centres, the granting of special permits to foreign workers and supporting the estabishment of educational courses in domestic subjects leading to the attainment of professional qualifications.[2]

Lucy Eyelesbarrow's success in her unusual job also indicated a more positive tone in Christie herself, with the pervasive disillusionment of *They Do It With Mirrors* and *A Pocket Full of Rye* becoming significantly modified in *4.50 from Paddington*. British society is still hardly vigorous, but with the exception of Alfred (known within his own family as 'Flash Alf') who is acknowledged to be a small-time gangster caught up in classic post-war racketeering, the various members of the Crackenthorpe family are feckless rather than crooked. It suits them all very well to have someone like Lucy Eyelesbarrow paid to provide them with comforts they have been used to but can no longer afford. They are occupied principally in waiting for the death of their father so that the family house can be sold off to property developers. Rutherford Hall, a monument to Victorian entrepreneurship set in its own large grounds, is described as 'an island bounded by railway lines … an anachronism … Bustling urban life goes on all around it, but doesn't touch it.' In its 'queer isolation' it is genuinely symbolic of the depressed mood of post-war Britain, with lethargy triumphing over energy, and an easy life preferred to hard work. Everyone knows that it makes more sense to have Rutherford Hall pulled down and the land sold for development rather than face the trouble and vast expense of trying to maintain it as a family home. Even the murderer is, technically at least, an outsider, perhaps making the point that the members of this particular family would be quite incapable of finding enough energy to indulge in such a decisive business as homicide. They, as with Britain itself, are suffering from a malaise, seemingly incapable of doing anything positive at all.

A similar note had been struck in *A Pocket Full of Rye* when Pat Fortescue describes the death of her first husband during the war. Then, she recalls, he had had all the qualities needed for such a life. He had been 'wonderful.' But, she also believes that had he survived, all such qualities would have been useless to him in peacetime. Throughout all of these post-war novels there is constantly present a feeling that the Second World War has represented for Britain a great peak of courage and daring, with little left to follow but a sad decline. Inspector Bacon in *Paddington* fairly assesses the type of individual involved, and the wider problem: 'In a way, we've given them a raw deal. Though I don't really know what we could do about it. But there they are, all past and no future, so to speak.'

That special kind of ruefulness in *Paddington* is well captured in the sharply observed portrayal of Bryan Eastley, a fighter pilot hero during the war, but who now, the widowed father of two young boys, appears himself to be a little boy lost, unable to find anything remotely as exciting to do in peacetime. It is notable that Christie's overall air of post-war pessimism was becoming sufficiently qualified for her to allow most members of the Crackenthorpe family to appear as charming as well as lethargic. At least, Lucy thinks that two of them are, though whether she is going to continue to remain her usual sensible self when it comes to choosing between them is left playfully in doubt at the close of the novel.

Left more seriously in doubt is whether Miss Marple herself could possibly have enough energy to handle another case. Already presented in *Paddington* by Mrs McGillicuddy with a mystery that she can't possibly ignore, Miss Marple is upset that she no longer feels up to the task: 'She was old – old and tired … She wanted nothing at all but to reach home and sit by the fire.' What success she does enjoy is made possible only by employing Lucy as her surrogate. Old age for Miss Marple now carries with it a weariness that is physically disabling. It is, though, one of the curiosities of most of these late novels that however weak physically Miss Marple is shown to be it does not prevent her from playing a very active role in the final tracking down of the various murderers. This was not a new thing. The dramatic endings, with Miss Marple suddenly becoming courageously involved in the unveiling of a murderer had been characteristic of pretty well the whole of her career. Not all of them are entirely convincing, and, in the later novels, especially, it might have been wiser to have had Miss Marple withdraw from them. But Christie probably felt it important to supplement the moral passion that becomes increasingly characteristic of Miss Marple with at least an element of physical recklessness. And physically involved Miss Marple remains to the end, in spite of her otherwise debilitating old age.

* * *

Five years were to pass before the publication of Miss Marple's next case, *The Mirror Crack'd from Side to Side*, and once again she is shown to have aged significantly. So much so that there is a pervasive valedictory air about the whole novel, a sense of tidying up and rounding things off; a sense, surely, of Christie's own uncertainty about just how much longer she could carry on. Thematically *The Mirror Crack'd* is still concerned with the nature of post-war Britain generally and housing in particular, but it is far more schematic than *A Pocket Full of Rye* and *4.50 from Paddington*, with events being introduced not simply to advance a plot or heighten narrative development, but to illustrate overtly, even justify, certain informing ideas or theories. Whether or not it was written as a probable farewell to Miss Marple's entire career, it does feels like that. It is certainly used to round off the batch of five post-war novels initiated by *A Murder is Announced* and to summarise the decade of doubt and uncertainty in which Miss Marple has struggled to understand the new Britain. Yet, with that said, in comparison with the overall tone of social decline and lethargy in the earlier four novels, *The Mirror Crack'd* offers a surprisingly optimistic analysis.

Not since *Murder at the Vicarage* thirty years earlier had one of the novels been set so completely within St. Mary Mead. *The Mirror Crack'd* opens with Miss Marple at home, gazing out of the window, regretting that she is no longer allowed to do any gardening. Or, officially, anything else of interest. She is confined to the house, looked after by a bossy professional home help, Miss Knight, and also by a young local housewife Cherry Baker, sensibly recruited by Miss Marple herself. The immediate explanation for her being so carefully protected is a recent attack of bronchitis, but those close to her know that she is really suffering from the frailty of old age. Cherry defends her against the fussy Miss Knight, and her old friend Dr Haydock encourages her to take an interest in the latest local murder. But much of the time she has to sit still and have information brought to her by willing helpers. With a mind still fully alert, she is in danger of becoming like Poirot or even Holmes, except that armchair detection was a delight to them. For Miss Marple physical inactivity is a penance. She is desperate to escape her housebound state, not just to hunt down criminals but for more personal reasons as well.

Her mind lingers uneasily on the changes taking place in St. Mary Mead. It was now ten years since she had acknowledged in *A Murder is Announced* that villages like Chipping Cleghorn and her own St. Mary Mead could not avoid being affected by what she saw as declining community values and individual alienation. Now she has to recognise that those same forces, powerfully reinforced by others that had received less prominence in the earlier book, are totally transforming St. Mary Mead. The 'old world core of it' may still be there, but the local houses are being bought by incomers and modernized. Colonel Bantry has been dead for several years, with his widow Dolly using the East Lodge of Gossington Hall as little more than a base from which to visit her children who have moved to distant parts of the world. The Hall itself is now owned by a famous film star Marina Gregg who has brought with her a complete Hollywood entourage as well as a spectacular murder case. Other things have changed as well. The shops in the old High Street have become glossily up-to-date, while at the corner there is a supermarket which is 'anathema to the elderly ladies of St. Mary Mead' but necessary to service the people from 'the Development.' That's what everyone calls it, just that and nothing else: 'It had an entity of its own and a capital letter.'

One of the most telling cultural observations in *A Murder is Announced* had been the way the villagers regarded an armed hold-up as a characteristically American happening, something they knew about not from personal experience but from their regular visits to the cinema. It was also treated as a solitary, attractive but odd, import. Now, ten years on, British life is totally dominated by America. People in St. Mary Mead and the Development read 'movie' magazines, chat endlessly about the personal lives of film stars, and consider having once shaken hands with Marina Gregg as one of the most important things that has ever happened to them. The influence of the film world can no longer be contained. Nor do many people want to see it contained. It is a key factor in the wider spread of American ways, along with home modernization, consumer goods, hire purchase, and convenience food piled high in supermarkets. Everything American is gleefully welcomed, especially by the young owners of the new houses that are now threatening to swamp St. Mary Mead.

All of this is filtered through Miss Marple's consciousness, not in any grumpy or reactionary way, but as careful observation. St. Mary Mead is simply 'not the place it had been' she muses, and then adds wisely that 'nothing was what it had been.' She knows that blame can be easily and variously attributed to 'the war (both the wars) or the younger generation, or women going out to work, or the atom bomb or just the Government.' She also realizes the pointlessness of thinking in this way. If she is discontented it is because her great age has all but removed her from the outside world. This is not passivity, but realism, a quality that Christie sets at the heart of *A Mirror Crack'd*. It is what prevents Miss Marple from following the example of her St. Mary Mead friend and fellow-gossip Miss Hartnell who is still alive and 'fighting progress to the last gasp.' Miss Marple, though, refuses to condemn things she hasn't experienced. In spite of the second-hand atmosphere of Hollywood glamour, she decides that the true nature of the social changes taking place is not to be found on the silver screen or in fan magazines. She is even beginning to doubt whether it can be understood from the standpoint of St. Mary Mead.

The answer, she decides, must lie in 'the Development' which appears to exemplify the dreams and aspirations of modern life. She has seen it from a distance, 'its Closes and rows of neat well-built houses, with their television masts and their blue and pink and yellow and green painted doors and windows.' But as she has never visited it, how can she know? So, Miss Knight is packed off on a series of unnecessary shopping errands, and Miss Marple plays truant, taking a brief walk but feeling like 'Columbus setting out to discover a new world.' The clichéd phrase is significant. Christie had always been willing to employ the language of corny hyperbole to evoke Poirot's ludicrous sense of self-esteem, but never before had she employed a similar technique with Miss Marple. It would not have been suitable for her to do so. Now, when the aged St. Mary Mead spinster is turned into a Christopher Columbus, it's for a clear purpose. No satire or even exaggeration is intended. Neither would have been appropriate for the Development. It is far too important a matter to be treated lightly.

Throughout these post-war novels, the most visible feature of social change is the rapid development of urban living and its impact on the countryside. This is at its most overwhelming in *Paddington* with Rutherford Hall, the handsome old-fashioned Victorian country estate, still intact but literally surrounded by the ever-growing town of Brackhampton. Everyone accepts that one day soon the town will engulf

Rutherford Hall and with it the way of life it once represented. And, in much the same way, St. Mary Mead will be absorbed by the Development. Here are to be found those people who have for so long been excluded from Miss Marple's daily world and about whom she readily admits she knows little. They had entered her tiny village world only as maids from the charity home and young men driving taxis or working in local shops. Although they were essentially no different from the people living on the Development, their circumstances had made them seem so. Now there are suddenly far more of them, arriving in large and organized numbers, bringing with them their own work skills, industries, and entertainments, creating as from nothing a large town just a short walk from St. Mary Mead. They are the people for whom the New Jerusalem was being built, and indeed places like the Development were sometimes described as New Jerusalems.

Miss Marple knows full well that the Development is not for her. She is too old ever to belong in any real sense to this emerging world, but should that worry her? She thinks not. After all, Cherry Baker, her current housekeeper comes from the Development, and Miss Marple is quick to admit that she is prettier, more efficient, livelier, smarter, friendlier, and a better housekeeper than any of the maids Miss Marple had spent so much of her life trying to train. If Cherry is the future, then the promise is bright. But Miss Marple still wants more evidence and she must seek it for herself. When she gives Miss Knight the slip and walks over to The Development, she *is* taking a voyage of discovery and she *is* brave to do so. And if she can also be made to seem a bit condescending, that is only natural, and always a factor when one type of society is felt to be totally supplanting another. And, in Miss Marple's case, not only is it honesty rather than condescension that is involved, she is perfectly right in believing that much of the future of England lies ready to hand, just a walk away from St. Mary Mead.

* * *

Of all the promises made in the general election campaign of 1945, the one that voters felt it most urgent to see fulfilled was housing. It was, as Kenneth O. Morgan points out, 'the most popular single theme for Labour candidates to emphasize.'[3] During the war something like three-quarters of a million houses in Britain had been destroyed or seriously damaged, and this quite apart from the appalling pre-war housing conditions endured by millions of people. Decent affordable housing was a prerequisite of the New Jerusalem and pressure on the Labour government for dramatic action was intense. Target figures were inevitably vague. In 1945 Churchill's Caretaker Government, which held power until the general election could take place, estimated that three to four million new houses would need be built in the next ten or twelve years. That was regarded as a highly optimistic aspirational figure and, in fact, it was to take seven years to complete the first million.[4] Ministerial responsibility for housing under the new prime minister Clement Attlee was handed first to Aneurin Bevan and later Hugh Dalton. After a worryingly slow start the pace of building began to accelerate but in 1947 Attlee was forced to admit that there simply wasn't enough money available to meet demand. In D.V. Donnison's words, 'the brakes were put on the housing programme' and what was regarded as a new manageable yearly target of 200,000 established.[5] Throughout the second half of the 1940s the government was beset not only by the financial crisis but by terrible weather and labour problems as well. Media publicity was also often against them. The rapid growth of prefabricated houses (or 'prefabs'), popular though they often turned out to be, seemed to suggest that a temporary solution was becoming accepted as a permanent fixture, while the squatting movement, in which homeless families simply went ahead and occupied empty properties, kept housing constantly and unfavourably in the headlines.

It was a long-term problem and therefore almost inevitably one that kept large numbers of people dissatisfied. Discontent over housing was a major cause of voter disillusionment in the general election in 1951, even though by this time the Labour government was successfully meeting its reduced target figures and building the 200,000 new houses a year it had promised.[6]

Now it was the incoming Conservative Party that was vowing not only to match the Labour's housing record but to improve upon it. The promised number bandied about was 300,000 per year. Once again hardly anyone believed this was feasible. We know something about the cynical attitudes behind these particular election promises because of the way they have survived to become a key part of modern Conservative Party legend.

When Churchill was forming his government in 1951 he summoned Harold Macmillan to offer him a place in the cabinet. As a loyal, ambitious Churchill supporter Macmillan was expecting to be given a prominent ministerial post. He was disappointed. In what was said to be a very emotional state Churchill urged Macmillan to take on the task of building 'the houses for the people.'[7] Macmillan stayed loyal to his leader and accepted the offered post which he regarded as probable political death, a view shared by those of his colleagues who were handed more immediately attractive ministerial portfolios.

Although Macmillan admitted he had no idea what was involved, he set about the job with the kind of missionary zeal that Churchill seems to have hoped for. Enthusiastically supported by a young junior minister Ernest Marples and strongly backed by Churchill, Macmillan enjoyed a spectacular success. Within two years the target figure of 300,000 new houses had been reached and passed. Housing was back in the headlines, this time as positive news. Macmillan had proved to be an efficient and unexpectedly ruthless minister. A popular one as well, blessed with a natural flair for publicity, a quality that his deputy 'Ernie' Marples (as he was now affectionately dubbed by the press) also possessed in abundance. Macmillan was soon receiving standing ovations at Conservative Party conferences. His political prospects were transformed.[8]

The rivalry between the Labour and Conservative parties over house-building targets was the new consensus politics in action. That didn't mean full political agreement. The ambitions may have been shared, but not how those ambitions were to be realized. Housing raised particularly complex ideological issues. Labour was committed to public housing, and although the Conservatives supported that commitment they also allowed for greater private initiatives. Furthermore, there were disagreements over the compulsory purchase of land, war-damaged and requisitioned property, and what constituted an acceptable 'house' or indeed a 'new' house. All such issues were often veiled by the talk of total targets reached or missed.

This was especially apparent in the plans to build a series of New Towns throughout Britain, a programme central to Labour's dream of a transformed British society and prepared for by the New Towns Act 1946. In addition to the provision of houses, the New Towns aimed to alleviate the poor conditions of many of Britain's crowded cities and create clean healthy urban environments in rural areas. Industries as well as families were encouraged to move to the New Towns, the plan being to create socially mixed communities, models for how life in Britain could be.[9]

By 1961 twelve New Towns had been designated, beginning with Stevenage in 1946 and Crawley the following year. With such complex planning involved, the movement was inevitably slow to take off and at first did little to help to ease the housing shortage. Peter Hennessy estimates that when the Conservatives returned to power in 1951 the first batch of New Towns were still 'building sites.'[10] This changed substantially over the following decade, though large-scale house building was never a main aim of the New Towns. But while the original ideal of creating holistic communities faded a little as the years passed it was not lost sight of entirely. The social drive behind the New Town programme could be plausibly regarded as the Welfare State in microcosm.

Christie would have watched these government policies with very special interest. Throughout her life, she had been fascinated by houses of whatever kind, from urban flat to country estate. She bought and rented houses repeatedly, not primarily as a financial investment but as homes and work places, temporary or permanent. Just before the outbreak of war in 1939 she owned eight houses. She loved to furnish and decorate them, and, where relevant, to maintain or restore their gardens. If they sold at a profit, well she enjoyed that as well. Dating back to her childhood, her fascination with houses can be interpreted in a variety of ways. It was a reinforcement of her desire for privacy and independence, as well as a determination to maintain a stable family and home, and can also be seen as a most unusual form of feminist assertion.

Gillian Gill has pointed out how important this interest in housing was to Christie. After all, she had no need to follow Virginia Woolf's advice and seek a room of her own: 'She was one of those rare women who can buy property at will, and buy it with money earned by their own work, not inherited or received from husband or lover.'[11] This fascination with houses and gardens can be seen being put to good use everywhere in Christie's novels, with a special importance attached to it in the post-war novels. From *A Murder is Announced* through to *4.50 from Paddington* rapid urban development is, as we have seen, a looming, threatening force. It is the proliferation of houses and the way that St. Mary Mead is being taken over and changed by them that disturbs Miss Marple and decides her to undertake her epic voyage of discovery.

That her visit to the Development succeeds in dispelling her apprehensions about England's future is a key part of the schema of *The Mirror Crack'd*. Miss Marple watches the young wives out shopping, wearing trousers or pretty dresses and pushing smart prams. She also stops to intervene decisively in a potentially sinister incident between a young engaged couple. When she falls in the street she is rescued, taken into a house and looked after by Heather Babcock whose gushing kindness to people will soon result in her becoming the book's principal murder victim. As for Miss Marple, she may know little about her new neighbours in the Development, but they know about her: 'I've heard about you. You're the one who does all the murders.' Miss Marple quickly formulates some village parallels for the occasion, relieved to find that the housing may be different but human nature hasn't really changed.

Impressed though she was, Christie didn't allow her basically favourable view of the Development to get out of hand. Not everyone who moved to the New Towns was happy with their decision or willing to stay for long. Christie picks up on this element of discontent and uses it for her own purposes. Cherry and Jim Baker are becoming concerned at the lack of privacy in their new rather flimsy house and ask if they can move into some unused rooms above Miss Marple's kitchen which will be quieter for them. In return they will look after Miss Marple. The old is united with the new, and for Miss Marple the servant problem is solved in a very welcome manner. Some readers claim to find this new relationship patronizing, but it isn't necessarily that. The relationship is by no means one-sided. It is actually Cherry who first advances the idea of her and her husband giving up their unsatisfactory Development house. It hasn't occurred to Miss Marple, though she certainly approves the plan. And why not? It is based on genuine affection, a desire on both sides to help others, with Miss Marple becoming unavoidably more dependent and Cherry moving to achieve greater independence not less. And Miss Marple's open admiration for Cherry's good qualities contains a similarly forward-looking element: 'Warm-heartedness, vitality, and a deep interest in everything that was going on.' It looks as though Cherry might be a Development detective in the making.

* * *

For those many Miss Marple readers who take a special interest in the admittedly vague topographical side of the novels there is an unexpected bonus to be plucked from looking a bit closer at the historical background of Christie's interest in post-war housing. Unexpectedly, it helps to solve a long-standing mystery in our knowledge of the spinster detective's personal life.

The Development is usually described by commentators, and by some characters in the novels as well, as a housing estate. But that is too general a term. The Development is clearly something quite different from a housing estate as we can see by its newness, size, variety, planned nature, careful mixture of shops, housing, light industries and outsiders being systematically moved to it. It is actually a New Town, though characteristically Christie never calls it by that name. She maintains the same policy that always allowed her to be vague about where exactly St. Mary Mead was situated, apart from it being roughly twenty-five miles south of London and roughly the same distance, when it was needed, from a seaside town like Danemouth. That closely matches Crawley New Town which was built in West Sussex, on the borders of Surrey, some thirty miles from the centre of London and twenty two miles from Brighton.

Of the New Towns, the Development has to be Crawley not only because the distances fit it so well. It was the only one of the original New Town sites to be placed south of London, and can be further connected with St. Mary Mead in that it was planned controversially to absorb a number of small Sussex villages along with the ancient market town of Crawley which gave the New Town its name.[12] But strong support for the case that Christie was quite consciously thinking of the Development along these lines is that the working title she used for *The Mirror Crack'd* was the 'Development Murder.'[13] The source of the word is highly relevant as well. Responsibility for the day-to-day planning of the New Towns was placed in the hands of specially appointed 'Development Corporations.' They were extremely powerful and received a lot of media publicity, but had only a restricted span of life. Once the New Town in question could be deemed to have reached a sufficient point of 'development' to be able to run its own affairs, the Development Corporation was wound up. Strangely enough, for Crawley this moment came in 1962, the same year in which *A Mirror Crack'd* was published. Its population had now grown to sixty thousand, and it could boast of having a large shopping centre, pedestrian walkways, and its own flourishing industries.[14] Future expansion was ensured by nearby Gatwick Airport which had been in existence since the 1930s, but in 1956 was designated London's second airport and upgraded to relieve pressure on Heathrow. In *4.50 from Paddington* (1957) Miss Marple says of St. Mary Mead: 'We're now quite close to an airfield, you know, and really the way those jet planes fly over! Most frightening. Two panes in my little greenhouse broken the other day.' A clue? Surely, and not the only one.[15]

The final evidence is essentially circumstantial but strong enough to solve the long-standing mystery of where exactly St. Mary Mead is to be found. The answer is on the fringes of Crawley New Town. And 'final' the clues to the mystery are in other ways as well, because no truly reliable information is ever given about the matter, even in *The Mirror Crack'd*, until *Nemesis,* the very last Miss Marple novel. It is obviously the case that Christie couldn't have thought of using Crawley New Town in this way until the 1950s. So, in the earlier novels she may have had some other place in mind, or more probably just the general area. It's impossible to say for sure. But nevertheless, Crawley does work perfectly for the later novels and the general area can be accepted for the earlier novels as well. The information given in *Nemesis* is undeniably specific.

Working for once in her life on an expense account which has been set up for her by the late Mr Rafiel, Miss Marple decides to be extravagant and use Inch's taxi service for a journey of about twenty-five miles. She estimates it will take one and a half hours, and, rarely indeed for Christie, we are given both map and timetable. They are especially useful because three different counties are involved. Miss Marple's destination is Alton in Hampshire, and she decides to stop for lunch at Haslemere in Surrey which is just across the border with West Sussex.[16] She must therefore be moving from East to West, not in a straight line across the Home Counties but with a detour for lunch. The starting point of her journey has to be in West Sussex and that is where Crawley New Town was situated, just a four-minute walk away from St. Mary Mead. Through the village, 'over the bridge' and along a path, the very walk that Miss Marple takes on her voyage of discovery to 'the Development' in *The Mirror Crack'd*.

Chapter 10

The Condition of England:
A Caribbean Mystery, At Bertram's Hotel

During the last ten years of her life Christie's fiction was as varied as ever, if slightly more uneven than in the past. There were signs of weariness and occasionally an all too obvious effort to keep up with changing times, but notable achievements as well. Poirot, Mrs Oliver, and Tommy and Tuppence all featured in new novels while in a category by itself was the experimental *Endless Night* (1967) which originated as an idea first aired in the Miss Marple short story 'The Case of the Caretaker.' But by far Christie's most sustained creative effort in these last few years was devoted to the writing of three Miss Marple novels: *A Caribbean Mystery* (1964), *At Bertram's Hotel* (1965) and *Nemesis* (1971).

Given the valedictory mood of *The Mirror Crack'd*, it is surprising that there were any further cases at all for Miss Marple. It is even more surprising that the three new novels Christie did produce should have displayed such originality, power, and energy. If *The Mirror Crack'd* had turned out to be Miss Marple's last case, as at the time it seemed it might, then the reader would have been left with a largely positive image of a woman who though very old and physically weak was comfortably settled in a rather unusual but happy domestic arrangement; who had triumphantly solved one more challenging mystery; and who, most significantly, was shown to have come to terms with certain important features of modern life. But the three novels that were still to come changed all of that. In the first two of them, the cosy domestic set-up made possible by Cherry Baker has temporarily disappeared from the scene and although Miss Marple remains old and prone to various debilitating illnesses she is no longer resigned to spending her last years confined, however comfortably, to St.

Mary Mead. Christie clearly intended not only to keep Miss Marple going but to present her with a more forceful and morally dominant personality than ever before.

This intention was announced in an oblique and odd manner. As John Curran points out, the title pages of the first editions of both *A Caribbean Mystery* and *At Bertram's Hotel* present themselves as: 'Featuring Miss Marple. The original Character as created by Agatha Christie.'[1] For *Nemesis*, the third and final Miss Marple novel, Christie returned to having just her own name on the title page. The reason why, at this late stage in her long career, one of the most famous English authors in the world writing about the world's most famous woman detective, should have treated these two novels with such an air of fake naivety has to be explained as a public dissociation of herself and Miss Marple from the sudden, baleful influence of Margaret Rutherford.

The first of the four films starring Margaret Rutherford as Miss Marple, *Murder, She Said,* came out almost at the same time, though coincidentally, as *The Mirror Crack'd from Side to Side.* This was late in 1961. The novel was dedicated to Rutherford 'in admiration,' a friendly act that appeared to confirm the existence of an amicable link between the Miss Marple novels and films. But at the time Christie had not seen Rutherford's interpretation of Miss Marple on screen and the dedication referred simply to the two women having met and liked each other. When Christie did get to see *Murder, She Said*, she loathed Rutherford's performance. Rutherford, though, knew nothing of this. She was personally moved by the dedication, taking it with relief as the author's approval of a role she had had great doubts about playing at all.

For Christie, the implications of Rutherford's interpretation of Miss Marple were extremely serious. One of the principal reasons why she had welcomed the film adaptations was because she hoped they might increase appreciation of her as a author. Now she feared they would have the opposite effect. As soon as *Murder, She Said* opened at a cinema in Torquay late in 1961, a family trip from Greenway was organised to see it. After the perfomance, they left the cinema shocked at what they had seen.[2] Unhappy as that experience was, *Murder, She Said* would actually turn out to be the highlight of the whole Rutherford episode. It had at least been based on a genuine Miss Marple story, *4.50 from Paddington*, with the plot tied reasonably close to the original. The films that now followed made no pretence of following the plots, characters, or the mood of Christie's novels.

Murder at the Gallop (1963) was a ludicrous adaptation of *After the Funeral,* a Poirot not a Miss Marple novel; *Murder Ahoy* (1964) an invented story that owed nothing to Christie or Miss Marple; while *Murder most Foul* (1965) ransacked another Poirot novel, this time *Mrs McGinty's Dead*, for a plot. Set slightly apart from these four films, though in a similar vein, was *The Alphabet Murders* (1966), starring the American comedian Tony Randall as Poirot in a loose adaptation of *The ABC Murders*, so loose that Margaret Rutherford, by now instantly recognizable as Miss Marple, could be brought on screen simply to share a passing glance of near-recognition with Poirot. Christie's long-term refusal to surrender to the wishes of her more fanciful readers and bring Poirot and Miss Marple together in the same story was thus overthrown whether she liked it or not.

Christie was helpless, trapped in circumstances that were partly of her own making and powerless to change anything. During her post-war struggle with the Inland Revenue she had agreed to the sale of the film rights of some forty of her books to MGM. The Rutherford films were the direct result of this agreement. They were American produced, but filmed at Pinewood Studios with a British director, writers and mainly British actors. The vacuous view of life they offered satisfied the films' American backers and would, anyway, have been willingly accepted by a largely pliant British film industry. The jovial generalizing approach to the Rutherford fillms was typified by Ron Goodwin's catchy theme tune that was featured in all four of them and employed to draw attention to the serial nature of the enterprise. The most notable British contribution came from the large number of fine actors and actresses who made what they could of their supporting character roles. They included Flora Robson, Ron Moody, Lionel Jefferies, Joan Hickson, and, in a rather special category, Robert Morley and James Robertson Justice, both of whom also shared the dubious distinction of closing their respective films by proposing marriage to Miss Marple.

There was nothing for Christie to admire in the films. Along with Rutherford's performance, she was appalled by the simplification of the plots, the conflation of Poirot and Miss Marple stories, and the overall tone of farcical comedy. This final worry was largely the responsibility of Rutherford herself who was treated as a star throughout. With the films a commercial success, her bumbling manner, blubbering lips, over-active double chin, bulging eyes and commanding voice became quickly accepted as suitable physical trademarks for Miss Marple, far removed though they were from the original. Christie's elderly, pensive detective, her mind open and curious enough to penetrate psychoanalytical theory during the war and to explore a transformed British society after it, was now obliterated by Margaret Rutherford's professional clownery. Dressed in a variety of fancy costumes, and placed in bizarre situations, this Miss Marple was full of unexpected, comically presented talents. At will, she became an expert horsewoman, small-bore markswoman, an experienced sailor and performer of dramatic monologues. There was no intention on the part of anyone involved of taking the films seriously. Quite the opposite.

For a variety of reasons, some known at the time, others totally unsuspected, it would actually have been impossible for Miss Marple to be portrayed as anything other than comic. Rutherford's own part was driven by complex motives and is still not fully understood. I have outlined the situation in more detail in an article about Margaret Rutherford and Miss Marple which is available to read on my website.[3]

Angrily provoked by the Rutherford fiasco, Christie was determined to establish a more intense image of Miss Marple. Against Rutherford's buffoonery she would assert Miss Marple's moral power, her intelligence, seriousness and religious beliefs. To counteract the outrageous film plots Miss Marple would reveal herself as more involved than ever before with the true, modern nature of British society. And, in the face of the ludicrous marriage proposals attracted by Rutherford, there would even be a hint, perhaps, that Christie's Miss Marple might just, after all these years, show herself as capable of inspiring something very like romance.

In all of the new novels there is apparent a very attractive mix of continuity and change. Miss Marple is still both detective and social commentator. She is also aware that she is nearing the end of her life, as, of course, Christie was as well. The three novels were almost certainly conceived of as a trilogy. They are most notably united by the friendship between Miss Marple and Mr Rafiel in the first and third of them, but there are other larger shared qualities.

All three draw on an identifiable change of mood in Britain. As memories of the Second World War began to fade and a teenage culture emerged that seemed to show little interest in Britain's immediate past, there was a growing feeling that a continuing preoccupation with the war was holding Britain back as a nation. It was time to stop being obsessed with the past and to begin looking positively to the future. In the Miss Marple novels of the 1950s Christie had identified the dominant mood in Britain as a deep-rooted social and political malaise. Ten years later she was just as quick to recognise the widespread desire that this negative attitude should not be allowed to continue. 'The essence of life is going forward,' Miss Marple announces in *At Bertram's Hotel*, 'Life is really a One Way Street.'

It was the prime minister Harold Macmillan who gave an instantly memorable form to the dangers of national stagnation in a celebrated speech to the South African parliament in February 1960: 'The wind of change is blowing through this continent … whether we like it or not … We must all accept it as a fact.' Macmillan's immediate reference was to the racial discrimination that was firmly entrenched in South Africa, and, more widely, to what he described as the rapid growth of 'African national consciousness.'[4] His words, though, were quickly given a much larger application and became attached to other nations and situations. At home, the phrase 'wind of change' was taken over to enforce the urgent need for Britain to adapt, wake up and move forward. Christie quickly picked up on the phrase and used it several times in just this way.

Each of the three final novels centres on a major problem of social re-adjustment in Britain. *A Caribbean Mystery* evokes an atmosphere of post-imperial uncertainty; *At Bertram's Hotel* examines a new phase of post-war crime; while *Nemesis* takes up the continuing worry about juvenile delinquency and its implications for young people. St. Mary Mead is entirely absent from the first two of these novels, while in

Nemesis it features only as a home base. Miss Marple's near immobility in *The Mirror Crack'd* has disappeared, so much so that she is on the move as never before. *A Caribbean Mystery* takes her to the West Indies where for the only time in her life she is involved in tackling a case outside of England; *At Bertram's Hotel* is set entirely in a contemporary London that is almost as alien to her as the West Indies; while in *Nemesis* she is sent on a coach tour of an area of England about which we are told little specific except that it is reached by 'taking a north-westerly route out of London.' None of these journeys and settings are invoked for local colour or effect. Their significance is thematic.

* * *

Although only referred to indirectly at the start of the novel, *A Caribbean Mystery* resonates with allusions to the rapid dismantling of Britain's world-wide Empire. St Honoré, where Miss Marple is being treated by Raymond and Joan West to yet another recuperative holiday, is a generic West Indian island, one of several that at the very time of Miss Marple's stay were in the process of attaining independence. Jamaica and Trinidad and Tobago had both achieved independent status in 1962.[5] Christie introduces the imperial theme through the hotel bore Major Palgrave who never stops talking about his experiences in Kenya. Trapped by him, Miss Marple notes that she is old enough to remember when he would have talked in the same way about India rather than Africa. And so he would have done. India, now very much the old empire, had obtained its independence as far back as 1947 and is of no topical interest. Kenya, on the other hand, was part of the more recent African Empire and current headline news, having only just, in 1963, attained its independence after the long and bloody Mau Mau campaign. None of this is mentioned directly. In classic Christie style, all such details are subordinated to the general atmosphere of the murder mystery.

Most of Miss Marple's fellow holidaymakers on St Honoré would be as much at ease in the Home County novels as on this exotic holiday island. They include a retired army officer, an elderly naïve clergyman with his devoted spinster daughter longing to have a good gossip with Miss

Marple; an English couple worried about paying their sons' school fees; a young husband and wife team trying to make a go of running the hotel; and a wealthy business man with his entourage. It's the holiday setting that makes them different and the fact that the tone of the hotel is established by a group of people in their thirties and forties. They are set apart from the older holidaymakers, as a distinctly post-war generation; comfortably off, able actively to devote themselves to leisure, and restlessly involved in steady drinking and casual sex. This West Indian island is hardly less occupied by the British than it would have been before independence, except that now they are now on holiday rather than administering a colony, happily taking advantage of the wonderful weather, beaches, and plentiful cheap labour which are St Honoré's main source of income. It is this transformed post-war, post-Empire generation that Miss Marple observes in *A Caribbean Mystery*.

For Miss Marple herself there is a new kind of freedom. It is as though towards the end of her life a long-standing, subdued characteristic had gained a sudden and unexpected prominence. Ever since the wartime novels Christie had made good use of a contrast between Miss Marple's fierce inner passion and her consciously maintained dithery external disguise. It was there in her ruthless use of Megan Hunter to trap the murderer in *The Moving Finger* and even more forcefully in *A Pocket Full of Rye* where she is introduced, on her way to avenge the murder of Gladys her former maid, sitting 'very upright, looking out of the window, her lips pursed together, an expression of distress and disapproval on her pink and white wrinkled face.' Inspector Neele had picked up on this feature of Miss Marple's character in *Rye* and had given it an appropriate definition. 'Miss Marple was very unlike the popular idea of an avenging fury. And yet, he thought that was perhaps exactly what she was.'[6] Now, a decade later, she begins to be openly transformed into just such a moral, or more correctly, a religious power. About half-way through *A Caribbean Mystery* she finds herself in 'militant mood' and the narrative steps up several levels.

Alone in a foreign Paradise – the Garden of Eden image is frequently evoked in this portrait of the West Indies – she can no longer rely on her police friends in England for help. Instead, she turns to the Bible.

Following the example of Isaiah (6:8) in response to the Lord's call for earthly support, Miss Marple yearns: 'Here *am* I; send me.' Her appeal is answered instantly. She is literally called, and the voice, though not actually God's is the next best thing. It belongs to Mr Rafiel who is aptly named, for Raphael was one of the Archangels, the messenger of God, and the patron saint of pilgrims and travellers. This Rafiel, though, is thoroughly earth-bound, a mortally sick financial wizard who sits in this island paradise giving orders, sending telegrams, effortlessly adding to his personal fortune. His message from God is passed to Miss Marple brusquely, comandingly, just like a man 'calling his dog' with the single word 'Hi!'

The alliance they form is a powerful one, with Mr Rafiel's wealth and worldly influence being placed at the service of Miss Marple's Biblical fervour. Ideas of God and Mammon are toyed with and in some senses inverted by Christie. To the Old Testament example of Isaiah Miss Marple adds that of Greek mythology, proclaiming herself to be Nemesis, the goddess responsible for administering appropriate punishments. For a while it looks as though she is building up her a part a bit too much. Perhaps she herself will end up a victim of *hybris*. But it is one of Mr Rafiel's roles to make sure that doesn't happen. The figure standing by his bedside in the middle of the night making her high-flown announcement looks to him very far from an awe-inspiring goddess of retribution. He sees a frail old woman who has just rushed from her own bed, framed romantically in the moonlight, with the important deflationary detail of her head being 'encased in a fluffy scarf of pale pink wool.' Mr Rafiel is amused and gently mocking: 'So you're Nemesis, are you?' The tone is affectionate, and possibly a little stronger than simply that.

In the American television film version of *A Caribbean Mystery* made by CBS in 1983, the part of Miss Marple was played by Helen Hayes who brought to the role a youthfulness that seemed at first viewing hardly appropriate. Her Miss Marple is a well-preserved, glammed-up pensioner, with prominent make up, smart hairdo, a taste for dancing, and a touch of flirtatiousness. She is clearly someone who, when not on holiday, would be more at home in Palm Beach or Miami than St. Mary Mead. Yet, misguided as Hayes's performance may seem, it does draw attention to an aspect of *A Caribbean Mystery* that more conventional dramatizations tend to avoid.[7] How exactly are we to interpret the relationship between Miss Marple and Mr Rafiel? Are they brought together simply on a crime-solving operation, or even in a crusading moral alliance against Evil? Or is there, potentially, a personal element involved? Was Christie playing with thoughts of a possible romance for Jane Marple, or even allowing her a romantic episode while there was still time, albeit one that is brief and undeclared?

The title of chapter twenty-two of the novel asks a question: 'A Man in her Life?' It's a good example of Christie's remarkable talent for laying multiple clues that few readers will recognize until it is too late to help them solve the crime. It also demonstrates the elaborate narrative playfulness to which Christie was so drawn in the later novels. She had employed the same phrase, and for similar reasons, in the still unpublished *Sleeping Murder* where the various 'men in the life' of the dead Helen Halliday are surveyed, with the cunning exception of the one who really matters. That omission was caused by customary assumptions about what constitutes a 'normal' sexual relationship. Once those assumptions are challenged the whole chapter needs to be re-read in a different way.

Chapter 22 of *Carribbean* works in a similar manner but is far more complex. The chapter title refers initially to Esther Walters' attempt to persuade Miss Marple that there is a a man in Molly's life other than Molly's husband Tim. Esther has been encouraged to believe this by Tim himself who has become, secretly, the man in Esther's own life. That is a second meaning, although at this point in the narrative, nobody, including Miss Marple and the reader, would be aware of it as a possibility were it not for Esther's querulous self-justifying manner as she tries to shift attention away from her own involvement. She becomes so confused that Miss Marple has to puzzle over 'the pronouns' Esther has been using. Is there a *man* at all in the case, she ponders, or is Esther hinting that the murders have been committed by a woman? That's a third potential meaning. In the same chapter there occurs one of the several moments in the book when Mr Rafiel interrupts Miss Marple's solitary musing to remind her that if she needs help she can 'count on' him. He therefore becomes the man in Miss Marple's life, crucially so because, as she herself admits, she can get no further with the mystery on her own. This fourth possible meaning of the phrase can itself be interpreted either straightforwardly in terms of a convenient alliance, or in a romantic manner, as it is both here in Esther's case and also in *Sleeping Murder*. Christie is careful to add a question mark to the *Carribbean* chapter title in order to prepare for it possibly not being a man in the case at all. But if it's a woman, the possibilities are no simpler. Which woman is being referred to? Molly, Esther, or, if a different relationship is considered, why not Jane herself? Perhaps Helen Hayes's jaunty interpretation of Miss Marple wasn't so misguided after all.

Much depends on how one interprets the bedroom scene already referred to when a dishevelled Miss Marple in dressing gown, slippers and the pink woollen scarf, wakes Mr Rafiel who is asleep in bed gently snoring, and urges him to fulfill his promise that she can always 'count on' him for help. They both joke about the unconventional nature of her behaviour which Mr Rafiel laughingly swears he will never forget. Here, and subsequently, the strength of the affection between them is very apparent. It is the only time anywhere in the Miss Marple novels that she is shown to be personally attracted to a man in any sense that might be interpreted as affection, let alone love. The bedroom scene is both serious and outrageous. Jackson, Mr Rafiel's manservant is openly astonished to find Miss Marple there at all. Clearly it was too outrageous a consideration for either American or British television producers. In the Helen Hayes CBS version the bedroom scene is omitted entirely – along with the woolly scarf and any reference to Nemesis – while in the BBC adaptation Joan Hickson is dressed in just the right manner for the confrontation with Mr Rafiel, but he is seated in his wheelchair wearing evening dress.

No explicit romantic declarations are made or expected. Not only are Miss Marple and Mr Rafiel both very old, they are also both aware that he is near to death. Even so, when Miss Marple flies back to England there is an emotional farewell scene at the airport, and everyone assumes that they should step aside and let Mr Rafiel be the last to say goodbye to her. He takes Miss Marple's hand and bids her farewell in a characteristically hammy manner with the words that gladiators were said to have used before facing possible death, '*Ave Caesar, nos morituri te salutamus*' ('Hail Caesar! We who are about to die salute you'). They have been warriors together and they have won the battle, but now he must die. That makes *A Caribbean Mystery* sound more like a tale of high adventure than a detective story, while the final lines of the book would be more suitable for a romance:

> She said no more. She knew quite well what he was telling her.
> 'It has been a great pleasure to know you,' she said
> Then she walked across the tarmac and got into the plane.

What she 'knows quite well he is telling her' is that he has little time left to live, but is that all? As with the phrase 'a man in her life,' in romantic fiction when a woman 'knows quite well what' a man is telling her it usually means only one thing, and it's not that he's about to die. Miss Marple responds to whatever private message Mr Rafiel may or may not be imparting to her with commendable Victorian reserve. And that, as far as *A Caribbean Mystery* is concerned, is the end. But it's not really, not quite anyway.

When Miss Marple next comes across Mr Rafiel's name it is to learn of his death from an announcement in *The Times*. This is at the start of *Nemesis*, published seven years after *Caribbean*. At first she has difficulty remembering him, but as her memory stirs, what she recalls is the excitement of that particular moment with him in the bedroom when they had acted so decisively together. She still insists to herself that they were nothing more than allies, but at the same time, and in Christie's most teasing allusive manner, Miss Marple calls to mind 'the title of that book they used to quote when she was young.' The book she is thinking of is Beatrice Harraden's *Ships that Pass in the Night*, a great bestseller of 1893, a bitter-sweet story of an unfulfilled and never properly declared love.

* * *

Of all the Miss Marple novels *At Bertram's Hotel* is the one that conforms least to the traditional pattern of the detective story. The single murder in the book comes towards the end of the novel and is by no means central to the narrative. Even though Miss Marple is supported by Scotland Yard, the exposure of a murderer is not her principal concern. In place of the standard final scene in which the innocent are dramatically exonerated and the guilty person publicly revealed, Miss Marple and Chief Inspector Davy interview the principal suspects and discuss, together and in private, the vexed issue of criminal responsibility. The reader is left in no doubt about the murderer's identity and is assured that retribution will eventually follow, but no charges are formally advanced, no name is stated, and no arrest made.

This comes over as a perfectly acceptable ending because Miss Marple has been trying throughout the book to understand the changing nature of criminality itself rather than to discover the perpetrator of a specific crime. Not truly a detective story, and only indirectly a crime novel, *Bertram's* is Christie's most sustained imaginative attempt to express her personal feelings about post-war England. It is perhaps best described by a term familiar to historians of early Victorian literature, a 'Condition of England' novel.[8] Once again Miss Marple is moved out of St. Mary Mead but whereas in *Caribbean* she had been sent off to the West Indies rather to her surprise and without having much say about it, in *Bertram's* the trip is very much her own deliberate choice. Bournemouth, perhaps, Aunt Jane? No, she would prefer London, a week at Bertram's Hotel which she had visited many years earlier with an uncle and aunt. Fourteen years old at the time, she had always remembered the experience with pleasure. Friends have told her that Bertram's has survived the war and is flourishing, miraculously unchanged. As she had earlier decided she must see the Development for herself, now she sets off for Bertram's in the expectation, if her friends are right, of some enjoyable nostalgia. Instead, she finds herself trapped in time.

There has long been a disagreement among Christie enthusiasts as to which London hotel was the model for Bertram's. For some it is Brown's, for others Flemings. Given the purposes to which Christie puts Bertram's it might be felt she was wise to leave its true identity vague and, anyway, the Bertram's Hotel of the novel is clearly intended to be symbolic rather than specific, a microcosm of modern Britain. There is also some uncertainty about when exactly the novel is set. On the opening page we appear to be told that the date is 1955, though later passing references to the Beatles and girls' fashions suggest we have moved on to the Swinging Sixties. There are also the significant references to Macmillan's 1960 'wind of change' speech to take into account. If some carelessness is observable here it may not matter very much, for as so often with Christie the precise date of a novel's setting is less important than the exactness of the prevailing mood. *Bertram's* is set approximately, from the mid-1950s to the mid-1960s, with the wind of change metaphor being placed at the exact centre of that span of time.

Miss Marple's friends turn out to be right about Bertram's. Outwardly at least nothing has altered. It is a perfectly preserved corner of Edwardian England, a delight for wealthy tourists (Americans especially) and for anyone else seeking reassurance that in spite of the previous half century of world wars and financial crises, everything, really, is still much the same. As the notebooks indicate, the American theme was always central to the book. For a while Christie thought of making the owners of the hotel two shadowy Americans who 'cash in' on their fellow countrymen by creating an authentic British atmosphere. She then considered making them simply the 'titular' owners, 'but really a façade for Henry.'[9] In the end it was wise of Christie to make the American connection less direct and its influence more culturally pervasive. After all, to function most effectively, Bertram's has to change from the inside. Its principal role in the novel is to portray post-war England as a community lacking an identity of its own, somewhere that strives to compensate for its present-day deficiencies by staging a show of past glories. In a Britain beginning to emerge slowly from austerity it is particularly pertinent of Christie to give a special emphasis to Bertram's flamboyant display of succulent everyday English food: the muffins oozing with butter, doughnuts squirting jam when bitten into, seed cake, and the full range of a traditional breakfast.

The amount of trouble the hotel management is willing to face in order to maintain the illusion of nothing having changed in the past fifty years reveals the hollowness of the whole proceeding. The hotel's traditional meals, punctilious service, warm and tastefully decorated bedrooms, all lose their attractiveness when it is learned why exactly such loving attention is paid to them. Unknown to the recipients, special cheap rates are charged to allow the kind of people to stay at Betram's who by their presence can help provide the desired old-fashioned image. Without this policy, Lady Selina Hazy wouldn't be there, nor would Canon Pennyfeather. Or, perhaps, Miss Marple herself. They are all in effect subsidised props used to create a suitably English atmosphere, just 'so much *mise en scène*' as Colonel Luscombe observes. The visitors are doubly fooled by being encouraged to think of England as luxuriously out-of-date while staying in rooms that meet the highest American standards of material comfort. Americans represent modern money and therefore everything must be done to pander to their wants and prejudices. Even the central heating in their bedrooms is adjusted to what is considered to be their national norm. And when they leave their miniature artificially created Americas and descend to the public rooms they are presented with an impeccably English breakfast or an equally impeccable English tea with seed cake or butter-soaked muffins. Around them they are guaranteed to find a smattering of unknowingly subsidised aristocrats, high-ranking clergymen, genteel old ladies and retired imperial administrators.

Bertram's elaborate subterfuge, though, shields a darker secret than merely this. Just as the fake gentility of the hotel is employed to symbolize a post-war England that has lost its sense of national direction, so crime features in the novel as virtually the only truly flourishing and imaginatively pursued activity. The hotel is actually a cover for a criminal organization which is itself based on fake outward images. In this particular world it is literally no easier to distinguish a genuine criminal from a genuine businessman than it is to distinguish a real bishop from an actor employed to play the role. The traditional setting of a Christie detective story, with the criminal operating largely within a domestic setting or circle, acting in defiance of moral codes which are accepted by most other characters in the novel and in society as a whole, has now gone entirely.

Instead, organized crime is rife in England and totally indifferent to the feelings, views and safety of ordinary people. At one point in the novel the reader is allowed privileged access to a conference of top officers in Scotland Yard. They are discussing the worrying growth of large-scale robberies: 'Bank hold-ups, snatches of pay-rolls, thefts of consignments of jewels sent through the mail, train robberies.' This is precisely the 'daring and stupendous' criminal activity that is master-minded from Bertram's Hotel and backed by influential individuals and groups throughout the country, including financiers in the City of London. Nor is it only Scotland Yard that is busily adapting its methods to deal with modern organized crime. Behind the police Christie acknowledges the work of both the Secret Service and an enormously powerful individual like Mr Robinson who appears in several of Christie's late novels, including *Bertram's*. A shadowy figure, he is linked with a similar network of people throughout the world. Although the exact nature of his business is never entirely clear and he is not above making a lot of money for himself, he is available as a force for social good, willing when called upon to help the agents of law and order. He deals in knowledge and information. In *Cat among the Piegeons* (1959) Colonel Pikeaway, the head of Special Branch, assures Poirot that 'there is a demand for such men in our modern world' and that dubious as Mr Robinson may seem, sometimes it is necessary to believe that he is 'on the side of the Angels.' Christie certainly grew to believe this ambivalent attitude was acceptable when it came to combating modern criminals. There is no alternative. As Miss Marple observes ruefully at a crucial moment half-way through *Bertram's* crime really does seem to 'have got above itself.'

There is some striking contemporary evidence to support Christie's instinct that this precise moment was crucial in the changing pattern of post-war crime in Britain. In 1961 the recently founded and much-admired Cambridge Institute of Criminology under the directorship of Leon Radzinovicz published a report *Robbery in London*. The authors were F.H. McClintock and Evelyn Gibson. They were concerned mainly with analysing trends to the end of the 1950s, but in order to make their report as up-to-date as possible they included the information they had gathered for the first six months of 1960. This produced some unexpected results. Their overall findings confirmed the view, already becoming generally recognised, of there having been a steady increase of crime during and after the war. But there there was also new evidence of very recent and drastic changes in the rate and nature of criminal activity. The report confirms statistically what Christie had grasped instinctively.

The number of robberies recorded by the police in the 1950s had almost doubled for the country as a whole and substantially more than doubled in London itself. But when the findings for the first six months of 1960 were included the level of crime unexpectedly soared. Not only was the number of violent crimes more than double that of ten years earlier, but the nature of the violence being used had also changed. When the figures for early 1960 were extrapolated to the full year they confirmed that darker trends faintly observable throughout the 1950s had now become frighteningly prominent. Criminals were 'more daring,' going for bigger hauls, with very large sums of money and bullion being targeted. They were not deterred by guards on business premises, were commonly armed, highly organized, and appeared to enjoy a worrying degree of immunity.

In his preface to the report Radzinovicz carefully balanced words of assurance for the ordinary citizen with a stern warning to the police about a new, highly skilled breed of criminals:

> The major increase has not been in attacks on defenceless people but rather in the lucrative and carefully planned operations of a relatively small group of seasoned professional criminals, who have been particularly successful in escaping the grip of the criminal law.[10]

Here, in 1961, Radzinovicz would have had in mind a number of spectacular mail-train and bullion robberies carried out in the recent past. Two years later that criminal trend was to be confirmed by the 'Great Train Robbery,' one of the most publicized and mythologized, crimes in British history.[11] It qualifies Radzinovicz's general argument to some extent in that the Great Train Robbery *did* involve an attack on a 'defenceless person,' he *was* seriously injured, and the criminals *were* quickly tracked down by the police. But all of this was rendered virtually incidental by the public and media interest in the train robbers, so much so that the efficient solving of the robbery became something of an ambiguous victory for the authorities. There was loudly voiced public discontent with what were felt to be the extremely heavy prison sentences handed out, and over the next few years the convicted men remained top news whether they were merely being held in prison, escaping from it, or avoiding it all together. Radzinovicz was being proved impressively right. Not only were crimes becoming bigger and more callously violent, there was also an increasing chance that whether or not the criminals involved were captured, they were likely to arouse a surprising degree of sympathy in the general public.

* * *

Christie's earlier reluctance to allow events in her novels to be identified too closely with real-life equivalents had now gone entirely. It seems more than likely that the fictional Irish Mail Robbery organised by the hotel-based criminals in *Bertram's* is at least an allusion to the Great Train Robbery which had taken place so recently. In addition, Christie's portrayal of Canon Pennyfeather in *Bertram's* might well have been prompted by the case of the Reverend Basil Andrews. He was an elderly, apparently respectable Church of England clergyman who had been paid by criminals to give false evidence in court.[12] Christie's Canon Pennyfeather is in no sense corrupt, but he is involved in a doppelgänger incident which is typical of the use of outward respectability to cover criminal activity employed by both the criminals working from Bertram's Hotel and by Basil Andrews.

Running throughout this concern to present a sociologically accurate picture of crime are the moral and social concerns about the changing nature of Britain that are characteristic of all of the post-war Miss Marple novels. In *Bertram's* these are strikingly conveyed through the mother and daughter relationship of Bess Sedgwick and Elvira Blake. Christie was too dedicated a storyteller to allow particular aspects of a novel to escape her control. Even so, there is an element of this in *Bertram's*. Bess and Elvira are, of course, carefully linked with the central themes of the novel, but their personal stories feel less integrated than other aspects of the criminal activity going on all around them. While these are all punctiliously concealed by the hotel's fake Edwardianism, Bess and Elvira's personalities aren't. They are in danger of taking control whenever they appear, demanding that what they stand for should be noticed. And what they stand for goes beyond modern crime as such, however highly organized.

Bess Sedgwick is an unusually outgoing and flamboyant character for Christie. She represents the unsavoury glamorization of crime and criminals in modern society. A compulsive headline seeker, Bess is attracted to crime by the sheer excitement of it. 'Danger,' she admits,' has become 'an addiction ... like that nice little dollop of heroin addicts have to have ... to make life seem worth living.' She is not driven by financial need or social deprivation, cares little about the money it can bring, and is careful to allow as little violence as possible into the jobs she plans. Her formidable criminal intelligence is revealed only late in the novel and by then she has been defined by her many other startling qualities. She is beautiful, classy, sexually attractive, amoral, physically daring, photogenic, loved by the newspapers and utterly self-centred. She is Christie's fictional contribution not only to the increasing glamorization of spectacular crime but also to what was just beginning to emerge as a celebrity culture.

One of the strongest marks of Bess's amorality is that she has early abandoned any maternal interest in her daughter. No money has been spared on Elvira's upbringing and she will inherit a fortune when she comes of age. But Bess has been so personally neglectful of her that at the start of the novel Elvira doesn't even know for sure who her mother is. Her personality clearly reveals the effects of this motherless upbringing. Like Bess she is amoral and self-centred, but she is also devious, a thief, and a compulsive liar. She has inherited her mother's beauty but not her charm and dynamic personality, or, more importantly, the defiant truthfulness that makes Bess so attractive a character and prepares the way for her dramatic exit from the novel. For Elvira, Christie had reserved a very different kind of fate. As a representative of modern youth she becomes the main target of Miss Marple's Old Testament fervour that is carried over here from *A Caribbean Mystery*.

It is Elvira who is being referred to specifically when Miss Marple invokes Psalm 37. This celebrates the Lord's power over 'evil-doers' who 'shall soon be cut down like the grass, and wither as the green herb' (verse 2). Chief Inspector Davy bemoans the fact that a modern court will not convict Elvira when confronted with all the 'sob stuff' about her 'unfortunate upbringing' that an 'experienced counsel' is bound to advance. And, he adds, 'she's beautiful you know,' meaning that that will also influence the law. Miss Marple will have none of this. The 'children of Lucifer are often beautiful' she acknowledges and they 'flourish like the green bay tree' (verse 35). This again is an allusion to Elvira, whose name surely embodies a play on 'evil.' When Elvira comes into the room she seem to justify all of Davy's fears. So beautiful is she that she 'looks like one of the angels in an early primitive Italian painting.' In phrases that echo throughout the novel, nothing here 'is quite what it seems'; everything 'is too good to be true.' Urged on by Miss Marple, Davy vows that Elvira will not be allowed to escape justice, while Miss Marple offers a final benediction: 'May God have mercy on her soul.'

The unusual ending to *Bertram's*, with its high religious tone has been prepared for by an earlier discussion between Miss Marple and Davy. She tells him that she expects 'evil of some kind to happen.' He replies: 'Evil is rather a big word.' And so it is for Davy but not for Miss Marple. He assumes she is talking about a possible murder, but she instructs him that crucial distinctions need to be observed. 'Evil' is something by itself. 'How shall I say? – it defies God.' Davy takes evil at its reduced everyday meaning as simply describing an act that is vicious or morally wrong. Miss Marple, though, uses it more accurately and in its primary religious sense. Always for her it implies the active opposition to good, the conscious attempt by the Devil to undermine the work of God. In English literature a classic expression of this definition is given by Milton's Satan. Christie actually refers to Satan and quotes the following lines in *An Autobiography*. She also links him with another highly relevant 'evil' figure in literature, Shakespeare's Richard III. The Milton passage reads:

> So farewell hope, and with hope farewell fear,
> Farewell remorse; all good to me is lost;
> Evil be thou my good (*Paradise Lost*, IV, 108-10*)*.

To the fallen Satan the destruction of good is all that can now give meaning to his life. The need to destroy good has itself become for him the only possible good.

When Christie began to be especially interested in the concept of evil in the years leading up to the 1939-45 war she was drawn, as we have seen, to the widespread practice of the day that related it to totalitarian regimes which were set on eliminating all forms of individual freedom. Later, as Miss Marple moves out into English society, weighing its strengths and weaknesses, she returns to the older religious meaning of evil as epitomizing those forces which are malevolently opposed to good. She is similarly meticulous in her use of 'wicked' which is also Biblical and was for long used as a fairly close synonym for evil. In *Caribbean* the evil she recognized had been Tim Kendal's ruthless manipulation and murder of gullible women, a perversion of love that for Miss Marple could not be left unchallenged. In *Bertram's Hotel* emphasis is placed on new types of criminality that are openly destructive of traditional moral values. These may be personal or institutional. At its most extreme, and surprising, Miss Marple finds it in modern youth, 'the children of Lucifer.' It was a theme to be explored further in Miss Marple's next and final novel.

Chapter 11

Emissary of Justice:
Nemesis

N*emesis*, published shortly after Christie's eighty-first birthday, really was to be Miss Marple's farewell performance, and is clearly offered as such. It is linked in a variety of pointed ways with other Miss Marple novels, most of them relatively recent but not always so. More directly, the novel closes on a moving, carefully modulated goodbye note. There is throughout a sense of Christie tying up loose ends, both narrative and personal.

Nemesis opens with an unusually detailed picture of Miss Marple at home in St. Mary Mead. It embodies a reference back to *The Mirror Crack'd* of 1962, the only other novel ever to have concerned itself in a similar way with the minutiae of Miss Marple's daily routine. Miss Knight, the irritating home help, has gone and the domestic arrangement made with Cherry and Jim Baker in *The Mirror Crack'd* is once again happily in operation. Miss Marple's health has improved since the earlier novel: at least, she is no longer regarded as sufficiently housebound for a local trip out of doors to be considered a reckless escapade. But she is feeling her age: 'I am old,' she replies when considering whether to undertake one more case, 'elderly we say, but old is a better word. Definitely old.' She is rheumatic, gardening is forbidden to her, and she spends her days fussed over by Cherry and devoting her energies to a meticulous reading of the two daily papers that are always delivered to her.

The movement back from *Nemesis* to *The Mirror Crack'd* and Miss Marple's previously fragile state of health, involved a leap over the two novels that had come between, *A Caribbean Mystery* and *At Bertram's Hotel*, though the presence of both is still felt in *Nemesis*. From them

Christie carries forward the image they had established of a resilient, crusading Miss Marple produced in the wake of the Margaret Rutherford travesty. In *Nemesis* Miss Marple is more than ever a woman driven by unshakeable moral and religious principles. In her own words she is an 'emissary of justice' or, even grander, Nemesis, the Greek goddess of justice, a label which she had first applied to herself in *Caribbean*. Once again, following the pattern of all of the novels in the final trilogy, the case to be investigated requires a journey to somewhere little known to Miss Marple. First it had been the West Indies; then London, and this time a coach tour of the Famous Houses and Gardens of Great Britain.

The connections between *Nemesis* and *A Caribbean Mystery* are particularly close. In a sense the later novel can almost be seen as a sequel to the former, so strongly is it concerned with the settling up of unfinished business, most immediately in the West Indies but also, and far more widely, in Mr Rafiel's and Miss Marple's lives. Also, perhaps, in Christie's as well. The two women are now so firmly associated that *Nemesis* can be seen as a conscious summation of both of their lives and ideals.

It is this unusual sense of Christie speaking out, whether through Miss Marple or in harmony with her, that gives *Nemesis* its distinctive narrative quality. Although more direct than usual, Christie still allows herself to communicate in the indirect ways she had developed over the years. So much so that *Nemesis* is also the most allusive of the Miss Marple novels, consciously literary, and unashamedly committed to the view of life it advances. There are times when Christie's determination to make her own, and Miss Marple's, moral and social views absolutely clear becomes too evident. But, as always, Christie's special genius for entertainment carries her through. If *Nemesis* is in some respects not only one of the most personal of the Miss Marple novels, it is also one of the most powerful as well.

* * *

The opening of the novel encapsulates, in carefully observed detail, a small but real moment in modern British social history. In addition, it is almost certainly evoking something of a regular routine that enabled Christie herself to keep up with the news and current affairs. Every day, Miss Marple takes two newspapers. In the morning she reads the *Daily Newsgiver* which to her great annoyance is gradually replacing solid news with gossipy general articles: it is on its way to becoming what would now be called a tabloid. Then, after lunch and a brief nap Miss Marple sets time aside to give a more 'leisurely perusal' of *The Times*. This part of her daily routine is also no longer what it once had been because *The Times* itself is 'no longer what it used to be.' The births, deaths, and marriages columns in which Miss Marple is particularly interested and which were once prominently on the front page have now been moved elsewhere in the paper. For a while they needed to be searched for, but have finally, Miss Marple is pleased to note, come permanently to rest on the back page. It had been in May 1966 that *The Times* had so upset Miss Marple and its many other long-time readers, including Christie herself one assumes, by printing news on its front page for the first time and beginning the general overhaul of the paper's traditional layout that Christie describes.

Even though she now has no difficulty finding the births, marriages and death columns, Miss Marple's pleasure is still reduced. At her advanced age, the births and marriages mean less to her. It's the announcements of deaths that most draw her attention. And that is how Mr Rafiel re-enters Miss Marple's life.

When she first sees his name listed among the deaths it means little to her but as her memory stirs she recalls their strange, ambivalent relationship from *A Caribbean Mystery*, trying to establish what exactly there had been between them. She muses that they hadn't been 'friends, or on terms of affection.' More 'allies,' she decides. But that's not quite right either. She goes on to remember his importance as an ally and what the experience had meant to her. She recalls the tropical night when she had rushed to seek his help, with that 'pink wool kind of shawl-scarf' which, when she was young they used to call 'a fascinator,' wrapped round her head, and how amused Mr Rafiel had been by the whole experience: 'Ah!' Miss Marple sighed, it had been, she had to admit it, all very exciting.' Throughout the day her mind keeps returning to Mr Rafiel. It is now she recalls Beatrice Harraden's *Ships that Pass in the Night*, the popular late Victorian romantic novel which suddenly feels so appropriate to her. She even adds the lines from the poem by Longfellow that had given the novel its title:

> Ships that pass in the night, and speak each other in passing;
> Only a signal shown and a distant voice in the darkness.[1]

That is as far as she will allow herself to go, and she decides 'she must put Mr Rafiel out of her head. She would probably never think of him again.'

But, of course, that isn't possible. By means of a formal announcement in *The Times* Mr Rafiel has spoken to her from beyond the grave and the communication continues, first in the form of a letter from his solicitors and then in two letters from Mr Rafiel himself. The title of the chapter containing his second letter is actually called 'Instructions from Beyond.' His own reminiscences of their adventure together in the West Indies are notably similar to Miss Marple's, with a down-to-earth common sense tempered by genuine affection. He had been inspired by their co-operation and particularly impressed by Miss Marple's 'natural flair for crime.' He addresses her as 'my dear, if I may call you that,' signs his second letter as from 'your affectionate friend,' and remembers her romantically 'as I saw you once one night as I rose from sleep disturbed by your urgency, in a cloud of pink wool.' Miss Marple has to accept or reject the challenge from Rafiel without knowing its exact nature, and from the moment she commits herself the dead man is never far from her. He controls her journey north, has arranged for her to meet the key people in whatever investigation may follow, and, knowing that he will probably be placing her in danger of her life, organizes for her what protection he can.

Behind his actions there are frequent hints that deeper, more spiritual forces are present. Mr Rafiel signs off his first letter to Miss Marple not as one of the archangels, as his name would entitle him to do, but by quoting from Amos, the Old Testament prophet: 'Let justice roll down like waters/And righteousness like an everlasting stream' (5:24). In *Caribbean*, it will be remembered, Miss Marple at a similar moment of uncertainty about how she should act had invoked Isaiah, with Mr Rafiel taking on the role of God and addressing her with an abrupt 'Hi!' as though he were calling a dog. Both Biblical occasions involve the two men being summoned to prophecy by God, though in very different ways. Isaiah's call takes place in the spectacular setting of a temple (6:8), while the humble herdsman Amos is summoned as he tends his flock (7:15). Both men regard themselves initially as unfit for the huge task given them, and their prophecies are much concerned with social justice and equality. Within Miss Marple's character there is a similar balance of the ordinary and exceptional, the mundane and the visionary. Above all, she is motivated by the urgent need to do whatever she is sure is right, as Rafiel's apt quotation from Amos expresses to perfection.

Religious imagery is used throughout *Nemesis* and, surely, with a clear purpose on Christie's part. Miss Marple makes an unequivocal statement of her faith: 'I believe in eternal life,' she announces to herself, and uses this to justify talking to the dead Mr Rafiel: 'I don't know exactly where you are, Mr Rafiel, but I have no doubt that you are *somewhere.*' Her choice for early morning reading in bed is 'a devotional work.' Mr Rafiel's religious beliefs are made less clear but they are hinted at. He is serious about hoping to communicate with Miss Marple after his death and, of course, it is his own unprompted decision to adopt the persona of Amos. One of the jobs he takes on is to make sure that there will be 'guardian angels' on hand to keep Miss Marple safe. There is also the significantly named Miss Temple, who is murdered to prevent her discovering the truth about the also significantly named 'Verity' Hunt. Miss Temple is identified immediately by Miss Marple as having 'the look of one who is on a pilgrimage' and she willingly accepts this description of herself. Miss Marple, however, later tells Archdeacon Brabazon that she prefers the word 'mission' to describe her own quest for the truth, emphasizing again the driven nature of her task.

As throughout the final trilogy of novels, and in *Caribbean* especially, Miss Marple is set up not simply to solve a particular crime, but to confront two great abstract forces, Evil and Justice. When it is reported to her that Mr Rafiel has said she had 'a very fine sense of evil' she is pleased with the compliment and says it is like being born with a keen sense of smell or the instinct to know when someone is telling lies. Her special power is to be able to identify the presence of Evil. And of all evils, injustice is the one that can allow for no compromise. When Cherry Baker asks her what she is thinking about so intently, Miss Marple replies that she is wondering if she 'could ever be ruthless.' Cherry is amused by this: 'Never! You're kindness itself.' But Miss Marple persists. Yes, she could be ruthless if 'in the cause of justice.' And in *Nemesis* we are given a ruthless Miss Marple.

In addition to the frequent Biblical and religious allusions, there is in *Nemesis* a clutch of references to literature and mythology which further serve to heighten the seriousness of Miss Marple's quest and her determination to carry it through. The most telling of these allusions are applied to the three Bradbury-Scott sisters who constitute the heart of the book's murder mystery. They remind Miss Marple of Chekhov (*Three Sisters)*, Shakespeare (the witches in *Macbeth*), and, Aeschylus (Clytemnestra, from the *Agamemnon*). All of these allusions are chosen with care. Christie takes from Chekhov the listlessness of the sisters, the sense of social stasis, and the long waiting for something unknown to happen which, in their case, will be resolved by the descent of Nemesis/ Miss Marple. The witches in Macbeth had long been a favourite reference of Christie's but on this occasion she hands responsibility for explaining what the allusion implies to Miss Marple. Considering how the witches should be presented on stage she derides the tendency to present them as 'like pantomime creatures.' Instead she insists that the true force of their 'menace' can only be felt by portraying them as 'three ordinary normal old women. Old Scottish Women.' And this is how Christie handles the Bradbury-Scott sisters, a mixture of *Three Sisters* and *Macbeth*, normality blended with menace. Hovering over the whole novel, with its underlying fear of there being no certainty that true justice ever can be relied on, is the popular classical saying, attributed among others to Solon and muttered by Miss Marple: 'Call no man happy until he is dead.'

If picked up by the reader, the early linking of Clotilde with Aeschylus's Clytemnestra may seem a clumsy, and relatively rare, example of Christie giving the murder-mystery game away. She was aware of this possibility and tries to get out of it. She notes that Clotilde 'would have made a magnificent Clytemnestra – she could have stabbed a husband in his bath with exultation. But since Clothilde had never had a husband, that solution wouldn't do.' It's an uncharacteristically weak argument, unless Christie is playing a double trick on the reader, as, of course, she was perfectly capable of doing. As the corpse in *Nemesis* is not that of anyone's husband, why make so much of Clotilde looking as tragic and ruthless as Clytemnestra? If it's a clue, it's a totally irrelevant one. But was Christie actually being more subtle and alluding to the fact that Clytemnestra stabbed her husband Agamemnon in revenge for his bloody sacrifice of their daughter Iphigenia? It is, after all, Clytemnestra's love for Iphigenia that allows her to justify the murder of her husband, a connection that links well with the relationship between Clotilde and Verity.

As if this particular puzzle from classical literature wasn't complicated enough, the three Bradbury-Scott sisters are identified collectively, and most forcefully and uncontroversially, with the Greek Fates or Moirai who were responsible for the span of individual human lives. The Greek goddesses were named Clotho, Lachesis, and Atropos. Christie carefully modernizes these names while preserving the original capital letters for Clotilde, Lavinia, and Anthea. Daunting as the original Fates were, even their power was not absolute. Ultimately they were controlled by Zeus, and, in certain circumstances, subject to the judgment of Nemesis, a goddess responsible for seeing that justice was evenly distributed. This clash between moral authorities is the central issue of *Nemesis*, with Clotilde/Clotho over-reaching her legitimate powers and being punished for doing so by Miss Marple/Nemesis. In the dramatic scene when Miss Marple sits in bed awaiting the murderer who now needs to get Miss Marple out of the way, she wraps a pink woollen scarf round her neck before calling on her guardian angels to save her. With this simple gesture she is re-enacting the moment in *Caribbean* when she arrived so dramatically, and similarly dressed, in Mr Rafiel's bedroom. She is confirming that she has kept faith with him and that she really does deserve the title of Nemesis.

* * *

For the main story in *Nemesis*, the conviction and imprisonment of Mr Rafiel's son Michael for the murder of Verity Hunt, Christie reached back much further than the final trilogy of Miss Marple novels, to *They Do It With Mirrors* (1952), the novel in which Christie had first broached the subject of post-war juvenile crime. It was there that she had openly expressed her discontent with the general policy, followed by successive post-war British governments whether Labour or Conservative, to abolish the stricter punishments for crime that had long been in operation. Instead they looked to psychological and environmental factors to explain, or rather to explain *away*, Christie and many other people would have said, criminal activity, especially that of young people. Over the years Christie's interest in juvenile crime had not diminished. There are many references to it in her novels of the 1950s and 60s, but it wasn't until *Nemesis* that Christie returned to the subject in any substantial way. Here it is central, another issue on which Christie wanted her opinion to be made clear, something she was now able to do without being encumbered by the narrative awkwardness of *They Do It With Mirrors*. A little of that earlier unease remains in *Nemesis* but it is softened by the unusually frank portrait of Michael Rafiel and the complexity of the 'love' relation that is at the heart of the novel.

The generally accepted view of Michael Rafiel is put unequivocally by Professor Wanstead, a 'pathologist and psychiatrist' who works in a consultative capacity for the Home Office. He has come to believe that Michael was not guilty of the crime for which he had been imprisoned and is working to have the verdict overthrown. The material he has to work on could hardly be less encouraging:

> This had been a boy who from his early youth
> had been completely unsatisfactory. You can
> call it by what term you like. A young delinquent,
> a young thug, a bad lot, a person of diminished
> responsibility... He was a criminal type. That was
> certain.

Michael has earlier been charged with, or suspected of having committed various crimes including theft, fraud, embezzlement, and rape. He has already spent two short spells in prison. Everyone, including his father, agrees that he seemed to have been born a criminal. Neither the money that had always been available to ease his way in life nor a good education has had any beneficial effect on his character. Even so, there is a doubt about his conviction for this particular crime and justice must act on his behalf. Whatever his past, the only relevant question now is did he murder Verity Hunt by strangling her and then beating in her face so severely that she could barely be recognized?

As Miss Marple, guided by the spirit of Mr Rafiel, moves north, the various forces for Michael's defence gather around her, notably Professor Wanstead (professionally interested in Michael's case and supported by the Governor of the prison where Michael is being held), Elizabeth Temple (Verity's former headmistress) and Archdeacon Brabazon (who had agreed to marry Verity and Michael). Only Miss Temple seems to have any real idea of what happened to prevent the marriage, and she herself is murdered before she can collect the final evidence. But she does leave behind her a vital clue. 'Why did Verity die?' she is asked by Miss Marple. Miss Temple replies with the single word 'Love' which echoes 'like the tone of a deep bell.' For the moment, she will add only that love is 'one of the most frightening words there is in the world.'

From now on Christie's passion for ambiguity takes over. If love is the answer, doesn't that confirm Michael's guilt? After all, he had claimed to be in love with Verity. She returned his love, was determined that they should marry, and was said to be pregnant by him. Given his dreadful reputation it was easy enough to see this as a love affair that had gone tragically wrong. For the defence, Wanstead, the psychologist, argues that whatever Michael's shortcomings, he wasn't capable of horribly mutilating the body of a woman he loved. Archdeacon Brabazon supports this view. His evidence is that he had personally observed the genuineness of the love the two young people had for each and this had persuaded him to marry them in church in spite of Michael's bad name.

Michael's love for Verity is set against that of the Bradbury-Scott sisters, especially Clotilde, with whom the orphaned Verity had lived for much of her life. Their love, too, seems to remove them from any thought of being involved in her murder, a line adopted early on in the investigation by Miss Marple. She confirms that the sisters had 'loved Verity dearly' and agrees with Wanstead that if Michael is innocent then they need to look for 'another man.' It has to be someone who 'wouldn't hesitate to bash in a girl's head after he had killed her. The kind of man who would be driven frantic with jealousy.' She adds knowingly: 'There are men like that.' Not mecessarily in this case though, and most certainly not if the frightening nature of love as identified by Miss Temple is taken into account.

* * *

In placing love, its many faces, distortions and perversions, at the centre of *Nemesis* Christie was restating a moral issue that had troubled her throughout her career. Again and again she had asked, and been echoed by Miss Marple and Poirot, what is it that women seek most in life? Her answer remained the same, although the terminology used to express it was kept neatly up-to-date over the years. Back in the 1920s it had been a 'rotter' or a 'ne'er do weel.' Here in the 1960s it is a 'bad lot.' Early in *Nemesis* Miss Marple arranges to meet up with Esther Walters from *Caribbean*. She thinks back on the Esther she had known earlier and decides she was 'a nice woman … a very nice woman … the sort of woman that would marry a murderer if she were ever given half a chance.' It sounds an extraordinary conclusion, but the two parts of that sentence do not really contradict each other as they might appear to do. In Christie's scheme of things, it is quite possible to be a very nice woman and to look to marry a murderer. That, of course, was precisely what Miss Marple and Mr Rafiel had prevented Esther from doing in *Caribbean*. Now, helped, no doubt by the very generous legacy she has received from Mr Rafiel, Esther has married a man 'a little younger' than herself. What kind of man exactly is left pointedly unspecified.

Verity Hunt in *Nemesis* is rather more than 'a very nice woman.' She is every bit as naturally good as Michael is naturally bad. Miss Temple describes her as a 'very lovely girl and a very sweet girl,' and everyone else who knew her would agree with that judgment. Yet this 'charming and beautiful girl,' this 'lovely girl' and 'a dear child too' falls in love with and is desperate to marry Michael Rafiel. 'She knew he was what was technically called a bad lot,' says Miss Marple, 'but that is not what puts any girl off a boy. No. Young women like bad lots. They always have. They fall in love with bad lots.' Miss Marple actually sets aside any thought that she is talking about an exceptional case, as, after all, with Verity and Michael she might well be. It is a general statement, a deep-rooted belief of Christie's about women that had appeared in novel after novel throughout her career. She even uses it at least twice as a kind of in-joke at the endings of novels when she challenges the reader to guess which of two suitors a particularly attractive woman character is likely to marry, the decent or respectable as set against someone who if not a fully fledged rotter is at least morally weak or raffish. The answer should be clear to anyone who has carefully followed Christie's (and Miss Marple's and Poirot's) ideas on the kind of men even the most admirable women are drawn to.[2]

The reasoning behind this belief of Christie's was that women are driven by an overwhelming desire for the excitement and danger of passionate love and will sacrifice everything else to experience it. Conversely, they are terrified of being trapped in a mundane unexciting marriage. Reason is easily brushed aside because women are certain they can change the unsatisfactory men they fall in love with. It is impossible to dissuade them from the belief that *their* love will be strong enough to overcome the moral weakness of the men they choose. In this they are invariably deluded. Rotters, ne'er do weels or bad lots, whatever they are called, are not likely to be changed by the devoted love of a woman. It is the woman who suffers in such relationships. This, it is assumed, is what would have happened to Verity. Archdeacon Brabazon is willing to marry her and Michael because he is convinced of the depth of their love for each other, but he does not believe Verity when she says that by marrying Michael she will be able to 'help' him. Brabazon's warning to her that she will never change him is brushed aside. Verity doesn't survive even to try to prove that her love will reform Michael, and Miss Marple and Brabazon are left still believing that the marriage would have resulted in Verity being terribly disillusioned.

Ironically, Verity is brutally murdered to prevent her marrying Michael or any other man. She is killed because of her longing to enter into a normal heterosexual relationship and to escape from being the object of a form of passionate love that she herself had regarded as abnormal and unacceptable. She is buried in a 'vault' prepared for her in the gardens of the Old Manor House, the last of the many gardens experienced by Miss Marple which reflect the moral state of the owners. Verity's tomb is covered with Polygonum, 'one of the quickest flowering shrubs which swallows and kills and dries up and gets rid of everything it grows over.'

The tendency, in some cases the eagerness, of women to choose, to seek out, unsuitable and dangerous partners which had been one of Christie's deepest convictions for so long, is given a new and ironic twist in *Nemesis* by being linked to the growing sexual independence of women. This again was something she had long observed, and she had developed a clever technique for those moments when her spinster detective was obliged to confront any of the issues involved. Miss Marple would make some kind of obligatory Victorian indication – a blush or lowered eyes or gentle cough – that this, really, was something on which she shouldn't be offering an opinion at all, and then proceed to show herself to be totally unshockable. And, given her deeply cynical view of human beings it is difficult to see what could shock her. Like Christie herself, she is always exceptionally broad-minded and non-judgmental about people's sexual behaviour. She is also punctilious about 'women sticking together' as Jane Helier, in 'The Affair at the Bungalow,' had pointed out long ago: 'She wouldn't give me away before the men. That was nice of her.'

For Christie, the problem was not women's independence as such, though her views on the matter were never very consistent. Her reluctance to endorse feminism came from her belief that many women had been better off and lived more comfortable lives before entering into open competition with men, in whatever sphere of life. At the same time she admired and strongly supported the increasing number of women reaching high positions in the professions. A perfect example of this is Elizabeth Temple in *Nemesis* 'the retired headmistress of a famous girls' school.' When Miss Marple first sees her on the coach she registers her as 'A Personality. Someone! Yes, she was decidedly someone.' To support her view, she recalls having once met Dame Emily Waldron, the Principal of an Oxford College,' and being so impressed that she had 'never quite forgotten her.'

The increase in the sexual independence of women, however, had introduced social and moral complications which Christie felt became particularly difficult when criminal activity was also involved. This again was something that runs throughout Christie's work, and Miss Marple's career. And inevitably so. They had both lived through and come to accept the sexual liberation of the 1920s, but as it entered a more expansive and challenging phase in the 1960s they became more worried about it and, at the same time, harder in their attitudes.

For Professor Wanstead, the admired criminologist and psychiatrist in *Nemesis*, it is axiomatic that the increase of sexual liberation for women has created a serious legal problem. He believes that girls have become more sexually active but less sexually responsible, a view he expresses in language that today, nearly fifty years on, is likely to be widely regarded as unacceptable. If things go wrong, he argues, 'girls ... are far more ready to be raped nowadays than they used to be' and very often their mothers will 'insist ... that they call it rape.' This same view is advanced by several different characters, including Mr Broadribb the solicitor: 'Well, we all know what rape is nowadays. Mum tells the girl she's got to accuse the young man of rape even if the young man hasn't had much chance with the girl at him all the time ... to sleep with her.' This is not an attitude that occurs only in late Christie. Many years earlier, Dolly and Arthur Bantry had argued about a closely related issue in the short story 'Death by Drowning.'[3] But by the 1970s the language to describe it had become much blunter, and the charges of irresponsibility by both mothers and daughters even more so. The problem is seen as further aggravated by fashions in the 1960s which are said to indicate an unwillingness of young girls to grow up, a stunting of maturity: 'They wish '*not* to become adult, *not* to have to accept our kind of responsibility.' Wanstead is talking to Miss Marple and she makes no objection to his opinions, even though, as the reader would well appreciate by this time, she is capable of openly disputing the views of any man, and has frequently done so in earlier novels. Here, there is every reason to believe she agrees with Wanstead.

* * *

Christie's ideas about crime and punishment had always been conservative rather than radical, and unsurprisingly that conservatism became more entrenched as she grew older. It was also, no doubt, further deepened by the feeling expressed in a number of the later novels that post-war Britain has lost its way in the modern world. In *Nemesis* Miss Marple makes this point very straightforwardly to Michael Rafiel: 'Our country's in rather a bad way just now, but you'll probably find some job or other.' Along with her edginess over sexual liberation and the moral dilemmas this has opened up for girls, she is worried by a number of other issues which are more directly linked to crime.

The shock she had registered in *They Do It With Mirrors* at the rise of juvenile delinquency and what she had felt to be the leniency of the State in dealing with it had not decreased over the years. Miss Marple's first response to having Michael's criminal childhood and youth outlined to her is 'if you expect me to feel sympathy, regret, urge an unhappy childhood, blame bad environment; if you expect me in fact to weep over him … I do not feel inclined to do so.' Professor Wanstead replies that he is 'delighted to hear it.' The same is true of the 'very nice woman' who acts as a part-time domestic for the Bradbury-Scott sisters. 'Killers are killers,' she tells Miss Marple when she brings the morning tea: 'And they won't even hang them nowadays.' She adds, as a possible reason for Michael not having been given the punishment he truly deserved, 'they'd abolished hanging by then – or else he was too young. I can't remember it all now.' Such views are held by characters in *Nemesis* regardless of their social position or their knowledge or personal experience of the subject.

Capital punishment had long had the support of Miss Marple. Forty years earlier than *Nemesis* in the short story 'A Christmas Tragedy' she had declared defiantly: 'I've no patience with modern humanitarian scruples about capital punishment.' The strength of her belief was reinforced by that being one of the few cases narrated by Miss Marple herself. She initiates the enquiry and is personally responsible for trapping the murderer who, as she says, will quite properly receive the justice he deserves. This view had not changed over the years, and in 1971 when *Nemesis* was published, the subject of judicial hanging had a very special topicality. Two years earlier it had finally been abolished by the UK parliament after a five-year period of suspension. Given the strength of feeling on capital punishment expressed in *Nemesis* it is worth stressing that Michael was innocent of the crime with which he was charged and if he had been hanged it would itself have been an act of injustice. Surprisingly, that is not a dilemma seriously considered by Miss Marple.

There is some rare evidence for Christie's own views on this subject to be found in *An Autobiography*. She had begun writing the book in 1950 and continued with it, on and off, for some fifteen or so years. The result of this irregular approach is that the early parts of the book are carefully written and well structured, but the later parts are more like unconnected notes, clearly added by Christie as they came to her. Her views on murder and its appropriate punishment appear late in the book and were probably written in the 1960s.

On murderers she says she can 'suspend' judgment and perhaps 'pity' them, but 'even then, I think, not spare them.' This is impossible for her because 'they are evil for the community; they bring in nothing except hate, and take from it all they can.' What is it possible to do with those 'for whom other people's lives go for nothing?' Surely they should be treated like wild beasts and destroyed. Imprisonment for life as an alternative is dismissed as being far crueller than death. One option she approves that was once employed but is now no longer possible is 'transportation' to some 'vast land of emptiness peopled only with primitive human beings' Among other suggestions are compulsory service for the community and the criminal being offered 'the choice between the cup of hemlock and offering himself for experimental research … human guinea pigs, who accepted a certain period of experiment in lieu of death, and who, if they survived it would then have redeemed themselves.'[4]

Miss Marple's no-nonsense support for capital punishment sounds humane when set beside Christie's personal musings here on possible alternative ways of dealing with convicted killers. And, of course, none of the options advanced by Christie is ever voiced, or even considered, by Miss Marple. Even so, she takes a hard line on crime and punishment in *Nemesis* and the views given to her are shared, as we have seen, with most of the other admirable or admired characters in the novel. Yet, forcefully expressed as these views are, it is remarkable that they do not seriously unbalance either the emotional or the narrative power of *Nemesis*. This is partly because Miss Marple's 'mission' is largely abstract in nature, an exploration of Justice itself, which, in effect, puts modern Britain on trial rather than any one individual; and partly because the presence of that kind of general context is never allowed to undermine the book's fundamental sense of humanity which centres on the unyielding personality of Michael Rafiel. It is only at the very end of the novel that Michael puts in a personal appearance. Up to this point he has never been seen, functioning only as disturbing presence, a 'bad lot'; discussed and judged by everyone, but not allowed to have views and feelings of his own.

* * *

The novel closes with a skilful blend of national and personal themes. It consists of three distinct vignettes, two of them fairly brief. First there is Miss Marple's formal exposition of the case; then a brief meeting between her and Michael Rafiel; and finally Christie's formal farewell to Miss Marple.

Miss Marple's invitation to give a full explanation of how she came to solve the Rafiel case is in a sense just another example of a standard detective story ploy regularly employed by Poirot as well as Miss Marple, in which any outstanding mysteries are clarified and loose strands tied up. But there is nothing conventional about the setting of Miss Marple's exposition in *Nemesis*. It is far and away the most formal, high-powered gathering she has ever addressed and indicative of the complexity and formality of the farewell Christie has planned for her. It takes place in 'an official Government building in London.' In addition to Professor Wanstead, there are four men present to listen to what Miss Marple has to say. They are all important, influential figures and represent between them the Public Prosecutor's Office, Scotland Yard, the prison service, and, for the government, the Home Secretary himself.

The verdicts they give on Miss Marple's performance are difficult to assess. Her distinguished listeners are impressed certainly, overwhelmed perhaps, but hardly complimentary: 'That old lady gives me the creeps' (the Prison Governor); 'So gentle – and so ruthless' (Scotland Yard); 'The most frightening woman I ever met' (the Home Secretary). The man from the Public Prosecutor's office recalls the response of Miss Marple's two 'guardians' finding her sitting up in bed, the pink fluffy shawl round her neck, waiting patiently for her would-be murderer to arrive: 'They said she gave them quite a turn.' That takes Wanstead back to Mr Rafiel's memories of Miss Marple in the West Indies, of Nemesis, of Justice in a pink woolly scarf, something Rafiel had said 'he'd never forget in all is life. Wanstead considers the image and decides he likes it, especially the 'pink woolly scarf ... I like that, very much.'

On the one occasion when Michael actually meets Miss Marple, he too is not at all sure what to make of her. Understandably muddled after being so suddenly released from prison, he thanks her for all she has done on his behalf, though not with enough enthusiasm according to Wanstead. Miss Marple isn't upset by Michael's apparent indifference, expecting, as always, little from people. She tries offering him as a gift the photograph of Verity Hunt that she herself had been given, and when he says he'd prefer not to take it but look forward in life rather than back, Miss Marple approves his attitude. Not that she carries any real hopes for him. No, she 'rather doubts' whether this time he will 'go straight' unless, she adds, he meets 'a really nice girl.' Wanstead accepts this as a perfect example of Miss Marple's 'delightfully practical mind.' But knowing Miss Marple's views on the probable outcome of relationships between really nice girls and bad lots it's likely that her mind is being portrayed as delightfully practical in ways that Wanstead himself isn't quite capable of understanding.

The final scene of *Nemesis* returns Miss Marple to the solicitors' office where her mission had started, and here we do see a truly practical side to her personality, one that had never been present before. For the first time in Miss Marple's long career, there is a substantial financial reward to be picked up at the successful conclusion of the case. It is in the form of a legacy left by Mr Rafiel to be paid after one year and is conditional on her accepting the task Mr Rafiel has set for her. Will she accept the money? Yes, she most certainly will, and gratefully so. She had decided this right at the beginning and had even then been clear about what she would spend the money on. Some favourite charities would be helped out, but she decides that Mr Rafiel had intended her to spend the money on certain personal tastes which she had not hitherto been able to 'indulge in or to afford.' And who could possible have guessed what those things might be? Occasionally a complete partridge for supper, a box of *marrons glacés*, and a visit to the opera at Covent Garden, with a hired car to carry her there and a night spent in a London hotel. Not the least surprising thing about Miss Marple revealed in *Nemesis* is this taste, carefully hidden from the reader over so many years, for culinary and cultural luxuries.

When she returns to the solicitors' office to settle her legacy, there is another attempt to get her to be more serious and she stubbornly rejects their advice. Some kind of investment perhaps? That's pointless at her age. How about putting the bulk of the reward in a deposit account? Certainly not, it is to go in her current account and be spent, not saved. But what about the proverbial rainy day? All she will need for that is an umbrella. Mr Rafiel, she tells them, would have wanted her to have fun, and that is what she is going to have. So Mr Rafiel, God's messenger on earth, who had sent Miss Marple/Nemesis on a mission to investigate the very nature of Justice itself, has decided that if she succeeds then she will have earned the right to enjoy some earthly pleasures before her own death. That is fully in keeping with Mr Rafiel's control of most of the novel's action.

And so, in a characteristically no-nonsense mood, Miss Marple takes her curtain call, though with the reader left in some uncertainty about how she should be regarded on such an auspicious occasion. Which one of her many different roles is to predominate? Most of them have been introduced, ironically or seriously, in *Nemesis*. A frightening woman, perhaps? Or 'ruthless'? A mythological embodiment of Justice wrapped in a pink woolly scarf, twittering away and fearlessly confronting possible death? One of God's avenging angels? Raphael's assistant? The advocate of capital punishment? Or, the humane, sympathetic clear-sighted analyst of human nature? Or perhaps, less grandly, the possessor of an eminently practical mind, just that and no more? The solicitors are too conventional to consider any of these options. From the start they have seen Miss Marple in the most traditional of her many roles. To them she is 'an old pussy from the country.' And that is how they continue to view her, the eccentric spinster, slightly dotty, fluffy, fluttery, and, in spite of their wise advice, determined to behave irrationally.

Even so, it is left to Mr Schuster who is slightly more imaginative than his partner Mr Broadribb, to give us our very last image of Miss Marple. As she leaves the office there comes into his mind, suddenly and quite unexpectedly, a memory from his own youth. It is 'of a young and pretty girl shaking hands with the vicar at a garden party in the country.' She was 'young, happy, going to enjoy herself.' That is a Miss Marple we have never before seen in any of the novels or stories. It comes as a complete surprise. The woman who throughout her long career had been denied any kind of youth or middle age is now transformed into a young, pretty and happy young girl eager to discover what life has in store for her. Once offered though, here at the very end of Miss Marple's life which has only ever been known by the reader for the remarkable achievements of the later years, it insists on being absolutely right, the perfect image to remember her by.

Notes

Chapter 1 What's in a Name?

1   The favourite candidate among fictional detectives has long been Hercules Popeau created by Marie Belloc Lowndes. There are certainly some marked similarities with Poirot. See Charles Osborne, *The Life and Crimes of Agatha Christie*, pp. 14-5. More recently claims have been made for the even less remembered Jules Poiret, created by Frank Howell Evans.

2   *Agatha Christie's Secret Notebooks*, p. 207.

3   'The Case of the Caretaker' (January 1942); 'The Case of the Retired Jeweller,' title later changed to 'The Tape Measure Murder' (February 1942); 'The perfect Maid,' title later changed to 'The Case of the Perfect Maid' (April 1942); and 'A Case of Buried Treasure,' title later changed to 'Strange Jest' (July 1944).

4   Curran, *Agatha Christie's Secret Notebooks*, p. 250.

5   *Agatha Christie: A Biography*, pp. 175-6.

6   *Miss Marple and all her Characters*, p. 143.

7   Pussy is a rare example of a colloquial, or rather slang, term strongly favoured by Christie that now sounds impossibly dated, so much so that it is liable to provoke in the modern reader a jokey response very different from anything she herself could have intended. It appears repeatedly in the Miss Marple novels and stories, early and late, and is used by young and old, men and women. In meaning it might seem to connect most obviously with Griselda's description of Miss Marple In *The Murder at the Vicarage* (1930) as 'the worst cat in the village' and from this, more generally, to a familiar stereotype of a gossipy, nosy, 'catty' old woman. But this isn't really the case. Sir Henry Clithering always talks, sometimes in gushing terms, of Miss

Marple as his very special pussy and is merely expressing innocent praise. In 'The Herb of Death' Dolly Bantry carefully explains that she uses the word descriptively to indicate someone who is not 'a cat' but simply 'a big soft white purry person. Always very sweet.' The problem for modern readers is, of course, that the word's sexual connotations, which go back a very long way indeed, are now widely and publicly used. So much so that the enormously popular, and enormously camp, television comedy *Are You Being Served?* which ran throughout the 1970s could raise a knowing laugh every week at the cat-loving Mrs Slocombe's tales of the great fun she had had overnight with her pussy. Given that kind of public licence Christie's fondness for the word became unacceptably naïve.

8   'Hercule Poirot – Fiction's Greatest Detective,' *Daily Mail*, 15 January 1938. Reprinted in *The Agatha Christie Official Centenary Celebration* edited by Lynn Underwood. John Curran reprints the original draft of the article in *Agatha Christie's Murder in the Making*.

Chapter 2 Enter Miss Marple

1   The issues and controversies are fully explored in the three principal biographies: Janet Morgan, *Agatha Christie: A Biography*, 1984; Jared Cade, *Agatha Christie and the Eleven Missing Days*, 1998; and Laura Thompson, *Agatha Christie: An English Mystery, 2007*. Also, see the revised and expanded paperback edition of Cade's *Agatha Christie and the Eleven Missing days* (2011).

2   *Agatha Christie: A Biography*, p. 175.

3   A good deal of credit for this turnaround is due to Jared Cade whose meticulous use of the correct dates of Christie's early publications contributed so much to *Agatha Christie and the Eleven Missing Days*. More recently, Karl Pike's chronology of all of Christie's short stories has further added to our understanding of this hitherto fraught situation. His chronology is usefully published as an appendix to the three-volume paperback edition of Christie's short stories, Harper 2008.

4   Cade, *Agatha Christie and the Eleven Missing Days*, p. 147.

5   Marion Shaw and Sabine Vanacker note that this first view of Miss

Marple is reminiscent of the image of 'the widowed Queen Victoria in woodcuts of the 1890s.' *Reflecting on Miss Marple*, p. 46.

6   See especially the photograph of 'Auntie-Grannie' at page 160 of *An Autobiography*.

7   For anti-Victorianism as it developed in the late Victorian period, see Peter Keating, *The Haunted Study: A Social History of the English Novel 1875-1914*, Secker and Warburg, 1989, pp. 91-151.

8   Just one example from many possibilities. Separated from Max during the war, she occasionally wrote in his library, producing, as she explained in a letter to him, 'lowbrow stuff in your highbrow sanctuary.' Quoted Morgan, *Agatha Christie: A Biography*, p. 243.

Chapter 3 Village Detection

1   Shaw and Vanacker place special emphasis on this topic, insisting that 'Christie's creation of Miss Marple must be seen against the background of social and literary concern with the spinster.' *Reflecting on Miss Marple*, p. 41.

2   Miss Marple is surely spelling out what Melchett hesitates to put into words. A few years earlier Christie had explained the situation more fully when Anne Beddingfield needs to carry with her a 'small pearl-handled revolver.' She quickly realizes that 'modern clothes are quite unsuited to the carrying of firearms. In the end I pushed it gingerly into the top of my stocking. It made a terrible bulge, and I expected every moment that it would go off and shoot me in the leg, but it really seemed the only place.' *The Man in the Brown Suit*, chapter 32. The plan works as well: 'In a flash I had whipped the pistol out of my stocking and was holding it to his head,' chapter 33.

3   For the long tradition of 'sleuthing twosomes' see the anthology *Detective Duos* compiled by Marcia Muller and Bill Pronzini.

4   Both women are treated with great respect by Miss Marple, impressively so given her usual habit of distrusting everyone until she is totally sure of them. They are even allowed to help her solve mysteries. Both women are married to vicars. 'Bunch' Harmon is one of Miss Marple's indeterminate number of godchildren and appears in *A Murder is Announced* and 'Sanctuary.' Mrs Dane Calthrop is to

be found in *The Moving Finger* and *The Pale Horse*. See Anne Hart, *The Life and Times of Miss Jane Marple*, pp. 115-8.

5   Michele B Slung, *Crime on her Mind*, p. xix. For an exceptionally wide-ranging survey of the field, see also Patricia Craig and Mary Cadogan, *The Lady Investigates: Women Detectives and Spies in Fiction*.

6   For Isabel Anders, the full Christian life that Miss Marple lives and epitomizes is the central point of her recent book *Miss Marple Christian Sleuth*.

Chapter 4 Rural Life and Minimalism

1   Raymond Chandler 'The Simple Art of Murder,' first published in the *Atlantic Monthly*, Boston Mass., December 1944. The article was reprinted in volume form, together with a number of Chandler's short stories, as *The Simple Art of Murder* (London 1950). The Chandler quotations given here are from this edition. Howard Haycraft's Golden Age of detective fiction referred to by Chandler, comes from his book *Murder for Pleasure* which was first published in New York in 1941 and in London the following year.

2   Quoted Morgan, *Agatha Christie: A Biography*, p. 267.

3   In a published interview with Christie some years later, Francis Wyndham spoke up for her and against Chandler in a rather unusual way. While agreeing with the view that Christie 'epitomises the "cosy" school of crime fiction,' Wyndham pointed out that Chandler's 'own school of romantic violence was equally artificial.' Francis Wyndham, 'The Algebra of Agatha Christie,' *The Sunday Times Weekly Review*, 27 February 1966, p. 25.

4   P. D. James, *Time to be in Earnest*, 1999, p. 13.

5   Ibid., pp. 126-7.

6   Ibid., p. 59.

7   *Snobbery with Violence*, pp. 169-71.

8   *Agatha Christie: An English Mystery*, p. 279.

9   Max Mallowan's attitude towards his wife's novels was usually respectful and sensible rather than enthusiastic, but here was one aspect of them that, as a classical scholar, he fully appreciated:

'Agatha has always scrupulously, though perhaps unconsciously, observed Horace's instruction – '*Ne coram publico Medea pueros trucidet*' – Medea should refrain from murdering her children on stage. An admirable precept.' *Mallowan's Memoirs*, p. 222.

10 See Peter Keating, *The Haunted Study : A Social History of the English Novel 1875-1914* (1989), pp. 330-1.

11 *The Life and Times of Miss Jane Marple*, p. 2.

12 Ibid.

Chapter 5 Interregnum

1 Martin Edwards, *The Golden Age of Murder*, p. 171. And, see Edwards for other aspects of Christie's work for the BBC. Also Peter Haining, *Agatha Christie: Murder in Four Acts*.

2 For full details of this, Agatha Christie, *The Grand Tour: Letters and Photographs from the British Empire Exhibition*, edited by Matthew Prichard, HarperCollins, 2012.

3 The formal name was the Simplon-Orient-Express, but it was very often abreviated to the Orient Express. Christie uses both interchangeably. See Axel Heimsoth, 'From Orient Express to Desert Bus: Agatha Christie's Travels in the Near East,' in *Agatha Christie and Archaeology*, edited by Charlotte Trümpler.

4 'Hercule Poirot – Fiction's Greatest Detective,' *Agatha Christie Official Centenary Celebration*, edited by Lynn Underwood, p. 32.

5 For all aspects of this episode, and the original story, see Curran, *Agatha Christie's Secret Notebooks*, pp. 425-452.

6 Quoted Morgan, *Agatha Christie: A Biography*, p. 228.

Chapter 6 Psychology, Psychoanlysis, and Shakespeare

1 The Poirot novels of this period do not fare much better in this respect, with the notable exception of *One, Two, Buckle my Shoe* (1940) which is given a contemporary setting. Hitler and Mussolini are both referred to by name, but only in passing and in very general terms. *Evil under the Sun* (1941), has an even more fleeting reference

to Mussolini, and there is also, of course, the strange case of 'The Capture of Cerberus,' discussed earlier in chapter 5.

2   *Agatha Christie: A Biography*, p. 148.

3   Ibid., p. 147.

4   Ibid., p. 159.

5   *Agatha Christie and the Eleven Missing Days*, p. 236.

6   *Agatha Christie: An English Mystery*, p. 272.

7   Ibid., p. 218.

8   Ibid., p. 272.

9   *Agatha Christie: A Biography*, p. 169.

10 See Joseph Schwartz, *Cassandra's Daughter: A History of Psychoanalysis*, chapter 10.

11 Janet Morgan is extremely unusual, but surely right, in recognizing an Agatha Christie who 'had always found intellectual speculation exciting.' Morgan shows Christie in the early 1960s eager to obtain copies of the Fontana *Modern Masters* paperbacks which would 'educate me to be up-to-date, and help my writing.' She also notes that Christie's discussions with 'Max and her family at Greenway had included Freud and Jung, Moore and Wittgenstein.' *Agatha Christie: A Biography*, p. 363.

12 *Memories of Men and Women*, p. 75.

13 Christie's letter is usefully included in the anthology *The Second Cuckoo: A new selection of letters to The Times*, edited by Kenneth Gregory, George Allen and Unwin, 1983. John Curran reprints Christie's original draft of the letter in *Agatha Christie's Murder in the Making*.

14 Quoted Thompson, *Agatha Christie: An English Mystery*, p. 323.

15 *The Times*, 3 February 1973, *The Second Cuckoo*, p. 232.

16 *Agatha Christie: An English Mystery*, p. 322.

17 As, for example, explored by John Sutherland in 'Poirot's Double-Death,' in *Where was Rebecca Shot? Curiosities, Puzzles, and Conundrums in Modern Fiction*.

Chapter 7 Miss Marple's Wartime Casebook

1   *Agatha Christie Mistress of Mystery*, p. 94. For the interview with Ramsey, see Morgan, *Agatha Christie: A Biography*, p. 340.

2   She makes a jocular reference to the ballad as early as 1925 in *The Secret of Chimneys*. A later example, very pertinent to the present argument, is to be found in *Crooked House* (1949): 'Oh grandfather wasn't taken in,' Sophia laughed. 'Grandfather was never taken in by anybody. He wanted Brenda. He wanted to play Cophetua to her beggar-maid.'

3   The text used here is taken from *The Legendary Ballads of England and Scotland*, edited by John Roberts, 'Chandos Classics,' London 1870.

4   Relationships of this kind, between a middle or upper-class man and a working-class woman were far from uncommon in the Victorian age. But they were usually conducted in secret and often highly organized, but one at least is exceptionally well documented. See Derek Hudson, *Munby: Man of Two Worlds*, Murray, London, 1972. Also, Diane Atkinson, *Love and Dirt: The Marriage of Arthur Munby and Hannah Culwick*, Macmillan, London, 2003.

5   *The Interpretation of Dreams*, first published 1899. The edition used here, translated and edited by James Strachey, Allen and Unwin, 1954, p. 354.

6   *The Life and Crimes of Agatha Chrisie*, pp. 375-6.

7   For this and further details of the Haymarket season of plays, see Jonathan Croall, *Gielgud: A Theatrical Life 1904-2000*, Methuen paperback, 2001, pp. 320-2.

8   *Agatha Christie's Secret Notebooks*, pp. 249-56.

9   *Agatha Christie: A Biography*, p. 284.

Chapter 8 Crime in the Welfare State

1   A. J. P. Taylor, *English History 1914-1945*, pp. 595-7.

2   'Agatha Christie talks to Julian Symons about The Gentle Art of Murder,' *Sunday Times*, 15 October 1961, p. 28. Symons described the interview in the 'Foreword' he contributed to *The Bedside,*

Bathtub, and Armchair Companion to Agatha Christie, edited by Dick Riley and Pam McAllister.

3   See especially Robert Barnard, *A Talent to Deceive*, pp. 97-9.

4   *Agatha Christie's Secret Notebooks*, p. 174. Craig and Cadogan choose a different turning point and see a more general decline: 'Narrative control began to slacken at about the same time as the mode became inappropriate to the spirit of the age. *4.50 from Pddington* is the last Miss Marple novel that can rank with the best of Christie,' *The Lady Investigates*, p. 170.

5   Terence Morris, *Crime and Criminal Justice since 1945*, pp. 34-5. These figures are for England and Wales and cover the years 1938-45. Edward Smithies estimates a lower increase of 57 per cent for the same areas but the slightly shorter period of 1939-45. He does, though, confirm the main point that as far as criminal activity was concerned 'the war saw a marked quickening of pace.' *Crime in Wartime*, p. 2.

6   Donald Thomas, *Villains' Paradise*, pp. 81-2.

7   Morris, *Crime and criminal Justice since 1945*, pp. 90-1.

8   Alistair Horne, *Macmillan*, volume 2, p. 64. The famous phrase actually predates the election. Macmillan used it in a speech given in July 1957, but the sentiment it expressed characterized the subsequent election campaign.

9   *Villains' Paradise*, p. 176.

10   The essay was first published in *The Lion and the Unicorn*, Secker and Warburg, London 1941.

Chapter 9 'Houses for the People'

1   David C. Marsh, *The Changing Social Structure of England and Wales 1871-1961*, p. 54.

2   For a full discussion of these post-war developments, see Pamela Horn, *Life Below Stairs in the Twentieth Century*, chapter 7.

3   *The People's Peace 1945-1990*, p. 40.

4   D.V. Donnison, *Housing Policy Since the War*, p. 12.

5   Ibid., p. 15.

6   Kenneth O. Morgan, *The People's Peace*, p. 40.

7   Alistair Horne, *Macmillan*, volume 1, p. 332.

8   Ibid., p. 339.

9   See Frank Schaffer, *The New Town Story*, 1970, with an introduction by Lord Silkin who had introduced the New Towns Act into parliament in 1946.

10   *Never Again: Britain 1945-51*, p. 173.

11   *Agatha Christie: The Woman and her Mysteries*, p. 10.

12   Frederick J. Osborn and Arnold Whittick, *New Towns: Their Origins, Achievements and Progress*, pp.134-7; Belinda Cole, *Crawley: A History and Celebration of the Town*, pp. 94-5.

13   John Curran, *Agatha Christie's Secret Notebooks*, p. 405.

14   Osborn and Whittick, *New Towns*, pp. 134-51.

15   In *Bertram's Hotel* Lady Selina Hazy tells Miss Marple that her second son had been stationed at an airfield near St. Mary Mead. This would have been Gatwick. In 1939 it was a very small commercial airport, but during the war it was requisitioned by the RAF and considerably expanded. See Belinda Cole, *Crawley*, pp. 89-91.

16   James Cresswell is the only commentator I know who even recognizes the unusual nature of Miss Marple's taxi trip in *Nemesis*. See *Miss Marple and all her Characters*, pp. 155-6

Chapter 10 The Condition of England

1   *Agatha Christie's Secret Notebooks*, p. 336.

2   Janet Morgan, *Agatha Christie: A Biography*, p. 328.

3   www.pjkeating.co.uk

4   Alistair Horne, *Macmillan*, volume 2, p. 195.

5   William Jackson, *Withdrawal from Empire: A Military View*, Batsford, 1986, p. 180.

6   Shaw and Vanacker offer this description of Miss Marple arriving at Yewtree Lodge: 'On her hat is a bird's wing. She appears as a cross between a stern nanny or governess and a supernatural being just alighted on earth, a goddess seeking justice, or a winged Fury,' *Reflecting on Miss Marple*, p. 80.

7   Here again Shaw and Vanacker are much to the point. They see Helen Hayes as a 'cuddly Miss Marple' with 'hints of romantic

interest called up both with the murder victim, Major Palgrave, who no longer has a glass eye, and with Mr Rafiel, never a dying man as he is in the novel but transformed into a sprightly, bouquet-swinging admirer,' *Reflecting on Miss Marple*, pp. 92-3.

8   The term is usually applied specifically to the work of a number of novelists in the 1840s, most notably Elizabeth Gaskell, Charles Dickens, Benjamin Disraeli and Charles Kingsley who drew public attention to the rapidly changing work and class relations, mainly in the industrial north of England.

9   Curran, *Agatha Christie's Secret Notebooks*, p. 337.

10   F.H. McCLintock and Evelyn Gibson, *Robbery in London*, p. ix.

11   For the spate of mail robberies at this time see Donald Thomas, *Villains' Paradise*, chapter 13.

12   Ibid., pp. 377-8; Morton, *Gangland*, pp. 59-61.

Chapter 11 Nemesis

1   The lines are from 'The Theologian's Tale: Elizabeth,' *Tales of a Wayside Inn* (1863) by the once enormously popular American poet Henry Wadsworth Longfellow. Miss Marple quotes only the first two lines of a quatrain. The third and fourth lines show fully the bitter-sweet nature of the verse:

> So on the ocean of life we pass and speak one another,
> Only a look and a voice, then darkness again and a silence.

2   See especially Emily Trefusis in *The Sittaford Mystery* (1931) and Lucy Eyelesbarrow in *4.50 from Paddington* (1957). Miss Marple seems to know which man Lucy will choose and so she should, given that Christie was quite clear in her own mind. See Curran, *Agatha Christie's Secret Notebooks*, p. 214.

3   'Dolly was all up in arms for the girl – you know what women are – men are brutes – all the rest of it, etcetera. But it's not so simple as all that – not in these days. Girls know what they're about.' Arthur Bantry to Sir Henry Clithering in 'Death by Drowning,' first published November 1931 and then in *The Thirteen Problems* (1932).

4   *An Autobiography*, pp. 438-40.

Miss Marple: A Chronological Bibliography

The main purpose of this listing is to identify the dates of the first publication in the UK of all of the Miss Marple short stories and novels and to present them in chronological order. Unless otherwise indicated the place of publication is London. Some additional details have been given, mainly relating to the different titles of novels in America and to first collected editions of the short stories, whether in Britain or America, but no claim is made for this information as being in any sense comprehensive. The reason is that the bibliographical situation, beyond the present limits, is extremely complicated, at times bewilderingly so. Most of the early Miss Marple short stories were also published in North American periodicals or newspapers at around the same time as their UK publication, sometimes with changed titles, and in a variety of different collections. The novels were invariably serialized in UK and/or North American newspapers or magazines, sometimes before, sometimes after the UK book publication. These serializations were often abbreviated versions of the books and occasionally carried different titles.

'The Tuesday Night Club,' *The Royal Magazine*, December 1927.

'The Idol House of Astarte,' *The Royal Magazine*, January 1928.

'Ingots of Gold,' *The Royal Magazine*, February 1928.

'The Bloodstained Pavement,' *The Royal Magazine*, March 1928.

'Motive v Opportunity,' *The Royal Magazine*, April 1928.

'The Thumb Mark of St Peter,' *The Royal Magazine*, May 1928.

'The Blue Geranium,' *The Story-Teller*, December 1929.

'The Hat and the Alibi' (title later changed to 'A Christmas Tragedy'), *The Story-Teller*, January 1930.

'The Resurrection of Amy Durrant' (title later changed to 'The Companion'), *The Story-Teller*, February 1930.

'The Herb of Death,' *The Story-Teller*, March 1930.

'The Four Suspects,' *The Story-Teller*, April 1930.

'The Affair at the Bungalow,' *The Story-Teller*, May 1930.

The Murder at the Vicarage, October 1930.

'Death by Drowning,' *Nash's Pall Mall Magazine*, November 1931.

The Thirteen Problems, June 1932. Published in America as *The Tuesday Club Murders*. Contents: 'The Tuesday Night Club,' 'The Idol House of Astarte,' 'Ingots of Gold,' 'The Bloodstained Pavement,' 'Motive v Opportunity,' 'The Thumb Mark of St Peter,' 'The Blue Geranium,' 'The Companion,' 'The Four Suspects,' 'A Christmas Tragedy,' 'The Herb of Death,' 'The Affair at the Bungalow,' 'Death by Drowning.'

'Behind Closed Doors,' broadcast on the BBC 11 May 1934 and printed in *The Home Journal*, under this title, 25 May 1935. Subsequently, always known as 'Miss Marple Tells a Story.' First collected with the changed title in *The Regatta Mystery and Other Stories* (New York 1939). Also included in *Miss Marple's Final Cases* (1979).

'The Case of the Caretaker,' *The Strand Magazine*, January 1942. First collected in *Three Blind Mice and Other Stories* (New York 1950). Also included in *Miss Marple's Final Cases* (1979).

'The Case of the Retired Jeweller,' *The Strand Magazine*, February 1942. Title later changed to 'Tape-Measure Murder.' First collected in *Three Blind Mice and Other Stories* (New York 1950). Also included in *Miss Marple's Final Cases* (1979).

'The Perfect Maid,' *The Strand Magazine*, April 1942. Title later changed to 'The Case of the Perfect Maid.' First Collected in *Three Blind Mice and Other Stories* (New York 1950). Also included in *Miss Marple's Final Cases* (1979).

The Body in the Library, May 1942.

'A Case of Buried Treasure,' *The Strand Magazine*, July 1944. Title later changed to 'Strange Jest.' First collected in *Three Blind Mice and Other Stories* (New York 1950). Also included in *Miss Marple's Final Cases* (1979).

The Moving Finger, June 1943. Published in America the previous year.

A Murder is Announced, June 1950.

They Do It With Mirrors, November 1952. Published in America as *Murder with Mirrors*.

A Pocket Full of Rye, November 1953.

'Sanctuary,' *Woman's Journal*, October 1954. This story had been published one month earlier under a different title in an American magazine. First collected in *Double Sin and Other Stories* (New York 1961). Also included in *Miss Marple's Final Cases* (1979).

4.50 from Paddington, November 1957. Published in America as *What Mrs McGillicuddy Saw!*

'Greenshaw's Folly,' *The Daily Mail*, 3-7 December 1956. It was collected in *The Adventure of the Christmas Pudding and a Selection of Entrées* (1960) together with a number of non-Miss Marple stories; then in *Double Sin and Other Stories* (New York 1961).

The Mirror Crack'd from Side to Side, November 1962. Published in America as *The Mirror Crack'd*.

A Caribbean Mystery, November 1964. Published in America the following year.

At Bertram's Hotel, November 1965. Published in America the following year.

Nemesis, November 1971.

Sleeping Murder, October 1976.

Miss Marple's Final Cases, October 1979. Contents: 'Sanctuary,' 'Strange Jest,' 'Tape-Measure Murder,' 'The Case of the Caretaker,' 'The Case of the Perfect Maid,' and 'Miss Marple Tells a Story,' plus two non-Miss Marple stories.

Select Secondary Bibliography

Place of publication is London unless otherwise stated.

Anders, Isabel, *Miss Marple Christian Sleuth*, Winchester, Circle Books, 2013.

Barnard, Robert, *A Talent to Deceive: An Appreciation of Agatha Christie*, Collins, 1980.

Brand, Christianna, 'Miss Marple – A Portrait', in Keating (ed.), *Agatha Christie First Lady of Crime*.

Bunson, Matthew, *The Complete Christie: An Agatha Christie Encyclopaedia*, New York, Simon and Schuster, 2000.

Cade, Jared, *Agatha Christie and the Eleven Missing Days*, Peter Owen, 1998.

Chandler, Raymond, *The Simple Art of Murder*, Hamish Hamilton, 1950.

Cole, Belinda, *Crawley: A History and Celebration of the Town*, Salisbury Wilts., Frith Book Co., 2004.

-- *Crawley: An Ilustrated Miscellany*, Salisbury Wilts., Frith Book Co., 2004.

Craig, Patricia and Cadogan, Mary, *The Lady Investigates: Women Detectives and Spies in Fiction*, Gollancz, 1981.

Curran, John, *Agatha Christie's Secret Notebooks: Fifty Years of Mysteries in the Making*, HarperCollins, 2009.

-- *Agatha Christie's Murder in the Making*, HarperCollins, 2011.

Cresswell, James, *Miss Marple and all her Characters*, privately printed, Cresswell, 2006.

Donnison, D.V., *Housing Policy Since the War*, Welwyn Herts, Codicote Press, 1960.

Edwards, Martin, *The Golden Age of Murder: The Mystery of the Writers who Invented the Modern Detective Story*, HarperCollins, 2015.

Fido, Martin, *The World of Agatha Christie*, Carlton, 1999.

Fremlin, Celia, 'The Christie Everybody Knew,' in Keating (ed.), *Agatha Christie First Lady of Crime*.

Fyvel, T.R., *Insecure Offenders: Rebellious Youth in the Welfare State*, Chatto and Windus, 1961.

Gill, Gillian, *Agatha Christie: The Woman and her Mysteries*, Robson, 1991.

Gregg, Hubert, *Agatha Christie and All That Mousetrap*, William Kimber, 1980.

Hack, Richard, *Duchess of Death: the Unauthorized Biography of Agatha Christie*, JR Books, 2010

Haining, Peter, *Agatha Christie: Murder in Four Acts*, Virgin, 1990.

-- *Agatha Christie's Poirot: A Celebration of the Great Detective*, Boxtree, 1995.

-- *The Classic Era of Crime Fiction*, Prion, 2002.

Hart, Anne, *The Life and Times of Miss Jane Marple*, Macmillan, 1986.

-- *The Life and Times of Hercule Poirot*, Pavilion, 1990.

Haycraft, Howard, *Murder for Pleasure: The Life and Times of the Detective Story*, Peter Davies, 1942.

Hennessy, Peter, *Never Again: Britain 1945-1951*, Cape, 1952.

Horn, Pamela, *Life Below Stairs in the Twentieth Century*, Stroud, Gloucester, Sutton, 2001.

Horne, Alistair, *Macmillan*, Volume 1, 1894-1956, Macmillan, 1988.

--*Macmillan*, Volume 2, 1957-1986, Macmillan, 1989.

Hurdle, Judith, *The Gateway Guide to Agatha Christie's England*, Oakland, California, RDR Books, 1999.

James, P. D., *Time to be in Earnest: A Fragment of Autoiography*, Faber, 1999.

-- *Talking about Detective Fiction*, Oxford, 2009.

Keating, H.R.F. (ed.), *Agatha Christie: First Lady of Crime*, Weidenfeld and Nicholson, 1977.

Light, Alison, *Forever England: Femininity, literature and conservatism between the wars*, Routledge, 1991.

Macaskill, Hilary, *Agatha Christie at Home*, Frances Lincoln, 2009.

McCall, Henrietta, *The Life of Max Mallowan*, British Museum Press, 2001.

Mallowan, Max, *Mallowan's Memoirs*, Collins, 1977.

Mann, Jessica, *Deadlier than the Male: An Investigation into Feminine Crime Writing*, Newton Abbot, Devon, David and Charles, 1980.

Marsh, David C., *The Changing Social Structure of England and Wales 1871-1961*, Routledge, revised edition 1965.

McCall, Henrietta, *The Life of Max Mallowan: Archaeology and Agatha Christie*, British Museum Press, 2001.

McLintock, F.H. and Evelyn Gibson, *Robbery in London An Enquiry by the Cambridge Institute of Criminology*, Cambridge Studies in Criminology volume 14, Macmillan, 1961.

Morgan, Janet, *Agatha Christie: A Biography*, Collins, 1984.

Morgan, Kenneth O., *The People's Peace: British History 1945-1990*, Oxford, Oxford University Press paperback, 1990.

Morris, Terence, *Crime and Criminal Justice since 1945*, Oxford, Basil Blackwell, 1989.

Morton, James, *Gangland Volumes 1 and 2*, Time Warner paperback, Omnibus Edition, 2003.

Muller, Marcia and Bill Pronzini (eds.), *Detective Duos*, New York, Oxford University Press, 1997.

Norman, Dr Andrew, *Agatha Christie: The Finished Portrait*, Stroud, Gloucester, Tempus, 2006.

Osborn, Frederic J and Arnold Whittick, *New Towns: Their Origins, Achievements and Progress*, Leonard Hill, third edition, 1977.

Osborne, Charles, *The Life and Crimes of Agatha Christie*, HarperCollins, revised edition 1999.

Palmer, Scott, *The Films of Agatha Christie*, Batsford, 1993.

Ramsey, G.C., *Agatha Christie: Mistress of Mystery*, Collins,1968.

Rawlings, Philip, *Crime and Power: A History of Criminal Justice 1688-1998*, Longman, 1999.

Riley, Dick, and Pam McAllister (eds.), *The Bedside, Bathtub & Armchair Companion to Agatha Christie*, second, revised edition, New York, The Continuum International Publishing Group, 2001.

Rivière, François, *In the Footsteps of Agatha Christie*, translated by Alexandra Campbell, Ebury Press, 1997.

Robyns, Gwen, *The Mystery of Agatha Christie*, New York, Doubleday, 1978.

Rowland, Susan, *From Agatha Christie to Ruth Rendell: British Women Writers in Detective and Crime Fiction*, Basingstoke, Hampshire, Palgrave, 2001.

Rowse, A.L., 'Agatha Christie' in *Memories of Men and Women*, Eyre Methuen, 1980.

Rutherford, Margaret, *An Autobiography as told to Gwen Robyns*, W.H. Allen, 1972.

Sanders Dennis and Len Lavallo, *The Agatha Christie Companion: The Complete Guide to Agatha Christie's Life and Work*, W.H. Allen, 1985.

Saunders, Peter, *The 'Mousetrap' Man*, Collins, 1972.

Schaffer, Frank, *The New Town Story*, MacGibbon and Kee, 1970.

Schwartz, Joseph, *Cassandra's Daughters: A History of Psychoanalysis*, Penguin, 1999.

Shaw, Marion and Sabine Vanacker, *Reflecting on Miss Marple*, Routledge, 1991.

Simmons, Dawn Langley, *Margaret Rutherford: A Blithe Spirit by her daughter Dawn*, Barker 1983.

Slung, Michele B., *Crime on her Mind: Fifteen Stories of Female Sleuths from the Victorian era to the Forties*, Joseph, 1976.

Smithies, Edward, *Crime in Wartime: A Social History of Crime in World War II*, Allen and Unwin, 1982.

Sova, Dawn B., *Agatha Christie A-Z: The Essential Reference to her Life and Writings*, New York, Facts on File, 1996.

Sutherland, John, 'Poirot's Double-Death,' *Where was Rebecca Shot?: Curiosities, Puzzles, and Conundrums in Modern Fiction*, Weidenfeld and Nicholson, 1998.

Symons, Julian, 'Agatha Christie talks to Julian Symons about the Gentle Art of Murder', *Sunday Times*, 15 October 1961.

-- *Bloody Murder From the Detective Story to the Crime Novel: A History*, Harmondsworth, Middlesex, revised edition, Penguin 1974.

-- 'The Mistress of Complication,' in Keating (ed.), *Agatha Christie: First Lady of Crime*, 1977.

--'A Portrait of Agatha Christie', foreword to Dick Riley and Pam McAllister (eds.), *The Bedside, Bathtub & Armchair Companion to Agatha Christie*.

--*The Great Detectives: Seven Original Investigations*, illustrated by Tom Adams, Orbis, 1981.

Taylor, A.J.P., *English History 1914-1945*, Oxford, Oxford University Press, 1965.

Taylor, Anna-Marie, '*Home* is where the Hearth is: The Englishness of Agatha Christie's Marple Novels,' in Ian A. Bell and Graham Daldry (eds.), *Watching the Detectives*, Basingstoke, Hants., Palgrave, 1990.

Thomas, Donald, *An Underworld at War: Spivs, Deserters, Racketeers and Civilians in the Second World War*, Murray, 2003.

--*Villains' Paradise: Britain's Underworld from the Spivs to the Krays*, Murray, 2005.

Thompson, Laura, *Agatha Christie: An English Mystery*, Headline, 2007.

Trümpler, Charlotte (ed.), *Agatha Christie and Archaeology*, British Museum Press, 2001.

Underwood, Lynn (ed.), *Agatha Christie: Official Centenary Celebration 1890-1990*, Belgrave, 1990.

Wagstaff, Vanessa and Stephen Poole, *Agatha Christie: A Reader's Companion*, Aurum Press, 2004.

Watson, Colin, *Snobbery with Violence: English Crime Stories and their Audience*, Eyre and Spottiswoode, revised edition, 1979.

Wilson, Colin, *A Criminal History of Mankind*, Mercury, revised edition 2005.

Wyndham, Francis, 'The Algebra of Agatha Christie,' The Sunday Times Weekly Review, 27 February 1966.

Yorke, R.A. *Agatha Christie: Power and Illusion*, Macmillan, 2007.

Index